THE ENCYCLOPEDIA
OF OUTDOOR SURVIVAL

BASED ON THE TRAINING AND TECHNIQUES OF THE SAS

THE ENCYCLOPEDIA
OF OUTDOOR SURVIVAL

BASED ON THE TRAINING AND TECHNIQUES OF THE SAS

Barry Davies BEM

Dedication: To my mother

Published in the United States in 2002 by
Lewis International Inc
2201 NW 102nd Place, #1
Miami, FL 33172
Tel: 305-436-7984 / 800-259-5962
Fax: 305-436-7985 / 800-664-5095

First published in Great Britain by Virgin Publishing
in 1999 under the title 'SAS Encyclopedia of Survival'

ISBN 1-930983-19-0

A catalogue record for this book is available from the British Library.

Designed by Design 23, London
Printed and bound in Great Britain by Butler and Tanner

Neither the author nor the publisher can accept any responsibility for any
loss, injury or damage caused as a result of the use of the techniques
described in this book, nor for any prosecutions or proceedings brought
or instigated against any person or body that may result from using the
techniques.

CONTENTS

SURVIVAL
ESSENTIALS
AIDS AND TECHNIQUES

ARCTIC

DESERT

JUNGLE

SEA AND COASTLINE

MILITARY

Note that units of measurement quoted in the text are given first in metric, followed by approximate Imperial equivalents – to convert 30 metres as 98.425 feet, rather than simply 100 feet, seems pointlessly pedantic. Similarly, most references to e.g. notional casualties in the medical section are in the male form; throughout, 'he','him' and 'his' should be read as including 'she' and 'her' – in the few cases where gender difference is relevant, it is pointed out.

INTRODUCTION

When I was a young soldier, about to join the SAS, I read a book called *The Long Walk* by Slavomir Rawicz. It recounts the trials endured by six men and one woman who, after escaping from a Soviet prison camp in late 1939, walked from the Arctic Circle across the Gobi Desert and south all the way to India. After 4,000 miles and 18 months four of them, including one American, survived. Their story instilled in me a never-ending thirst for all matters relating to human powers of survival.

The need to improvise in the Western world has diminished due to the easy availability of most items required to answer our every need. Food, drink, clothing and tools are cheap, commonplace items plucked from the shelves of any supermarket. The real need to improvise in the cause of survival is only faced by those who, by misfortune, find themselves in an isolated and uninhabited area. They may or may not have fellow survivors to assist them or to care for; either way, improvisation becomes the shopping basket, and the will to live the means of filling it.

We are creatures of comfort, with television, central heating and social amenities providing for our every need and appetite. In a survival situation these ever-present amenities will be replaced by perilous threats to life – pain, thirst, starvation, stress, loneliness, and boredom which may threaten the balance of the mind. In such a predicament the will to live must overcome the desire to lie down and give up. In order to do this we must look back at how our ancestors lived and survived, and the lessons they learnt from nature.

In many cases, if the need to survive presents itself we should be well equipped. Clothing to suit the environment, shelter, sufficient food and water and communications are essential items for those venturing into uninhabited regions, or for soldiers operating behind the enemy lines. In the event of an accident, when individuals are thrust unprepared into remote and hostile surroundings, the means to survive can still be found. Survival skills are common sense, requiring the minimal amount of equipment, much of which can be improvised from wreckage or from the natural surroundings.

Survival has one simple rule: work in harmony with nature rather than trying to adapt it to modern-day urban expectations.

Why build shelter if it is not cold and there is little chance of rain? Why carry water when surrounded by lakes and rivers? Animals have no tools, yet they build homes, find food, and survive.

Research for this book

This book is designed to provide a wide variety of information to cover every aspect of survival. The first section on Survival Essentials covers the basics that apply in any situation, in any terrain or climate. This provides information on medical emergencies, shelter, fire, water, food, travel and rescue. This is followed by sections on the specifics of survival in the Arctic, Desert and Jungle. The section on Survival at Sea includes information not only on surviving in an open boat or raft, but also on the problems and opportuniteis faced after landing on islands or mainland coastlines. Finally, the Military survival section deals with those aspects associated with captivity, escape and evasion.

Adding the new developments in the world of survival to the vast amount that already exists has meant the curtailment of some subjects. These curtailments have been made in the areas of plant and animal food; and in the military section, given that servicemen and women are already familiar with basic techniques such as camouflage and concealment. Where possible all duplication has been avoided, by placing subject matter in its most logical context – e.g., hypothermia is to be found in the Arctic section under the heading 'Medical Hazards', even though it also obviously applies in survival situations in most other regions.

Research for this book was carried out by visiting some of the world's best survival schools, in America, Europe and the Far East. Additionally, through the kind offices of BCB International Ltd of Cardiff, UK – the world's largest survival equipment manufacturer – and many other similar companies, this book displays the most modern survival equipment available both for civilian and military personnel.

A complete list of those who contributed can be found at the end of this book.

Barry Davies

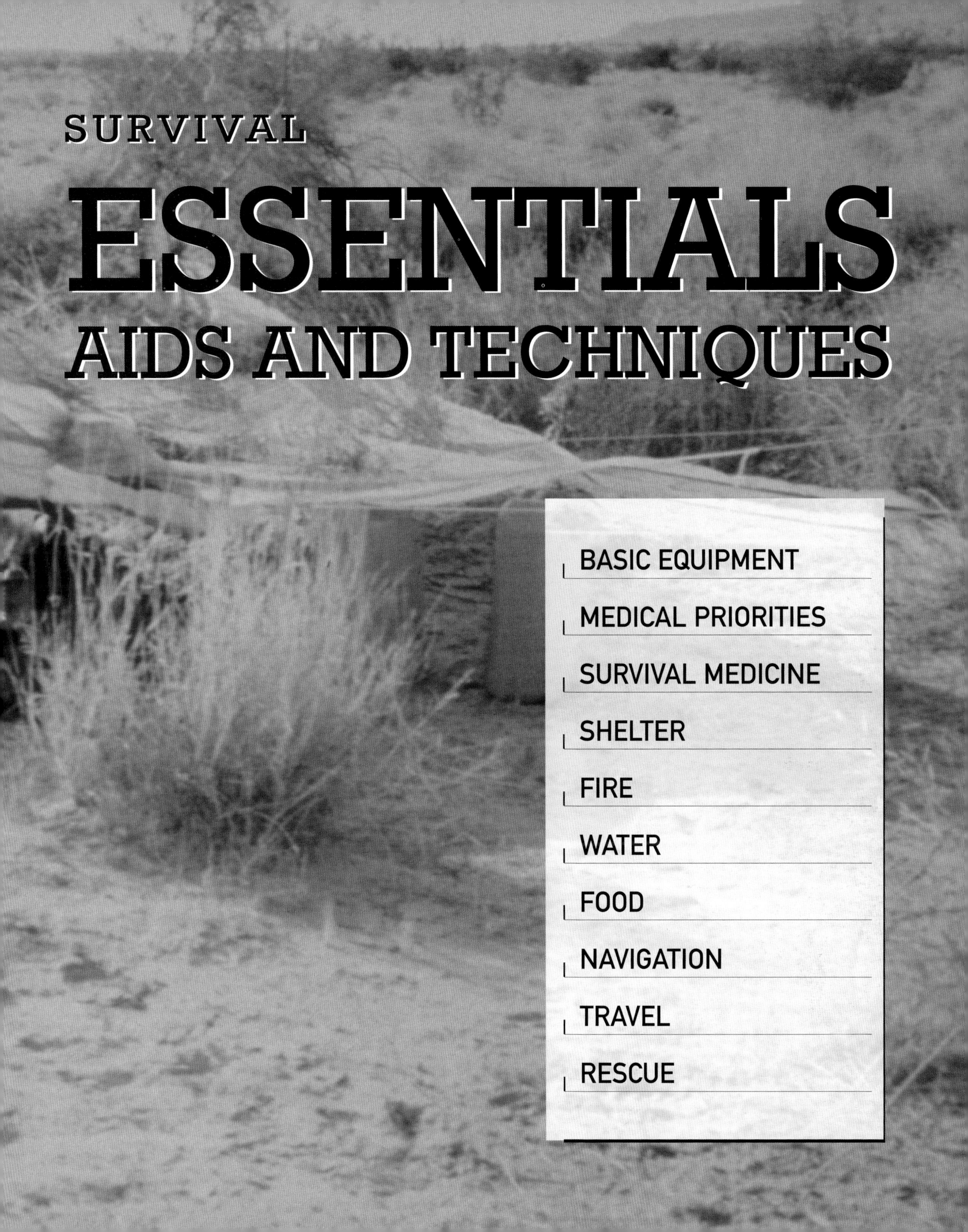

SURVIVAL

ESSENTIALS

AIDS AND TECHNIQUES

BASIC EQUIPMENT

MEDICAL PRIORITIES

SURVIVAL MEDICINE

SHELTER

FIRE

WATER

FOOD

NAVIGATION

TRAVEL

RESCUE

BASIC EQUIPMENT

Anyone venturing into an uninhabited and potentially hostile area should carry a survival pack. The contents of the pack should be dictated by the type of terrain you are entering, and should provide the means to protect life in the event of a survival situation occurring.

Escape and survival equipment is issued as a matter of course to military pilots and Special Forces units; but the development of specialist survival equipment for civilian use has also increased dramatically over the past decade. This equipment varies from the basic items supporting such 'global' techniques as making fire, contructing shelter, and navigation, to those varying items required for survival in specific terrain and climatic conditions.

An important factor is that every item included in a survival kit has to be of real use, and its usefulness must be judged against its size and weight. Ultimately, each item must increase your chances of survival in and rescue from situations in which you may initially have no other resources apart from the clothes you stand up in.

Fire

Candle A candle will prolong the life of your matches by providing a constant flame (as long as you can protect it from wind and rain); it will help start a fire even when the tinder is damp. Additionally, a simple candle provides light and comfort to your surroundings. Choose a candle made from 100% stearine, or tallow (solidified animal fats) – this is edible and may therefore serve as an emergency food (do not try to eat candles made of paraffin wax). The candle wax can also be used as a multi-purpose lubricant.

A flint and steel, mankind's basic fire-lighting tool for thousands of years although now greatly improved by including a small magnesium bar.

Flint & Steel Matches, if not protected, are easily rendered useless by wet weather, while a flint and steel will enable you to light countless fires irrespective of the conditions. The flint and steel is a robust and reliable piece of apparatus, but its usefulness is vastly improved when combined with a block of magnesium. Sparks generated by the flint will readily ignite shavings scraped from the magnesium block onto kindling materials.

Matches Ordinary kitchen matches will not be of much use unless they are made waterproof. This can easily be done by covering them

Water bottle; the newer types on the market come fitted with a built-in filtration and purification system – you simply fill them, and drink from them.

A survival kit suitable for packing in a tobacco tin.

Wind and waterproof matches

completely with melted wax, or coating them with hairspray. Special windproof and waterproof matches can also be purchased; each match is sealed with a protective varnish coating, and manufactured using chemicals which will burn for around 12 seconds in the foulest of weather.

Tampon Due to the fine cotton wool used in its manufacture, the tampon has proven to be the most efficient tinder and fire-lighting aid. It works best if the white surface is blackened with charcoal or dry dirt first, as it accepts the sparks and ignites more readily. British RAF and Special Forces packs contain two tampons as standard issue. The cotton wool can also be used in medical emergencies to clean wounds.

Water

Condoms A non-lubricated, heavy duty condom makes an excellent water carrier when supported in a sock or shirtsleeve. The water must be poured in, rather than the condom being dipped into the water supply; shake the condom to stretch it as it fills up. Used in this way a condom can hold about 1.5 litres (2.6 pints). Condoms will also protect dry tinder in wet weather; and are strong enough to make a small catapult.

Water Purification The means of water purification come in a number of different forms, from tablets to pumping devices. For inclusion in a survival kit you are best advised to choose tablets (about 50), as they are light to carry and quick and convenient to use. One small tablet will purify about one litre (1.75 pints) of water, although it will leave a strong chlorine taste. Tablets cannot clean the water or remove dirt particles, but they do make it safe to drink.

A stainless steel wire saw can cut through most materials, including steel.
'Para cord', a material with a score of uses in a surival situation; and hooked bungees for shelter construction.

Clothing & Shelter

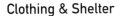

Needles & Pins Several different sized safety pins should be included in any survival kit. They make good closures for makeshift clothing, or can be baited as large hooks to catch fish or birds. Large sailmaker's needles, such as a Chenille No 6, have a large eye which makes threading easier, especially if the hands are cold or if you are using thread improvised from sinew. They will also be able to cope with heavier materials such as canvas, shoe leather or rawhide. Another good use for a needle is as a pointer in a makeshift compass, although it will have to be magnetised first.

Parachute Cord Parachute cord is an extremely strong alternative to plain string,

having a breaking strain of about 250 kilogrammes (550 pounds). It can be used for lashing shelter frameworks and many other necessities; and the inner strands of thinner cord also make good thread for sewing or fishing lines. A survival kit should contain a minimum of 15 metres (50 feet).

Razor Blades Hard-backed razor blades make useful cutting tools, for gutting fish, cutting sinew, or when making a weapon. Despite its small size, if used with care the blade will continue to cut for up to a month.

Its life can be prolonged by not trying to cut materials which are obviously beyond its capabilities.

Survival Bag Loss of body heat potentially leading to

hypothermia is one of the most commonplace but deadly threats encountered in a survival situation. A simple survival bag made of polythene protects the body from both wind and rain and minimises the risk. Two bags separated by a layer of moss, bracken, grass, hay, etc, will form a basic sleeping bag. The survival bag also has many other uses, including an improvised rucksack, a waterproof layer when making a shelter, a solar still, and when extracting water from plants.

Wire Saw A good saw, similar to those issued to the military, is made of eight strands of stainless steel wire; it is capable of cutting through wood, bone, plastics, even metal. A wire saw can be used when cutting timber to

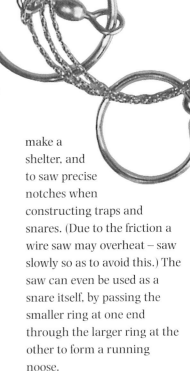

make a shelter, and to saw precise notches when constructing traps and snares. (Due to the friction a wire saw may overheat – saw slowly so as to avoid this.) The saw can even be used as a snare itself, by passing the smaller ring at one end through the larger ring at the other to form a running noose.

Navigation & Signalling

Air Marker Panels Air marker panels can be made from any lightweight fluorescent material, although orange is the standard recognizable colour. It is advisable to carry a sheet two metres (at least six feet) square, which can either be folded into different shapes (see under Signalling, page 135), or split into three 30cm (12in) wide strips. Do not split the sheet until there is an absolute need to do so – e.g. you have spotted a search aircraft – as the whole sheet is useful for other functions such as a makeshift shelter.

Compass A compass provides the means to establish direction and position, the two vital elements if you are forced to travel or need to give your co-ordinates during rescue. A small button compass is designed primarily as an emergency escape and evasion tool for the military, its use being restricted to

Air marker panels can be made from any fluorescent material.

direction-finding only.

The liquid-filled 'Silva'-type compass is more commonly associated with navigation by map, and together these offer the means of precise position-finding.

Flares & Smoke A wide variety of signal flares and smoke canisters are available on the market. If you decide to add them to your survival kit you

'Silva' type compass.

would do best to choose a standard flare pack containing a launch pistol and nine different coloured flares. Although it is a good idea to know which colour is traditionally associated with which intended signal, firing any colour will attract attention. When firing the flares take great care that the launch pistol is aimed skywards. In an life-threatening emergency flares can be used to start a fire.

Survival Bags

One or more strong polythene sheet bags, big enough to climb into wearing your clothing and boots, will provide you with:

• Protection from rain, wind, and hypothermia

• The basis for an insulated sleeping bag or matress

• A shelter roof

• The means of collecting water

• The means of distilling water

• The means to keep your clothing and kit dry when wading rivers

• If brightly coloured, as ground signal panels to attract SAR aircraft

Even the simplest survival bag is extremely valuable for a number of survival purposes in both hot and cold conditions.

The Global Positioning System (GPS) utilising the network of navigation satellites in Earth orbit is of limited value in most survival situations; although it may allow initial positioning, in the absence of a power source its batteries do not last long.

A waterproof watch with high nighttime luminosity is the best choice.

The above watch has the added survival benefit of a compass.

Global Positioning System (GPS) GPS is relatively new to the survival market, but its popularity is growing. This state-of-the-art instrument is a navigational aid capable of plotting your precise position on the surface of the Earth. This is obviously of particular value in the Arctic, where a normal compass can become erratic. However, GPS has cer-tain drawbacks in most pure survival situations; away from any other power source it relies on batteries, making its usefulness shortlived.

Heliograph Modern heli-ographs are small, light, and easy to use. They operate by reflecting the sun's rays pre-cisely towards aircraft or other rescuers. On a clear, sunny day their reflection can be spotted up to 30 kilometres (18.5 miles) away. It is a good idea to familiarise yourself with the operating instruc-tions prior to any rescue attempt.

Radar–Reflective Balloon Radar-reflec-tive balloons are not new to survival, but in recent years they have improved dramatically. The principle is to inflate a balloon made from a special foil which can be detected by search-and-rescue

While a purpose-made heliograph is best, any mirror can be used in an emergency.

radar from ranges of up to 38 kilometres (24 miles). Some are tethered to a length of line and flown like a kite, while others are inflated by gas; the latter will stay aloft for up to five days even in strong winds.

Strobe Designed for military rescue situations, the strobe is a bright blue light which flashes with great intensity and can be seen many miles away. These are perfect for location at night or in the darkness of the Arctic winter. Although the strobe is water-proof, in cold conditions it should be kept close to the body to preserve the battery strength. The strobe should only be operated when the sound of a rescue aircraft is positively identified.

Survival Radio Although there are a vast number of survival radios on the market, some are limited in range and capabilities. If your work or pastimes often take you into

isolated areas then you are well advised to carry a radio telephone which is capable of world-wide communications. In the event of any accident requiring the emergency ser-vices your chances of sur-vival will be greatly enhanced. Many surviving parties have been successfully rescued by telephoning the emergency services directly. While most mobile phones will only work where there is an established network, com-munications are improving all the time as global satellite phones are introduced.

Watch Although not a direct part of your survival kit, a watch can be an excellent navigational aid – providing that it is of the analogue type, i.e. not digital.

Whistle Modern survival whistles are compact and can have a range of up to 1000 metres (3/4mile) on a clear day. Its main usefulness is for localised communication, i.e.

between members of the survival party, or when the weather is so bad that only surface rescue is possible. Every life-vest carries a whistle for location after a disaster at sea. In the same way, an injured and immobile person can signal their location on land.

Food

Emergency Food Food is not an immediate requirement in a survival situation, as the body can do without solids for several weeks before it starts to deteriorate. However, morale plays an important part in survival, and this can be lifted by maintaining some normality. Having the means to make a hot drink produces this normality. Any food pack should be kept to the minimum: two fuel tablets, two tea or coffee

sachets, sugar, etc.

Meat stock cubes contain salt and flavouring and make excellent hot drinks; they can also be used to flavour plants and food from the wild.

Fishing Equipment A survival fishing kit should consist of the following basic components: five hooks (size 14 or 16), approximately 30m (100ft) of line, 10 iron or brass weights, and swivels. A float can be made from a cork (which when charred will also provide hand and face camouflage). If there is room, include a plastic, luminous lure, and a small fishing net.

Snares Purpose-manufactured snares work best, but if you cannot get these then carry at least 5 metres (16.5 feet) of brass wire from which they can be constructed.

Next to a rifle, snares are perhaps the most effective way of catching game. Brass wire can also be used for fishing traces, and when building shelters, making bindings for snowshoes or improvised packs.

All survival packs should contain basic fishing kit, which has a high usefulness-for-weight value. The pocket knife below is specifically designed for fishing.

Emergency food pack. In most situations only the minimum of food items justify their bulk and weight in the survival pack.

Food

• Except in extreme cold conditions, fit adults can live without solids for weeks.

• Food can add more heavy bulk to survival packs than it is worth

• For short-term survival conditions, pack only small, high-energy rations

BUT

• Hot drinks lift morale, and morale affects survival chances

• Ingredients for hot drinks are light and low-volume, so are worth packing

Knife

Along with your survival kit you should select a good knife. For many reasons this may be the most important item you carry; it is therefore essential to choose a knife of high quality which is best suited to your needs.

There are several types of blade to be considered in this context, such as those found on pocket knives and multi-functional tools, and purpose-made survival knives.

Pocket knives range from the simplest single-bladed type to multi-bladed, multi-function knives. Whichever knife you choose, always carry it on your person as a matter of course. Single-bladed knives offer little more than a simple cutting tool. If you decide on a pocket knife you will be better off with a multi-function, 'Swiss Army' type. This will provide the survivor with a versatile range of tools, including scissors, saw and screwdriver.

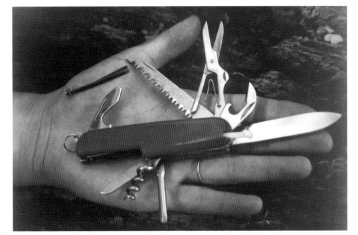

Pocket knives range from simple blades (above), through the slightly more versatile jacknives (bottom right), to the multi-purpose 'Swiss Army' type (left). Some are small enough to fit in a tobacco tin survival kit (bottom left).

There is a wide range of knives on the market, some excellent and some inadequate although superficially impressive.

Survival knives tend to be much larger than pocket knives and are usually carried in their own sheath. Most of the better knives have a sharpening stone in a pocket on the sheath, and many have a hollow handle or a pouch on the sheath in which a basic survival kit can be carried, although the nature and number of items in the kit

will depend on the price of the knife model. A large number of relatively cheap, poor quality survival knives have flooded the market in recent years. These tend to have a weak point where the blade meets the handle, which is likely to fail when the knife is most needed. Check the knife's construction and any attached survival items carefully before purchase, and certainly before venturing into the wilderness.

Multi-functional tools serve endless applications, from shelter building to making improvised clothing and travel gear. In a survival situation the multi-function tool is likely to prove more productive than an ordinary knife. The better-known names such as Leatherman and Gerber are well made and should last a lifetime. Most types include pliers, wire cutters, cutting blade, saw, screwdrivers and files. Because of its importance the tool should be attached to the body by a length of cord to prevent loss.

The next step from the 'Swiss Army' knife is the multi-function tool such as the Leatherman or Gerber, whose increased size and length gives extra leverage and weight to its applications.

Keeping a Sharp Edge

The knife is a vital survival aid; do not misuse it by throwing it into the ground or at trees. Keep it clean, and know where it is at all times.

A knife with a blunt edge is nothing more than a useless piece of steel. Granite or dark, hard sandstone are best for sharpening a blade. Find a flat piece the size of an open palm; rubbing two rocks together will produce an even surface. Wet the stone surface and work the blade edge over it with a smooth action, always working the blade away from you across the stone. At first use a clockwise circular motion over the surface, then an anticlockwise motion. Learning to sharpen a blade is a skill that can only be achieved through practice. Grinding the blade at the correct angle will produce a long-lasting cutting edge. If your intended travel will involve a lot of cutting then you will be better off carrying a sharpening stone or steel with you.

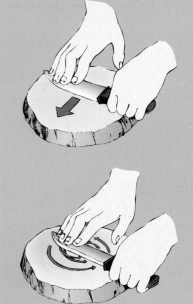

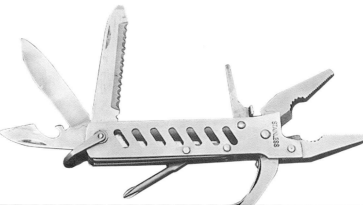

The most impressively macho knife is not always the most practical

SURVIVAL MEDICAL PACK

Knowledge of even basic first aid skills is a useful and valuable accomplishment in everyday life, but in a survival situation these skills take on immeasurable importance. Even when medical training and equipment are limited or totally non-existent, it is always possible to save life if the priorities of first aid are administered.

It is important to put together a small emergency medical kit, based on your own personal medical skills. Obviously, if you are not trained as a medic, you should only include basic items, as detailed below.

Antihistamine Cream Antihistamine cream will soothe the severe irritation that insect bites or allergies can cause. Antihistamine tablets can be carried as an alternative, but beware – some cause drowsiness.

Antiseptic Potassium Permanganate crystals (see below) are easy to carry and provide an all round sterilizing agent, antiseptic and antifungal agent. A tube of general purpose antiseptic cream is also very handy.

Aspirin Aspirin will relieve mild pain and headaches and reduce a fever. Carry a strip of about a dozen soluble aspirin tablets.

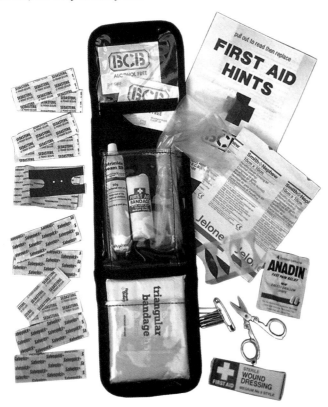

Dressings Include at least one large wound dressing in your medical kit. As any soldier will tell you, always have it ready for immediate use. Note – the inside of a wound dressing contains cotton wool which makes excellent tinder, so make sure to retain all used dressings.

Electrolyte Drinks Most survivors will inevitably suffer from dehydration; this can occur in both hot and cold climates, and is mostly attributed to diarrhoea. While replacing fluid loss is the priority, body salts and minerals can also be replaced by adding an electrolyte drink.

Magnifying Glass In survival situations a magnifying glass is traditionally associated with fire-lighting by focusing the sun's rays on dry tinder; however, it is also useful for finding hard-to-see objects such as splinters and thorns. Short, sharp burns are also effective for removing leeches and ticks from the body.

Mosquito Repellent The chances of contracting malaria and other mosquito-borne diseases can be reduced if the correct precautions are taken. Anti-malarial tablets, as prescribed by a doctor, need to be taken; but it is just as important to deter the insects from biting you in the first place, so it is recommended that you include a mosquito/insect repellent in your kit.

Plasters Carry various sizes and shapes of waterproof plasters. Larger plasters are best, as they can always be cut down if necessary. Keep your plasters together in a waterproof sachet.

Potassium Permanganate A small tube of this crystalline chemical has many uses, and is carried in military survival kits. If mixed with a glycol-based substance such as anti-freeze it can be used to light a fire. A small amount added to water will make a sterilizing mouthwash, and a more concentrated mixture can be used to treat fungal diseases.

Surgical Blades Two surgical blades take up little space and are best left in their protective sterile wrapping. In use they can either be held between the fingers, or a handle can be fashioned from a small stick. Do not discard used surgical blades; sterilize them by boiling, and re-wrap. When a blade is no longer viable for surgery it will still make an excellent arrowhead.

Salt Salt is essential when travelling in tropical climates. Carry a small amount to make sure that the salt balance in the body is maintained. Try to reserve this resource for medical uses only and refrain from using it for culinary purposes. Salt water is also helpful in treating fungal infections.

Suture Plasters If you are unable to administer stitches, butterfly sutures will prove successful in closing small wounds.

MEDICAL PRIORITIES

The first task for any survivors is to establish the priorities for treatment of the injured. Casualties are usually sorted into categories. Those who require urgent assistance to prevent immediate death – mainly those suffering from varying asphyxia disorders – must be given priority. Shock caused by major injuries and severe haemorrhaging must be assessed; after a major disaster many may be hopelessly injured and thus cannot qualify for immediate assistance. The task is to identify the injury and establish how long the casualty will live without assistance; and to decide if any assistance that can be given will prove beneficial.

Breathing

Check a casualty's breathing by placing your ear close to the nose and mouth and looking down over the chest and abdomen. If they are breathing you should be able to both feel and hear the flow of air, and to see chest and abdominal movement. If these signs of breathing are absent, immediate action must be taken.

First make sure that the airway is clear:
Tilt the casualty's head back gently while lifting the chin with the other hand. Doing this will automatically open the airway, and will also lift the tongue from the back of the throat so that it will not cause an obstruction. Supporting the head in the tilted position with a hand on the forehead, check inside the mouth for any object or substance which may be causing a blockage, e.g. dentures, vomit, etc. If any of these are present gently remove them, without touching the back of the throat, as this may cause a swelling of the throat tissues.

In many cases these actions alone may be enough to enable the casualty to breathe again. If this is the case, and they also have a pulse, then place them into the recovery position (see illustration on page 25) and maintain a periodic check on their condition.

Any visible injury to the front or back of the head may also indicate that the casualty has damaged his neck or spine. In such cases maintaining an open airway will still be a priority over their other injuries. However, it is recommended that a collar or head support be improvised in order to keep the head properly positioned.

Artificial respiration If the casualty is still not breathing, then extra steps must be taken to ensure that they get some oxygen into their body. This can be achieved through still beating by feeling the carotid pulse point in the neck. It is no use providing the patient with oxygen if their heart is unable to pump blood to the necessary

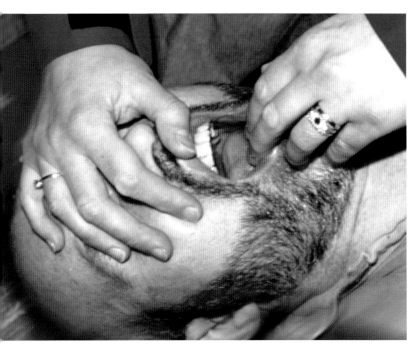

Check that the airway is clear.

mouth-to-mouth resuscitation, as the air we exhale still contains 75% of the oxygen we inhaled.

With the casualty's head still tilted back so that the airway is clear, pinch his nose to prevent air loss.

Breathe in deeply, and then seal your lips over the casualty's mouth. Gently blow into their mouth and watch for the chest to expand. It will take about two seconds for the chest to expand to its maximum capacity. Move your mouth away and wait for the chest to fall fully.

This should be repeated nine times before checking that the casualty's heart is

organs. If the heart has stopped, chest compressions (see below) must be administered.

In cases where mouth-to-mouth resuscitation is impossible or undesirable, e.g. when there is a serious lower jaw injury, mouth-to-nose ventilation may be carried out instead, but making sure that the mouth is firmly sealed first.

Artificial respiration should be carried out until the casualty is once more able to breathe unaided. Once the breathing rate is steady, place the casualty in the recovery position and monitor their condition every three minutes.

Chest Compression If the heart has stopped, it must be artificially pumped so that the oxygen carried by the blood can reach the vital organs. To do this a technique called chest compression is used.

Before beginning this procedure it is vital to make sure that a pulse is entirely absent. If the heart is still beating, however weakly, then chest compression will cause damage.

Place the casualty flat on

Mouth-to-mouth resuscitation.

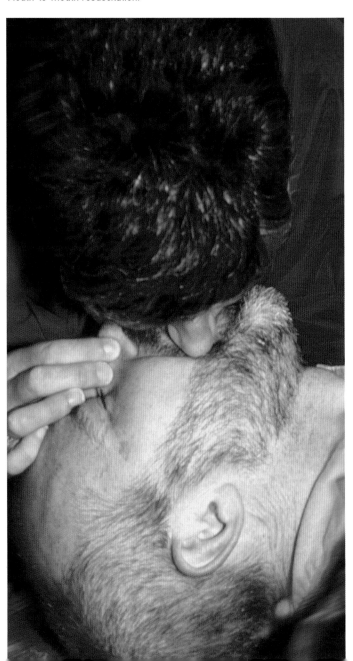

his back on a firm surface. Kneel beside him and locate the bottom of his breastbone – this is found where the bottom two ribs meet. Place the heel of one of your hands about three fingers' width up from this point; place your other hand on top of this, and interlock the fingers.

Lean forward over the casualty, making sure that your elbows are rigid and that your weight is pressing vertically on

LIFESAVER

The human body needs a constant supply of oxygen to function. If we stop breathing even for a few minutes the brain will start to sustain damage; the longer we go without air, the greater the damage. If casualties are unconscious, choking, or having trouble breathing, then they must be treated urgently.

In the case of an unconscious casualty, check for breathing and also for a pulse. If one or both are indetectable then emergency treatment must be given immediately. Urgent assistance must also be given to anyone who is choking or showing other obvious signs of breathing difficulties.

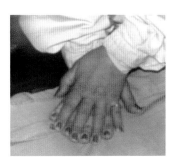

Chest compression.

Immediate First Aid Checks

• Check for breathing and pulse

• If no breathing, check if the airway needs clearing

• If still no breathing, begin mouth-to-mouth respiration

• After nine breaths, check carotid pulse for heartbeat

• If certain there is no heartbeat, begin chest compressions

• Check for a pulse every 15 compressions

• If alone and casualty displays neither breathing or pulse, alternate the treatments – two breaths, then 15 compressions, then two breaths, checking breathing and pulse at one minute intervals

the casualty's chest. The breastbone should be depressed by about 4-5cm (2 inches). Release the pressure by leaning back, but without removing your hands. Chest compressions should be repeated at a rate of about 80 per minute, pausing for a pulse check every 15 compressions.

Generally, if the heart has stopped then breathing will also have stopped. In order for the casualty to have a chance of survival both artificial ventilation and chest compressions will have to be performed at the same time. If you are on your own, the correct procedure is to first give the casualty two assisted breaths, followed by 15 chest compressions. Continue with this cycle for one minute before checking on heartbeat and breathing.

If neither are present, continue with the alternated breaths/chest compressions until either until the casualty's heartbeat is restored, help arrives, or you become too exhausted to continue.

Artificial respiration when there are two people available.

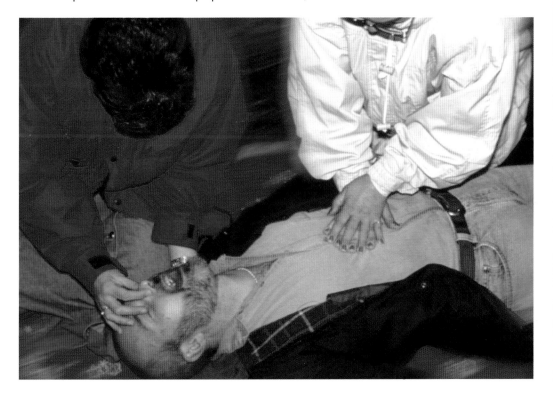

Many commercial survival medical kits contain a mouth-to-mouth recuscitation device. This is a one-way valve which prevents cross contamination.

Resuscitation by two people

If a second person is present and able to help, one should assist the casualty's breathing while the other manipulates the chest compressions. To begin with, four assisted breaths should be given followed by five chest compressions. Subsequently, the correct procedure is to give one assisted breath for every five chest compressions. There should be no pause between the end of the chest compressions and the beginning of the assisted breath.

After one minute check for pulse and breathing; if neither are present continue the alternating breath/compression cycle and check every three minutes. Continue until either heartbeat and breathing are re-established, help arrives, or both helpers become too exhausted to continue. If heartbeat and breathing do return, check for any other injuries and place the casualty in the recovery position.

Choking

Choking is a serious condition requiring immediate assistance, as the airway is blocked and therefore no air is getting through to the lungs. Choking can be recognized by the casualty suddenly being unable to breathe or speak, grabbing at their

If the casualty is conscious, try to get them to cough it up. If this does not work, make a visual check of the mouth to see if the object can be cleared with a finger. If not, bend the casualty as far forward as possible, preferably so that the head is below the level of the lungs. Give five sharp slaps between the shoulder blades with the heel of the hand, and check to see if the obstruction has been dislodged. This is

Aiding a casualty who is choking.

Attempt to remove any obstruction by slapping between the shoulder blades.

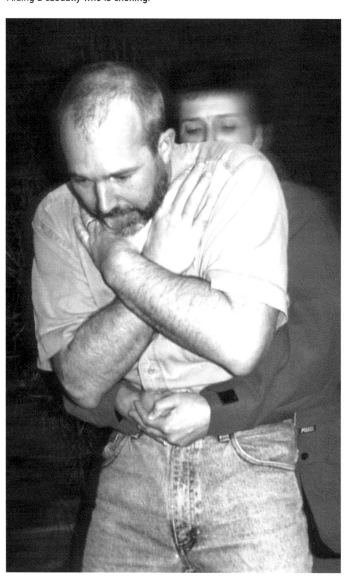

throat or their skin turning pale blue.

The first priority is to try to remove whatever is causing the blockage in the windpipe.

usually enough to remove the object, but if it does not work and choking continues you will have to try to clear it by using abdominal thrusts.

To do this, stand behind the casualty and put your arms around him. Ball one of your fists and lock it in place with the palm of your other hand, making sure that one thumb is pressing into the abdomen. Pull your hands sharply inwards under the casualty's ribs. Repeat up to four more times before checking whether the object has been expelled. If this does not succeed at first, give five more

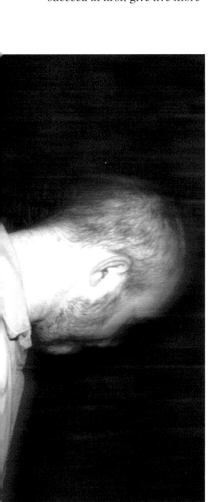

back slaps and then five more abdominal thrusts. Keep trying until the object becomes dislodged. It is very unusual for this procedure to fail.

Choking when unconscious If the choking casualty becomes unconscious, first lie him on his side with his abdomen supported against your knee, and give four to five back slaps. If this does not dislodge the object, turn the casualty onto his back, kneel astride him, and perform the abdominal thrusts described above.

To do this, locate the heel of one hand just below the ribcage and cover it with the other hand. Press sharply inwards and upwards with the heel of the hand, up to five times. Check in the mouth to see if the object has been expelled. Continue alternating back slaps with abdominal thrusts until the obstruction is removed. If the casualty begins to breathe normally, place him in the recovery position and check breathing and pulse rates every three minutes.

If breathing does not recommence and/or there is no pulse, start immediately with assisted breathing and, if necessary, chest compressions.

Self-help when choking If you find that you are alone and choking, find something like the back of a chair or a tree trunk, and push it inwards and upwards into your abdomen to expel the air and, hopefully, the blockage. You could also attempt to use your own hands made into a fist to achieve the same effect.

Expelling the air in your abdomen by coughing can release any blockage and stop choking.

The Recovery Position

An unconscious casualty with a regular heartbeat and who is breathing normally while showing no sign of serious injury should be placed in the recovery position. In this position the head is slightly lower than the body, thus preventing the tongue from blocking the airway and allowing any liquids such as blood or vomit to drain freely from the mouth.

Kneel to one side of the casualty and turn his head towards you. Straighten the nearest arm alongside the body, with the other folded across the chest. Cross the ankles and roll the casualty towards you. Gently bend the upper arm and leg so that they safely maintain the body in the position. Keep the head, neck and back in a straight line.

If the casualty has spinal injuries or wounds the position may have to be slightly modified. In such cases use improvised padding, such as towels or rolled clothing, for extra support.

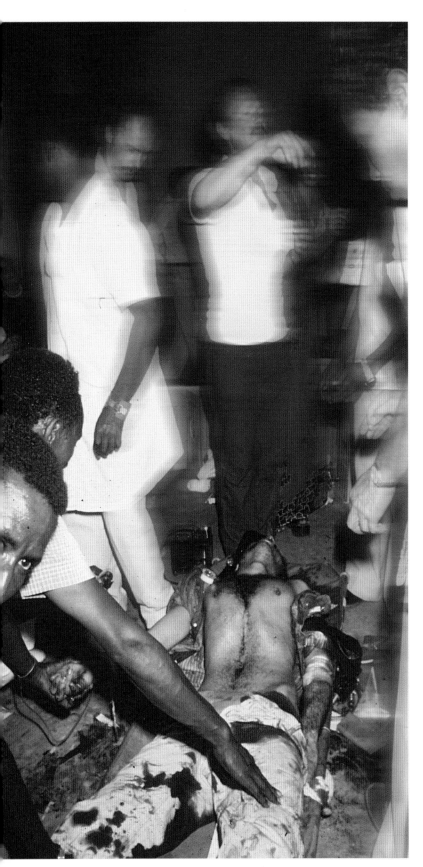

Excessive bleeding induces shock which can be fatal .

Bleeding

Once breathing and circulation are restored the next priority is bleeding. Bleeding may be external or internal.

Internal bleeding is almost impossible to treat with first aid, but external bleeding can be controlled.

Wounds present two main problems. Firstly, extensive bleeding can cause shock to develop, and will, if not controlled, lead to death. Secondly, any break in the skin will let infection in, so it is imperative that the wound site be kept as clean as possible. There are three procedures with which to stop the bleeding:

Direct Pressure Use a sterile dressing if you have one; if not, find a clean piece of cloth. Place the dressing on the wound and press on it gently but firmly. If you have no dressing available then you may have to use your hand, but bear in mind the dangers of infecting the wound. Use only dressings that are large enough to cover both the wound and part of the surrounding area. It is possible that the first dressing will become soaked through with blood. If this happens, lay a second dressing over the first and, if necessary, a third over the second.

By tying a bandage around the wound and dressings you will be able to keep the dressings in place with a continued firm pressure. It is important, however, that the bandage is not tied too tight, as this will restrict the flow of blood to the whole area.

Some large wounds will tend to gape. If you have suitable dressings you may use these to bring the edges of the wound together; otherwise you may have to use your hand. Blood flow from a large wound may be stopped by applying firm pressure, preferably with a pad of dressings, to the site of the greatest bleeding.

Using pressure on the wound helps the body's own mechanisms to slow down and finally to stop the bleeding. The damaged ends of blood vessels will shrink and start to retract in order to slow down the blood loss. Clotting agents are released so that the escaped blood eventually begins to thicken, and will eventually form a plug over the wound.

Sometimes these mechanisms will be enough to stop the bleeding on their own. However, the casualty may still be in danger of going into shock. It is therefore vital that they rest; and reassurance, too, is important – if the casualty is anxious it will only serve to raise his heart rate and blood pressure, which is not desirable. An injured limb should be elevated above the level of the heart, as long as it is comfortable for the casualty and not

Identify which type of bleedir

liable to make any other injury worse. This elevation not only reduces the flow of blood to the damaged area, but also helps the veins to drain blood away. This helps reduce blood loss through the wound. The elevated limb should be supported if possible, either by you or by padding.

Indirect Pressure If, due to the severity of the bleeding, the techniques described above do not work, then indirect pressure should be tried. However, this only works on arterial bleeding, so it is important to identify what type of bleed you are dealing with.

Arterial bleeding takes place from vessels which are carrying filtered and oxygenated blood away from the heart and lungs. It has no impurities and is therefore bright red. It will also spurt out of the wound in time with the heartbeat.

Venous bleeding takes place from vessels which are carrying blood full of impurities away from the tissues towards the heart and lungs to be filtered and re-oxygenated. As venous blood is low in oxygen it is dark red in colour. It runs steadily or gushes from a wound at a steady rate.

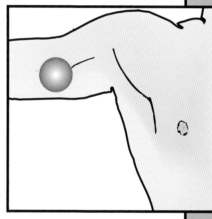

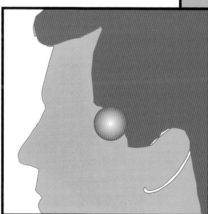

Applying direct pressure to stop bleeding.

Pressure Points

Indirect pressure works by using pressure points. These are found where an artery crosses a bone near the surface of the skin. For survival purposes it is best to concentrate on the four points which flow to each limb.

❶ The pressure points in the arm are found down the centre of the inner side of the upper arm, on the brachial arteries.

❷ The main pressure point in the leg is on the femoral artery, located down the inside of the thigh. The pressure point for this artery is in the middle of the groin. It is often easier to locate if the knee is bent so as to create the groin crease. Press firmly at this point against the bones of the pelvis.

❸ Locate the pressure point and, placing the thumb or fingers on it, apply enough pressure to flatten the artery against the bone. This should stop the blood flow.

❹ Pressure must not be kept on for any longer than ten minutes, or else other healthy tissue will be damaged through lack of blood. While using indirect pressure the wound may be dressed more effectively; however, do not use a tourniquet, as this may cause tissue damage.

ou are dealing with, arterial or venous, before deciding on your best course of action

Applying a Tourniquet

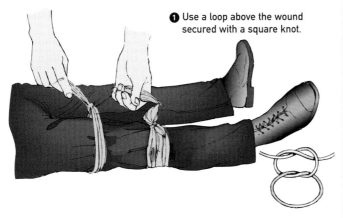

❶ Use a loop above the wound secured with a square knot.

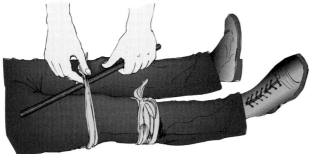

❷ Insert a strong stick or similar under the loop to act as a tightening device.

❸ Twist the stick, tightening sufficiently to stop bleeding.

❹ Secure the stick to prevent the tourniquet becoming loose.

Tourniquets The aim of first aid is to save life. If the damage to a limb is so severe that it plainly requires amputation, or if part of the limb is missing, and direct pressure will not stop the bleeding, then you may need to employ the third procedure by applying a tourniquet.

The tourniquet can be made from whatever cloth is at hand, but avoid any thin material that will cut into the flesh. Place it around the extremity, between the wound and the heart, 5 to 10cm (2-4ins) above the wound site.

Never place it directly over the wound or a fracture. Use a stick as a handle to tighten the tourniquet, but tighten it only enough to stop blood flow. Clean and bandage the wound.

The tourniquet must be slowly released every 10-15 minutes for a period of 1-2 minutes; however you should continue to apply direct pressure at all times. It must be stressed that applying a tourniquet to prevent blood flow is a dangerous procedure, and should only be attempted when all else has failed.

Fractures

Fractures normally occur during an accident in which a body has stumbled unrestrained or has been hit by a flying object. Not all fractures are readily apparent, but a casualty may have a bone fracture if he has difficulty in moving a particular part of the body normally. The reason for a fracture is fairly evident, and it is followed by a sharp increase in pain when movement of the affected part is attempted. Pronounced swelling, bruising, distortion and tenderness at the site of the injury are also good indicators of a fracture. An injured limb may look deformed or shortened, and a distinctive grating sound may be heard while attempting to move the limb. Signs of shock may be evident, especially if the injury is to the ribcage, pelvis or thighbone. The casualty may also have felt or heard the bone break.

In a survival situation the scope for treatment of a fracture is limited to immobilisation of the injured part.

Splints should be applied before the casualty is moved unless there is some form of imminent danger which requires immediate evacuation. If conscious, fracture casualties will be experiencing pain, so handle them with the greatest of care so as not to cause increased distress. If the fracture has also caused a wound, this must be treated and stabilised before any splints are fitted.

Splints Suitable splints can be improvised from small branches, sticks, or suitable pieces of equipment; rolled clothing or bedding can also be used in an emergency. Make sure that the splint is padded and that it supports the joints both above and below the fracture. In the case of a leg fracture, if no suitable substitute for a splint can be found in your environment then immobilise the injured leg by tying it to the good leg instead.

Sometimes a fractured limb may become twisted, shortened or bent in such a way that immobilisation proves impossible. Gentle traction to re-align the limb can be used as long as the casualty can tolerate the pain. Pull gently in a straight line with the bone until the limb has been straightened. If this is done properly the casualty may find that the pain and any bleeding at the site of the fracture are significantly reduced.

Once you have done all you can to straighten the limb, apply the splints. If possible, elevate and support the fractured limb as this will help to reduce both any swelling and the danger of the casualty going into shock.

Make sure that the casualty receives plenty of rest.

Fractures

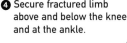

1 Complicated fracture where broken bone has damaged blood vessel.

2 Open fracture where bone is exposed.

3 Closed fracture where bone is not exposed.

4 Secure fractured limb above and below the knee and at the ankle.

5 Use plenty of padding with foot injuries. Elevate the foot to reduce swelling.

6 A splint to support a broken arm can be improvised using a rolled up newspaper or magazine. Never use metal to splint a limb in cold climate.

7 Imobilising a broken arm to speed healing and avoid further injury can be done with a large triangle of cloth. Pad the sling with rags or leaves to provide further protection.

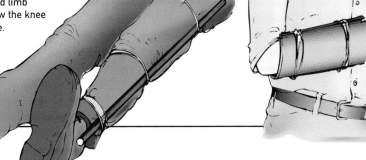

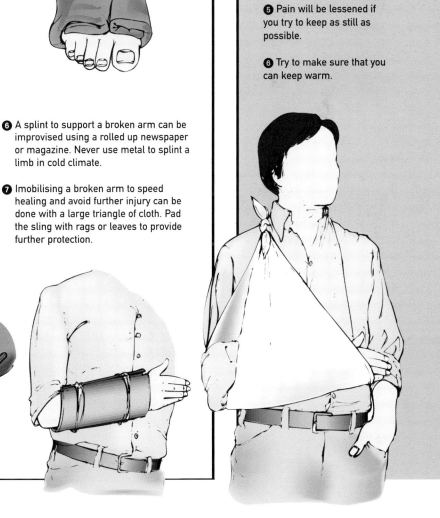

Self-Help

It is possible that you may become injured while you are on your own, and in this case it is sensible to have thought out a self-help routine:

1 Try to rest. Lie down somewhere, but preferably out of the wind.

2 Use direct pressure on your wound to control the bleeding. If possible apply a dressing, sterile or improvised.

3 If available, use a bandage to maintain pressure. Tie it firmly but not so tight as to restrict circulation.

4 If possible, elevate the injured part and support it.

5 Pain will be lessened if you try to keep as still as possible.

6 Try to make sure that you can keep warm.

Splints can be improvised with composite materials as well as single objects.

Open Wounds

Cleaning Open Wounds The purpose of washing a wound is to remove as much bacteria as possible, thus giving the body's own defensive system the best chance of finishing the job. All exposed wounds, no matter how small, need to be cleaned. This is best done with water which has been sterilized by boiling, but clean, pure drinking water will suffice if boiling is not possible.

Deeper wounds can be washed out more efficiently by making some form of irrigation device which will deliver a strong jet of water into the wound. A small plastic bottle or a polythene bag can be pierced with a pinhole so that the water jets out when it is squeezed.

Adding a very small amount of soap or potassium permanganate to the water will assist in flushing out the wound. The amount of potassium permanganate crystals added should be barely enough to tint a pint of water; similarly, only enough soap should be added to barely cloud the water. If in doubt, err on the side of weakness.

Debris and Foreign Bodies
Before starting any cleaning or irrigation, open the wound to its fullest extent and examine for debris – bits of clothing, glass, dirt, or any other foreign body which may have been forced into the wound at the time of injury. If these are small and not deeply impacted, remove them; if no properly sterile instruments are available, wash your hands with soap and water and use your fingers. (Instruments and wound dressings can be sterilized by boiling for five minutes.) Once the wound is open and foreign bodies have been removed, scrub it briskly while irrigating at the same time – this is a job best done by two people. Work quickly, as this will be very painful for the casualty. Once finished, apply a clean sterile dressing, and arrest any fresh bleeding by direct pressure. Check the wound on a daily basis.

Unless they are life-threatening, larger foreign bodies deeply impacted should be left in place, as pulling at them may cause more serious damage. Control the bleeding by direct pressure, squeezing the wound along the line of the foreign body. Next, form a padded ring which will fit neatly over the protruding object, and secure it with a dressing.

Sucking wounds If air is allowed to enter the lungs from puncture wounds to the chest or back then a sucking wound will develop. Always check for sucking wounds if missiles or debris of any form have penetrated deeply, or if a rib is protruding from the chest or back. The lung on the affected side will collapse, and as the casualty breaths in so the sucked air will also impair the efficiency of the good lung. If the condition goes untreated the result will be a lack of oxygen reaching the blood stream, which could cause asphyxia.

If a sucking wound is suspected, immediately cover the area with your hand. Support the casualty in a lop-sided sitting position with the functioning lung uppermost. Cover the wound with a clean dressing and place a plastic sheet over the top so that the plastic overlaps the dressing and wound; tape it down so as to form an airtight seal. If a foreign body is present in the wound, do not remove it, but pack with a ring as described above and fit an airtight seal.

LIFESAVER
No matter what your situation, if you intend to handle open wounds or burns – whether on yourself or other casualties – you should reduce the risk of further infection by sterilizing your hands. Wash them with water, snow, alcohol, or anything that will disinfect them.

Dislocations

Dislocations are caused when bone joints become separated and get out of alignment. This can be extremely painful, as the nerves and blood flow are affected. The best way to relieve this pain is to re-align the joint as quickly as possible. Although this is a simple process the joint will be swollen and extremely tender and the limb will suffer from a lack of mobility.

Dislocations are treated by reduction or 'setting' the bones back into their proper position. There are two basic methods available to the survivor, depending upon whether they are alone or not. In either case the appropriate action should be taken as quickly after the dislocation as possible. Both, if successful, will bring about a lessening of pain and restoration of the circulation. Once reduction is completed the limb should be immobilised, using splints if possible, and allowed to recover.

Use a well-padded splint above and below the injury site. Always check the circulation below the dislocation after completing the splint. Remove the splint after a week and start gentle exercises until the limb is fully functional.

Unassisted reduction The lone survivor will need to improvise some form of weight, e.g. a large rock or log, to which they can attach a cord from the limb. The idea is to stretch the limb slightly by countering against the weight, and aligning it back into place.

The procedure requires the body and/or limb to be rotated in order to set the joint while at the same time comparing it to the joint on the opposite side. All movement must be kept to a minimum, yet must be positive rather than hesitant.

The procedure should be performed lying down if possible, as it is extremely painful and the manoeuvre will require a great deal of will-power on the part of the survivor.

Assisted reduction The same basic procedure of stretching and re-aligning the limb is followed, but it has the advantage of being more often successful, since manipulation is usually more positive and precise when the casualty does not have to deliberately inflict pain on himself. Where possible one person should hold the casualty in a comfortable position while a second manipulates the limb into alignment. Again, this procedure is best done with the casualty lying down.

Concussion & Skull Fractures Skull fractures and concussion are also common after major accidents.

Concussion is a temporary disturbance of the brain, normally due to a severe blow or shaking. If conscious, the casualty should be made to lie down with their head and shoulders supported. If unconscious, make sure that they are breathing and have a pulse – if not, carry out artificial ventilation and chest compressions immediately.

If the casualty is unconscious but the breathing and pulse are normal, turn them into the recovery position and maintain a close check on their vital signs.

In either case, make sure that the casualty is kept warm and quiet and handled carefully. Apply a light padding to the injured area and hold it in place with a dressing. If blood is being discharged from an ear, lightly cover it but do not block it. Concussion is normally only a temporary disturbance from which the chances of recovery are good.

Using a weight to assist reduction of a dislocation when there is nobody else available to help.

A skull fracture or concussion must be suspected if any or all of the following symptoms are present:

❶ An obvious head wound, a bruise or a soft or depressed area on the scalp.

❷ Unconsciousness, even for a short period of time.

❸ Clear or watery blood coming from the ears or nose.

❹ Blood in the white of the eye.

❺ The pupils of the eyes are unequal or unresponsive.

❻ A steady deterioration in responsiveness to external stimuli.

Burns

Naked flames, boiling water, electrical devices, friction, acid, liquid oxygen, freezing metal and the sun all cause skin burns. The severity of the burn and the amount of body area affected will determine the casualty's survival chances.

Cooling Burns caused by naked flame should be cooled immediately to limit the damage caused by heat to the skin tissues. Either pour cold water slowly over the affected part, or immerse it totally in clean cold water.

This should continue for at least ten minutes to stop further tissue damage and to reduce pain and swelling.

Dressing Once the burn has been cooled, a dressing should be applied immediately to limit the possibility of it becoming infected. Do not attempt to remove any charred fibres that have stuck to the burn, but remove any restrictive clothing around the site to prevent further swelling. The dressing should be sterile and made of a non-fluffy material. Avoid adhesive dressings, which will only aggravate the injury and cause more damage.

In a survival situation sterilization of cloths, bandages and dressings can be achieved by scorching the cloth with a candle, as this will kill most bacteria. Do not be tempted to burst any burn blisters which form, as these provide a protective layer. A solution containing tannic acid derived from boiling oak or beech bark can be used to clean the burn; make sure that any such concoction has cooled before using it. If polythene bags are available they can be used to cover the burnt limb and help stop further infection.

To reduce the possibility of shock setting in, lay burn casualties down and keep them warm and comforted. If the casualty is unconscious, turn him over into the recovery position and monitor his breathing and pulse closely

Blistering is the body's natural protection and should be left intact.

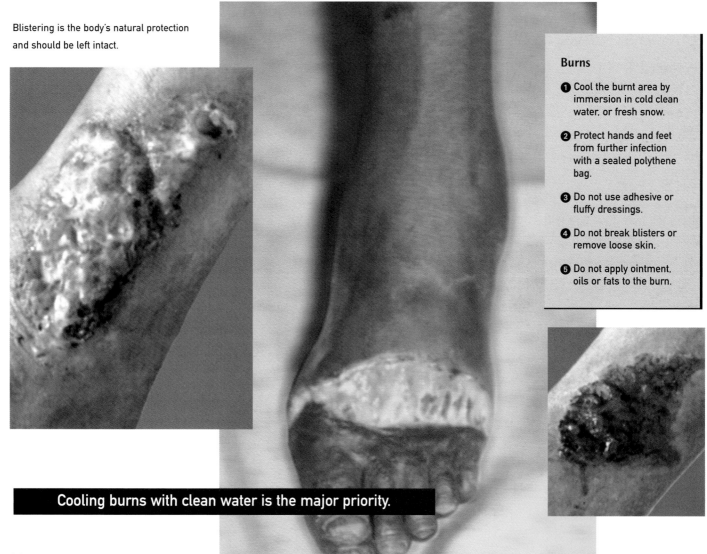

Cooling burns with clean water is the major priority.

Burns

❶ Cool the burnt area by immersion in cold clean water, or fresh snow.

❷ Protect hands and feet from further infection with a sealed polythene bag.

❸ Do not use adhesive or fluffy dressings.

❹ Do not break blisters or remove loose skin.

❺ Do not apply ointment, oils or fats to the burn.

SURVIVAL MEDICINE

After the immediate priorities for first aid have been identified and acted upon, survivors in remote and uninhabited regions will face the need to monitor and safeguard their health under challenging conditions, perhaps for a relatively long period.

In a survival situation it is obviously important to maintain health while awaiting rescue – and this is absolutely central to preserving the survivors' option to make an attempt at travelling across country themselves.

Personal Hygiene When ill, weakened or injured, the first priority is not medicine but a good standard of personal hygiene.

Proper hygiene, care in preparation of food and drink, waste disposal, insect and rodent control (and, of course, prior immunization) will greatly reduce the causes and number of diseases and infestations to which the survivor may fall victim. The importance of prevention of disease during any survival situation cannot be overstated, and physical hygiene is important if you wish to protect yourself.

If possible, wash daily with warm water and soap. A small amount of water can be used to sponge the face, armpits, crotch and feet at least once a day. Regular washing, especially after defecation, is a necessity no matter how bad you are feeling.

Eat as often as you can to keep up strength, but stick to simple, easily digested and nourishing foods – a vegetable soup is ideal. Make sure that your water is pure and that you wash food before cooking it. Raw food should be avoided as it is not only harder to digest in most cases, it is also a possible source of contamination. Make sure that your liquid intake is sufficient – water or a herbal tea is the best drink for a body in a weakened state. Although these points are common sense, they will aid the body to heal itself or to fight off an illness or infection.

Underclothing collects dirt and sweat, so keep it dry and clean, especially if you are unable to change it regularly. If clothing cannot be washed it should be shaken vigorously and exposed to the sun and air at least once a day. The sun is a useful agent against disease, as few bacteria or viruses can survive exposure to ultra violet light.

Wash sensitive areas at least once a day.

Infections cut survival chances – hygiene cuts infections

Keeping the teeth clean reduces the risk of serious stomach upsets.

Lice & Ticks Along with ticks, lice are also carriers of typhus, which is transmitted through their faeces.

Clothing should be checked regularly, and if any of these pests are discovered they should be removed either with a delousing powder if available, or by boiling, or by exposure to direct sunlight for a few hours. Louse bites should not be scratched, no matter how irritating, as this leaves the skin vulnerable to infection with typhus through the louse faeces. Instead, wash the skin with weak antiseptic or a strong soap.

When a tick bites into skin it embeds its head in the flesh. For this reason they should never be simply pulled off, as they may leave the head behind and this will cause an infection. Smothering their bodies in smoke, iodine, paraffin, petrol, etc will only make them vomit – thus, again, causing infection. The best way to remove a tick is to pinch the surrounding skin with tweezers, pulling the tick with the flesh. Apply thumb pressure to the small hole and it will stop bleeding and soon heal.

The juice from crushed nettles mixed 50/50 with fresh water can be used as a body wash which will reduce lice infestation. The same concoction also makes an excellent shampoo for keeping the hair free of head lice.

Hair Hair can attract lice, and is best kept short. It is easier if another member of the party does this, using any available scissors rather than a knife. During any long-term survival situation (more than one week) all members of the party should crop their hair. Do not discard any cut hair – it can be used as tinder in fire-making. Shaving should not be encouraged during cold weather survival as it leads to cracked skin.

Teeth Teeth can be cleaned with an improvised tooth-brush made by chewing the end of a stick to separate the fibres; use the stick only once, then discard it. Lye slurry, soap, sand and salt can be used instead of toothpaste. The inner strands of paracord or the fine fibres on the inside of tree bark can be used as dental floss. A mouth-wash can be made from salt water, or pine needle tea. Painful cavities can be filled with candle wax to help relieve the pain. A compound of fennel and mistletoe will also reduce toothache.

Feet Feet require constant maintenance; blisters or ingrown toenails can be extremely painful, and may prevent a survivor from walking. Foot blisters are usually caused by ill-fitting boots, poor quality socks or loose laces, combined with long periods of walking over rough, uneven ground.

Stop and treat small blisters immediately by covering them with surgical tape. A severe blister is often filled with fluid, and can be made more comfortable if the fluid is drained. Large blisters which look as if they are about to burst should be punctured with a sterilized needle and thread. Run the needle through the blister

So called 'second skin', found in many commercial survival packs and excellent for foot care.

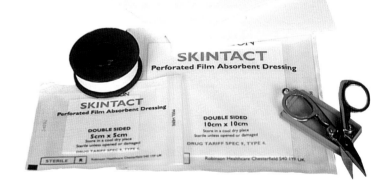

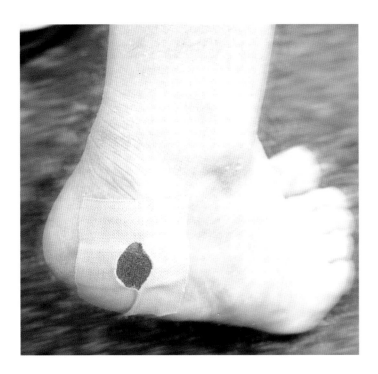

If you have to travel across country then how well you take care of your feet may be the factor which decides whether or not you survive.

Charcoal slurry for treatment of diarrhoea.

Diarrhoea

Charcoal powder can be purchased and added to your survival medical pack, or produced in the field when required. Small amounts can be taken dry, but it is best administered mixed with water into a slurry.

As with most foreign travellers, survivors will suffer from bouts of continuous diarrhoea. Although unpleasant they pose no threat to life, and the disorder is usually self-limiting. In the case of the survivor diarrhoea will normally develop as a result of consuming contaminated food or water, although malaria, cholera and salmonella produce similar symptoms.

Diarrhoea is detected when the number of daily bowel movements increases by a factor of two or more, the stools being soft and watery.

A small amount of charcoal slurry will settle the stomach, as charcoal absorbs toxins from the gut. Take charcoal from a cold fire, grind it to a powder and mix it with water. The thickness of the slurry is determined by its usage: for diarrhoea a light mix is required, about 10 grammes (0.35 ounce) of charcoal to a cup of water; for stomach poisoning the mixture should be 50 grammes per cup.

from side to side, then clip off the thread leaving a short length hanging out each side of the blister. This will ensure that the fluid drains without creating a large break in the skin. Make sure that the surrounding area is kept thoroughly clean and dry.

Ingrown toenails should be treated as soon as they become apparent. Without removing the nail the best method is to shave the top centre of the nail with a razor blade from your survival kit. Skim the middle third of the nail, shaving from the bed towards the nail tip. Place a thin piece of plastic under the nail to prevent accidentally cutting the toe. When the nail is thin enough it will buckle into a ridge and relieve the outward pressure. Removing the nail altogether should be avoided, as this will require a dressing and may prevent the patient from walking for several days.

Herbal Medicine

Herbal medicine has been practiced worldwide since before recorded history, and many modern medications are derived from refined herbs. Although many herbal medicines and ancient treatments are effective, they should only be used when medical supplies are not available. The subject of survival medicine would fill many volumes, but a few of the more popular methods and remedies are listed here. Most herbal medicines are mild in their effects and therefore quite slow-working, unlike today's powerful pharmaceutical drugs. They work with the body, encouraging its natural healing processes and strengthening the immune system. Most herbal remedies are safe to use, especially if the casualty is in a weakened physical state, and will not cause side effects. Any allergies to the herb will become apparent before any serious damage occurs. However, do bear in mind that not all plants will have a positive effect; some plants with medical properties, such as foxglove, should never be used by the medically untrained.

Herbal medicines do not need to be complicated mixtures of different plants. Often one plant substance alone will have the desired healing effect. Try using one plant on its own and for a matter of days to register its effects.

Use only one herbal remedy at a time to monitor its effectiveness.

Fluid loss

Fluids must be replaced using sterile (boiled) water mixed with a little salt. Check medical packs for any electrolyte powders. A juice made from potassium-rich fruit – such as apples and oranges – will help, as will honey if it can be found.

Safe Medicinal Plants

As with edible plants, medicinal plants should only be considered if they have first been positively identified.

It is vital to know how to use the plant correctly and for what ailments. If the plant has a medical reputation but is also poisonous, leave it alone. The smallest mistake in dosage could kill or irreversibly damage major organs in the body. Potency will also vary in a plant from one location to another, so a correct dosage of a poisonous plant is almost impossible to judge in its wild state. Plants that have an edible as well as a medicinal use are the best to use.

Making Medicines

Whether for internal or external use, clean fresh herbs and plants are required for medical purposes. Internal use will require the plant being prepared either by infusion, decoction, maceration or powdered. Infusion is simply a mater of pouring boiling water over the plant or plant parts and leaving them for around 5 minutes (a little linger if the plant is tough). Decoction means boiling the plants or plant parts in order to extract the most from the plant. Maceration means crushing the plants or plant parts and leaving them for several days in water. Powder is obtained drying the plant or plant parts followed by crushing and grinding. The powder can be used to form a brew by adding water or moistened and rolled into small tablet sized balls, the latter will be very strong. External use is either via a compress which has been soaked in a decoction or infusion and then applied to the wound, or a poultice made by crushing the plant or plant parts which are applied directly to the wound.

Giant Puff Balls can be used to treat weeping wounds.

Aloe Vera has a multitude of medicinal uses.

Aloe Vera This amazing plant can be used for a number of different ailments, from soothing bites, stings, and minor burns to calming fever. The gel-like juice is extracted by crushing, and can be used for external applications in its raw state. The gel can be partly sun-dried and thickened by continuous stirring, the resulting balm being used to heal most skin abrasions.

Fennel and Mistletoe To treat toothache, crush together an equal amount of fresh mistletoe leaves and fennel. Cover your finger with the juice and rub onto the gum around the affected tooth. This concoction was used in medieval times and is very effective.

Giant Puff Ball This large fungus should be cut into segments and rubbed into a powder. This can then be used on wet sores and weeping wounds. Cutting the ball into slices 3cm thick will produce a number of wound pads. Two hundred years ago puff balls were often harvested prior to battles purely for the purpose of field dressings.

Plantain Add fresh plantain leaves to the water when washing your clothes; this stops lice infestation.

Lining your grass bedding with the same leaves will also help keep ticks and lice at bay.

Willow Willow provides the means to make an effective pain relief. Cut out a large patch of willow bark, making sure that the white inner skin is attached. Remove this skin in strips and boil it in clean water for about an hour. Allow to cool before drinking. Putting more of the inner skin into the concoction or boiling for longer can increase the

Using crushed laurel leaves to soothe an itchy rash.

Dock leaves.

Remedies

• The bulbs of wild garlic can be crushed and used directly on a wound, or may be boiled to extract the oils and applied as an antiseptic.

• A handful of salt added to a litre of boiling water and allowed to cool will produce a solution that will kill bacteria.

• Sphagnum moss is a natural source of iodine, and makes a useful dressing. It is found in bogs all over the world.

• Remove the paper and tip from a cigarette and chew the tobacco until your mouth has produced enough saliva to allow swallowing. The ingested nicotine will kill most stomach worms. Repeat the process for several days until the infestation has stopped.

• The addition of hot peppers to your food diet will create a parasite-free digestive system.

Wild garlic.

strength. The stronger the brew, the less you need to take. The process involves trial and error, but this is an extremely effective remedy.

Garlic All members of the garlic family such as garlic mustard, chives, leeks and hedge garlic etc, can be used to treat a wide variety of ailments. As a general rule of thumb all those plants that smell of garlic when the root is crushed are part of the same family and safe to eat. (if unsure carry out the edibility test) Garlic contains an antibiotic called allicine together with concentrates of vitamins A,B and B2. Eating garlic will help protect you against food poisoning, amoebic dysentery and typhoid. The plant root bulbs should be cleaned and the first layer of skin removed, thereafter they can be eaten raw of used to flavour soups and stews. Garlic is one of the few plants that can be consumed in large quantities without and side effects. The most common found is mustard garlic, the whole plant can be eaten.

Remedies

Antiseptics Wounds may become infected quite easily, but luckily there are certain plants which have natural antiseptic properties. If you have time, take the plant material and make an infusion with which the wound can be washed. In an emergency the same plant material can be chewed to make a pulp which can be applied to the affected area. Examples of some plants which may be used in this way are: selfheal (prunella vulgaris); greater plantain (plantago major); birch (betula pendula); dried burdock (arctium lappa), and thyme (thymus vulgaris).

Bites & Stings Apart from being irritating insect bites, in particular, can leave the skin open to infection. Some insects are also the carriers of dangerous and debilitating diseases and parasites. It is important to be aware of the dangers and to take advantage of the several lines of defence that are available.

Bee, wasp, hornet, spider and scorpion stings should be removed if visible and the wound dressed with a cold compress of mud. Slow-burning, smoky fires will drive insects away; it is best to light one on the windward side of camp. A ring of ash around your sleeping area or camp site to deter most crawling insects.

The pain of stings from plants such as nettles can be reduced by rubbing them with a fresh dock or burdock leaf.

Treatment with Maggots

There has been much speculation about the use of maggots in wound treatment. They do have a value; however, they can be a double-edged weapon, and their use must be carefully monitored. They should only be applied when antibiotics are not available. Despite the hazards involved, maggot therapy should be considered if a wound becomes severely infected and ordinary debridement of rotting tissue is impossible.

❶ Remove any bandages to expose the wound to flies, which will deposit their eggs on the rotting flesh.
Warning: The flies are also likely to introduce bacteria into a wound, causing additional complications. Limit the number of flies accessing the wound – one exposure should ensure enough maggots. Live or hatching maggots will naturally find their way into the wound, at which stage the wound should be covered with a clean dressing.

❷ The dressing should be removed daily to check for maggots; if none are found within three days expose the wound to the flies once more. If there are too many maggots, remove the surplus with a sterilized instrument, leaving no more than a hundred in the wound.

❸ Monitor maggot activity very closely each day. The maggots produce a frothy red fluid which must be sponged away with a sterile cloth in order to keep track of the maggots' progress. The time taken by the maggots to clean the putrefying tissue from the wound will depend on several factors: the nature and depth of the wound, the number of maggots present, and the type of fly which layed the eggs.

❹ Many people believe that maggots will only feed on dead tissue, but this is not the case – they also eat living tissue if nothing else is available. Maggots eat at an alarming rate, so the wound should be checked on a regular basis or whenever the patient feels any sharp increase in pain; this, and any fresh blood flow, are good indicators that the maggots have eaten all the dead tissue and have started to invade healthy flesh.

❺ At this stage all the maggots should be removed by flushing the wound with sterile water or fresh urine; it should then be carefully sponged dry. The wound should be left open, and checked every few hours to ensure that it is completely free of maggots. Once all of the maggots have been removed, bandage the wound and treat as normal.

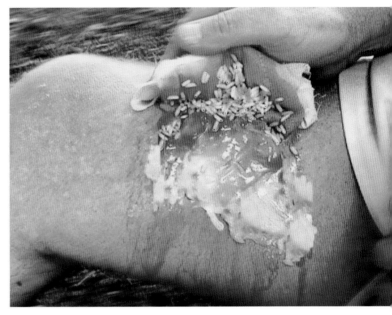

Maggot activity should be monitored closely.

Coagulants The body has remarkable powers to stop bleeding on its own; however, there are also plants which can assist or speed up the process. As they are rarely around when you most need them, it is a good idea to collect them whenever you come across them, dry, powder, and store them against need. Useful herbs to stop bleeding include bistort (polygonum bistorta), yarrow (achillea millefolium), shepherd's purse (capsella bursa-pastoris), horsetail (equisetum orvense), and marigold (calendula officinalis).

Digestive Disorders The most common digestive disorder that a survivor may encounter is diarrhoea (see box on page 35). Fortunately there are many plants which have astringent properties helpful in easing this condition. Remember that any diarrhoea or vomiting will also deplete the body's fluid levels, so it is important that any fluid loss should be replaced. A simple infusion of the following herbs will replace fluid and administer medicine at the same time: blackberry leaves (rubus fructicosus); strawberry leaves (fragaria vesica); dog rose petals (rosa canina), and bistort (polygonum bistorta). Bistort root is especially recommended for severe cases of diarrhoea, such as in dysentery. Upset stomachs can be calmed by infusions of meadowsweet (filipendula ulmaria) or peppermint (mentha piperita).

Headaches Survivors often suffer from headaches, especially during the first few days of their ordeal. A good remedy is to drink a soothing mint tea while applying crushed mint leaves to the forehead and temples.

Other effective teas can be made from rose hips and/or petals, and feverfew (chrysanthemum partenium).

Mosquitoes As mosquitoes breed in stagnant, sluggish water or swampy ground you would be well advised to avoid camping near any of these, aiming for higher ground where possible. They bite mainly during the late evening and night – although those which carry dengue fever also bite in the daytime. Use any available insect repellent. Make sure that exposed skin is covered as much as possible; tuck trouser legs into socks and sleeves into gloves. Cover your body with mosquito netting, parachute material, handkerchiefs, or anything else that you can improvise. Smearing mud over any exposed areas of skin will reduce the number of bites that you will suffer.

Poisoning If you are forced to live on wild plants your chances of being poisoned are greatly increased.

The danger can be averted by eating only those plants or fungi which are easily recognizable. If poisoning is suspected, the patient must be made to vomit. A glass of water mixed with salt followed rapidly by gagging should produce the desired result. Use you fingers or a smooth cold instrument such as a spoon handle to stimulate the throat. After vomiting is completed give the patient a drink of charcoal slurry, which should help absorb any remaining poison.

Stings from Sea Creatures. Sea creatures can leave a painful stings which, in some

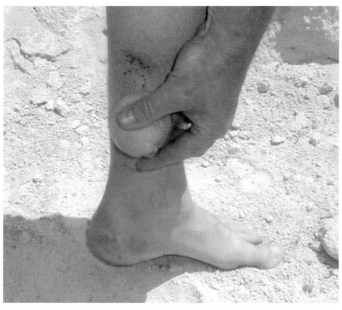

Stings from sea creatures such as jellyfish and stingrays can be remedied with a mild acid such as lemon juice.

cases can be fatal, but are generally they are short lived.

Stings from sea creatures such as jellyfish, stingrays, weaver, lion and zebra fish can be extremely painful, while those of the Portuguese man-o-war can also bring on paralysis and breathing problems. If any sea creature stings you, try to isolate the venom by placing a tourniquet between the wound and the heart. Don't worry about time the tourniquet is applied as the venom is short lived and it can be released after ten minutes. Use hot water on and around the wound area as this will help neutralise the venom, as will any form of mild acid such as lemon juice or vinegar. Use tweezers to remove any tentacles or spines visible in the flesh, do not touch with bare hands. Those patients who are having trouble breathing

or who are unconscious due to a sting should be given mouth to mouth resuscitation and cardiac massage for a period of at least fifteen minutes as the venom is short lived.

Rashes Avoid scratching any rash. As a basic rule of thumb, dry rashes should be kept damp and wet rashes kept dry. A dry rash is best covered with a clean cloth compress that has been boiled in a concentrate of tannin or aloe vera. A small rendering of boiled animal fat and crushed charcoal rubbed into a dry rash will help prevent the skin cracking and promote healing. Fungal infections are best exposed to direct sunlight whenever possible, and should be kept dry. All skin rashes that become infected should be treated as open wounds and dressed accordingly.

Survival Soap

Good hygiene prevents disease and illness, and is never more important than in a survival situation. Survival soap is easy to make and will help clean wounds and wash clothes.

❶ Melt animal fat by cooking it in water while constantly stirring. Drain off the grease into a flat tray to harden (a metal wheel hub is ideal).

❷ Take a clean sock or shirt sleeve and fill it with cold, crushed ash from the fire; soak the whole sock in water, and hang it up so that the water and charcoal drip out – this liquid is potash or lye.

❸ Remelt the grease and add the lye, mixing two parts grease to one part lye. Boil the mixture until it thickens to the consistency of porridge, then allow it to cool.

❹ It can be used in its liquid form, but is best left to go solid and cut into blocks.

MALARIA AND RABIES – WORLDWIDE KILLERS

Malaria

Malaria is the world's most widespread disease; 300-500 million people are infected, and 1.5-2.7 million die of it each year. The vast majority of cases occur in the Third World, particularly in sub-Saharan Africa but also in Central and South America and all over Asia. Isolated cases occur in advanced countries, particularly in the vicinity of airports, carried by travellers returning from danger areas.

If sensible precautions are taken it is very rare for Europeans and North Americans to die of the common strain Plasmodium vivax, although cerebral malaria (Plasmodium falciparum) can kill within 24 hours through obstruction of the blood vessels in the brain.

The parasites which cause malaria are transmitted by the bite of female anopheline mosquitoes. The parasites migrate to the victim's liver, where they multiply. After nine to 16 days they return to the bloodstream, breaking down the red cells and causing anaemia.

The Malaria Virus

❶ The Anopheles mosquito transmits sporozoites to the liver.

❷ The virus multiplies and re-enters the bloodstream

❸ It is then caried in the mosquito's gut to infect further victims.

At this point the outward symptoms appear: fever and chills, headaches, and joint pain. These symptoms may be mistaken for flu, food poisoning, or even jet lag. In danger regions, always assume that fever means malaria unless you have good reason to think otherwise. Untreated, Plasmodium vivax can lie dormant in the liver for many years, causing recurrent bouts of illness.

Treatment

For many years the drug chloroquine was an effective preventative; this is now true only in some areas of Central America, the Caribbean, North Africa and the Middle East.

Elsewhere malaria has evolved resistance to it, and other drugs (e.g. mefloquine, doxycycline, etc) will be needed. These are claimed to be about 97% effective, but resistance is growing all the time; for instance, in northern Thailand along the Burmese border there is already a strain of malaria which is wholly resistant to all known curative drugs. Elsewhere, which drug is effective depends on local circumstances; it is important to take medical advice on the right drugs for your emergency kit before travelling to a particular area.

Rabies

Rabies is a viral infection of the central nervous system, contracted from the saliva of infected animals – most commonly, dogs, cats, jackals, foxes, wolves, racoons, skunks, mongooses, bats, etc. Much less commonly, it can be transmitted by scratches (if an infected animal has been licking its claws); and by licking on broken skin or mucous membranes (e.g. the mouth, eyelids, etc). In very rare cases it has been contracted by respiration when in bat-infested caves. The virus travels from the puncture to the brain, and thence down the nerves to many different organs.

Dog rabies is quite common in Central America, India, Nepal, Sri Lanka, Vietnam and Thailand; it is also found throughout South America, Africa, and the rest of Asia, and is not unknown in southern Europe. Assume any bite suffered from a warm-blooded animal in the Third World is dangerous, even if the animal had no obvious symptoms (classically, drooling at the mouth coupled with agitated body movement and noises, and unprovoked agression or over-friendlyness).

In humans the symptoms are fever, headache, sore throat, nausea, loss of appetite, followed by pain or numbness at the infection site, skin sensitivity to temperature changes, depression and insomnia. As the virus attacks the central nervous system extreme pain is suffered when swallowing, leading to 'foaming at the mouth' through inability to swallow saliva, and terror at the sight of water (hydrophobia). Dementia or paralysis follow, and sometimes coma, always leading to death.

The great danger lies in the long incubation period between infection and the appearance of symptoms – this can vary from five days to more than a year in some cases, the average being two months.

Once symptoms appear in the infected human there is no cure, and a very distressing death is inevitable. It is therefore vital to take strict precautions before and after suspected exposure.

Treatment

Pre-exposure vaccines are available, but immunization must be planned well ahead. A course of three injections is given over 28 days; these can be intradermal or intramuscular. The former causes less discomfort, but does not give effective protection until 30 days after the final dose. **Its effect may also be impaired if you are taking antimalarial drugs.** Some individuals may be allergic to compounds in one or other of the three types of vaccine (RVA, HDCV and PCEC). For all these reasons, get qualified medical advice in good time.

If caught soon enough, rabies is curable during the incubation period, so treatment should always be sought even if some time has passed since the bite. Treatment will be in the form of a series of intramuscular injections, which are often given into the stomach wall. They can be painful, but are infinitely less so than death from rabies.

If in doubt whether an animal which has bitten you is rabid, there may be some circumstances in which you can capture it and watch it to see if it develops (further) symptoms; handle it with extreme care to avoid further infection. A rabid animal will normally become obviously sick within about three days of inflicting an infectious bite. If you are far from any realistic hope of post-exposure treatment, it will at least reassure you if the animal does not develop symptoms. If treatment may become available, cut off the animal's head and pack it carefully – its salivary glands can be tested when you reach help.

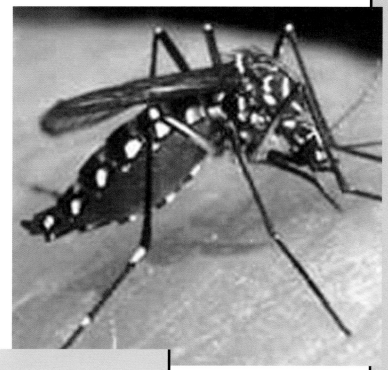

LIFESAVER
Rabies
Although it is vital to seek proper treatment as soon as possible, the virus is unstable, and in many cases it can even be washed out of a wound immediately with copious amounts of soap and water.

Malaria Danger Areas

• 90% of malaria cases occur in sub-Saharan Africa.

• 6% occur in Brazil, Colombia, India, Sri Lanka, Vietnam, Thailand, and the Solomon Islands.

• Malaria also occurs in the southern republics of the former USSR.

• Malaria is not confined to rural areas; travellers to major cities should take full precautions.

Protecting Yourself Against Malaria

• Before travelling to danger areas, check which antimalarial drugs are recommended for specific destinations, on the web site of the Centers for Disease Control at www.cdc.gov/travel.

• Seek medical advice on your intinerary; you may need several different antimalarial drugs.

• Take the drugs regularly throughout your trip.

• Follow all the advice in this book on avoiding mosquito bites: use repellents, smoke, etc; cover your skin; avoid stagnant water particularly after dark.

• Most antimalarial drugs should also be taken for four weeks after you leave a danger area. Obey the instructions.

• If symptoms strike after you leave the area – fatigue, weakness, light-headedness, fever, chills, nausea – get immediate medical help. Tell your doctor where you have been travelling.

SHELTER

Once you have assessed your situation, you must judge the urgency of your need to make or find a shelter. This need will be particularly urgent in both hot and cold climates. The weather conditions that pose the greatest threat to survival are cold, wind, rain, snow, and excessive exposure to the sun. Apart from the last, all these factors can lead to the rapid development of hypothermia – which can kill long before the effects of any lack of food or water. The need for protection against such conditions is therefore paramount.

Hot climates can also pose a danger to the survivor without a shelter, as too much exposure to the sun can cause overheating of the body and a loss of body fluids leading to severe dehydration, sunburn and sunstroke. Although the effects of heat upon the body are slower to inflict damage except in extreme desert conditions, without adequate protection they can still cause death.

Shelter Location

If you have a tent or commercially produced shelter then this should be used in preference to building a makeshift structure. If you do not have a tent, check whether the natural features in your surroundings might provide temporary shelter. Do not waste time and energy in building a shelter or windbreak if naturally occurring protection can be found nearby. Look at the possibilities afforded by trees, bushes or natural hollows. Caves and rock overhangs will also give shelter – but check for signs of dangerous rock falls from above.

The type of shelter you build, and where it is sited, will depend very much upon the terrain, climate and your personal situation. Nevertheless, there are general guidelines which can be applied in any situation, and these should be carefully considered before you start to construct your shelter:

If there is no natural cover and you have to construct one from scratch, build it so that its entrance or open side is on the leeward side (i.e. facing away from the wind). A shelter on a hillside may be warmer than one on a valley floor, where colder air tends to sink; but a hillside location may also prove too exposed. The ideal shelter should be built close to a source of firewood and building materials in a wooded area, near a fast-flowing stream which contains fish.

Building Materials

Foliage Foliage, particularly if it is large-leafed, will make an excellent waterproof covering for a shelter, and should prove quite durable. Branches, bark, large-leafed plants, straw, moss and grass can all be used as a covering, while thin trees and saplings make excellent frameworks.

Turf Trees and shrubs may be in short supply in some areas, e.g. flat, open grassland. In such a site turf can be used to construct shelters and to roof

Foliage is a versatile building material, providing both cover and good insulation.

Turf rolls and bricks are damp, but they keep out wind and rain.

In the absence of vegetation rocks and stones were used to build shelters by pre-historic man.

them over. The local populations of many countries use turf as a roofing material, and 'sod houses' partly dug into earth slopes provided homes for many early settlers on the North American plains.

Rocks and Stones Rocks and stones provide very acceptable building material in places where the ground is too hard to dig or where a more permanent shelter is required. In many desert areas where there are few trees or shrubs, piled rocks provide the obvious means to make a quick shelter.

Snow, Sand and Mud Snow blocks can be cut and formed into a number of different shelters (see Arctic Survival); and although not so easy to use, sand can also provide protection. Mud, when mixed with dry grass, straw and/or animal droppings, can be

Any type of forest area will provide the material to make a good shelter.

formed into practical sun-dried building bricks . Mud can also be used to fill cracks, insulate and prevent drafts.

Sheeting Plastic or canvas sheeting of any kind can be used in the construction of a shelter – ground sheets, parachutes, plastic sacks, jute sacking, tarpaulins and blankets can all be used in some way. Wreckage from

vehicles and aircraft can all be put to use providing excellent weatherproof shelter.

Dangerous Shelter Sites

Always check shelter sites for possible dangers:

• Shelters too close to low-lying water may be in danger of sudden flooding.

• Coastal sites may be in danger from high tides or storms.

• An area of fallen trees in a forest may indicate shallow soil: in high wind falling trees could crush you.

• In mountainous areas, beware mud slides, rock falls and avalanches; check for visible evidence of previous slides.

• Outside Europe, do not camp too close to established animal trails.

The ideal site will provide protection from the elements and safety from other natural features.

Tree-line Areas

Forested areas provide many opportunities to make a shelter. Fallen logs offer the means to fashion an especially simple type. Move two fallen logs until they are close to one another and parallel; then dig a trough between them. Roof the area between the tops of the logs with branches and foliage. If there is only one log to hand, a low earth wall can always be thrown up to provide the second side of the shelter, or else it could be used as the basis for a small lean-to.

Lean-to The lean-to pattern of shelter is the most commonly built, and one of the simplest to construct.

The only important thing to remember is to build it so that the roof slopes down into the prevailing wind. The frame itself could be covered by any material that is available – plastic sheeting, foliage, a groundsheet, wreckage panels, etc. Turf blocks or layer of firm, dried mud on top of foliage provides an excellent cover – it is both waterproof and windproof, and will not blow away. Once the roof has been established, the sides can also be filled in using a similar mud, foliage or turf fabrication.
Construction time: 1 hour.

If you have a good supply of cord in your equipment, you could consider building a variation on this basic lean-to. This version is especially suited to areas with short, shrubby vegetation. First, cut four or five very long, pliable stakes, and push their ends into the ground in a circular pattern so that they will stand firm.

Bend the tops inwards at an angle of 45 degrees, and tie them together. If there are any suitable saplings growing in the immediate area, consider saving yourself some time and energy by incorporating them into the design as they stand – they will also give much more strength and stability to the shelter.

Once the basic framework is in place, weave twigs, branches and foliage between the struts to form a rigid structure. Add more foliage until it is totally covered, and finally complete the roof with a layer of firm mud or light turf.
Construction time: 1 hour 30 minutes.

Quick Tree Shelter Any small tree can form the basis of a quick and simple shelter. After selecting the tree, cut or saw part way through the trunk at about shoulder-height. Once you have cut most of the way through, push on the upper portion so that it falls and

A quick tree shelter can be fashioned in half an hour by anyone with the means to cut through a thin treetrunk.

rests on the ground while still being supported by the intact part of the trunk. Break the up-standing branches on the outside of the trunk so that they hang down and form the sides of the shelter. Cut out the branches from the underside to make room for you to get underneath, and weave them into the shelter's structure.
Construction time: 30 minutes.

Turf Shelter 1 If trees are in short supply or entirely absent and you are on grassland, it is still possible to build a shelter from cut turf bricks. Once the sides are built to the desired height try to find material to make 'rafters' to support a turf roofing layer; small sticks or boughs are ideal for this if any are available.

Otherwise, use any sheet material that you have in your equipment, anchoring it at the sides with turf blocks.

If none of these are available, make the shelter small and narrow enough to roof it over with long turf strips; use them in pairs so that they support each other. Whatever roofing method you use, try to give the roof a pitch of anything up to a 45-degree angle so that rain will run off it better.
Construction time: 1 to 2 hours.

Turf Shelter 2 Soft ground (but not wet) will provide the

Utilise fallen trees and natural shelter hollows.

A one-pole tepee. If you are carrying some form of sheeting the simplest form of shelter can be constructed, ensuring a dry night's sleep.

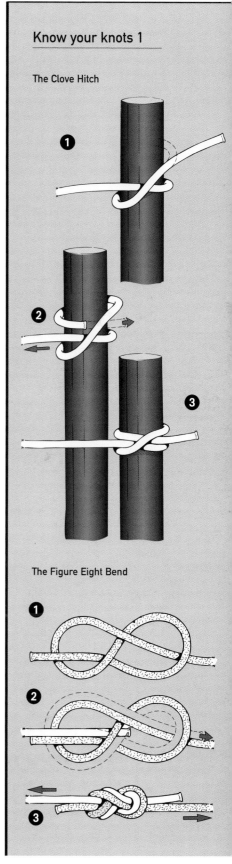

Know your knots 1

The Clove Hitch

The Figure Eight Bend

Turf Shelters

1 Turf shelter built with two walls of blocks of different heights, to provide the roof with a run-off slope.

2 Even simpler shelter made from single wall of turf blocks and a lower earth wall.

A shelter frame ready for thatching can be made even when long poles are scarce.

opportunity for a slight variation on the design of the above shelter. Build the wall up along the edge of the slit trench produced by the digging or cutting of the turf pieces. This not only saves effort by combining the digging and the building, but will also increase the height of your windbreak. If you do decide to adopt this method, ensure that the slope of the land and the shelter will drain rain water away from the trench and not into it. Underground shelters are also preferable in hot conditions, as they provide a cool space.

Construction time: 1 hour.

Parachute Tent A parachute, if you are lucky enough to have one, will be a valuable asset in building a shelter, as it can easily be made into a bell tent. First, the paracord rigging lines should to be removed; keep the cord, which is extremely valuable in a survival situation. Take hold of the centre of the parachute and tie a long length of cord to it. At the other end of the cord tie a heavy stone or log, and throw it over a suitable tree branch. Pull on the cord to raise the parachute to its full height, and then secure it to the trunk of the tree. Then

Parachute tent.

spread out the skirt of the parachute into a circle, and peg it into the ground. This should provide you with a shelter that is windproof and rainproof (as long as the material is not touched); however, the fabric is not robust enough to keep out very heavy rain.

Construction time: 20 minutes.

Tepee If desired, the parachute can be used to form the covering of a more traditional tepee. This will require a minimum of five thin poles which are at least 4 metres in length. Lay the poles side by side on the ground and lash them together at one end. Drape the parachute over the poles, passing the hole in the apex over the lashed-together pole tips and tying it securely to them. Get underneath the canopy and lift all the poles together until they are standing vertical. Splay the poles out in a circle until it becomes self-supporting.

Gather the surplus material at the skirt of the parachute and fold it up around the legs until you have formed a tepee. Cut a 'door' into the lee side of the tent in such a way that it can be fastened closed if necessary.

Secure the parachute skirt with stones to prevent drafts. (This type of shelter is ideal for the use of a Yukon Stove – see page 159).

Construction time: 1 hour.

Snow used to anchor the edges of a shelter

A well prepared and organised camp can provide comfort for a long period.

Foliage used to provide additional insulation to a shelter.

Long Term Camp Routine

Long term camp routine implies that you will be permanently in one place for an unspecified length of time. To alleviate boredom and maintain a sense of personal discipline and hygiene certain routines need to be established, both for the individual and any group of survivors.

• In order to improve your existence you must become a scavenger and improviser. The world is full of rubbish discarded by thousands of travellers. From the inner forests of the Amazonian basin to the peaks of the Himalayas, and even in the vast wilderness of the polar regions, you will find the pollution of discarded man-made artefacts. To the survivor all this rubbish has a value.

• Long term camps sites can easily become contaminated with urine and faeces, and a strict routine should be organised as soon as your shelter and fire are finished. Dig toilet holes until a more permanent structure can be built. Collect your water upstream, and locate your washing point at least 50 metres downstream.

• Organise your day around the priorities of rescue, health and survival:

• Check your signal fires and markers, and always have your heliograph and signal flare with you at all times – Sod's Law dictates that you will be out of camp when the search aircraft flies over.

• Establish a disciplined pattern of working to prevent boredom and the consequent drop in morale. Get up early; make a warm drink; check your traps; collect firewood; make something useful.

Finding and Making Cord All survival kits should include a length of parachute cord; but many survival situations will also reveal several ways in which cordage can be produced. Parachutes contain at least 100 metres of excellent cord, from which the thin, inner strands can be extracted. Electric cable and control lines are also a valuable source of material for making lashings. Many military combat belts are made up of a series of strong cotton strips, and the material can be unravelled to make cordage.

Natural materials such as animal sinew and gut make ideal cordage. These are best dried and separated into the required thickness. Wetting them before use will allow for easy manipulation, while their hardening when dry will hold any knot firmly in place. The bark of some trees can be used, either in its natural state or split into stringy fibres.

Making cordage – this is a central necessity for most survival tasks, from mending clothing and shoes to constructing packs, traps, tools and shelters.

Knots Knots and lashing are best kept simple, and require little or no explanation. If the survivor is unable to tie a secure knot then his chances of survival are fairly limited. It should also be remembered that any knot or lashing is only as strong as the material used in its construction. Knots and ropes are used in climbing, shelter construction, and a whole host of survival applications. A knot can join one or more ropes together, either permanently or for quick release depending on the requirement.

Utensils

Billy Can A 'billy can' is perhaps the most important utensil for the survivor – a container which can be used to collect water and plants, and also for cooking. Any metal container, such as a commercial-sized baked bean can, makes one of the best,

with a wire handle attached for carrying.

Bamboo Bamboo has many uses, as jungle tribes have discovered over millenia. It can be used to make rafts, construct homes, build traps, and – because of its sectional nature – to make carrying, cooking and eating utensils.

Birch Bark Containers Containers made from birch or cherry bark will not burn through when heated over a moderate fire, provided that you fill them with sufficient water. Cooking on a fire of glowing embers produces a much better meal and extends the life of the bark container. Shoes can also be produced from such bark.

Eating Utensils If you have a penknife, you can construct a simple spoon from a flat piece of wood. Mugs can be made from a section

Birch bark makes waterproof containers which can even be used for cooking.

After a knife, a billy can of some sort is probably the most constantly used item in a survival situation.

Improvised Tools

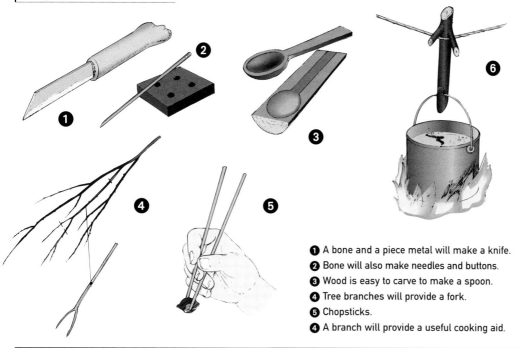

❶ A bone and a piece metal will make a knife.
❷ Bone will also make needles and buttons.
❸ Wood is easy to carve to make a spoon.
❹ Tree branches will provide a fork.
❺ Chopsticks.
❹ A branch will provide a useful cooking aid.

Spoons, awls, forks, pothooks, and other camping utensils can all be carved or fashioned from natural materials with a little imagination and patience.

A tyre doing service as a latrine seat.

of bamboo, a carved-out piece of wood, or a folded piece of birch bark. Many naturally occurring items can be fashioned into simple but adequate eating and drinking utensils with a little ingenuity and experimentation.

Tyres In survival situations brought about by vehicle accidents the survivor may well have access to tyres, which are a valuable resource. Tyre rubber can be cut up to make shoes and belts, and the reinforcing wire can be stripped out for traps and snares. Burning tyres create large amounts of black, acrid smoke which is excellent for signalling; for this reason they should normally be kept for use in rescue beacons rather than used for everyday fuel. (However, they could be used in an emergency when fire was a question of life or death, after e.g. falling through ice.) A tyre set in the middle of a three-pole frame makes a comfortable toilet seat; its value to morale should not be dismissed, particularly where survivors are suffering from digestive disorders.

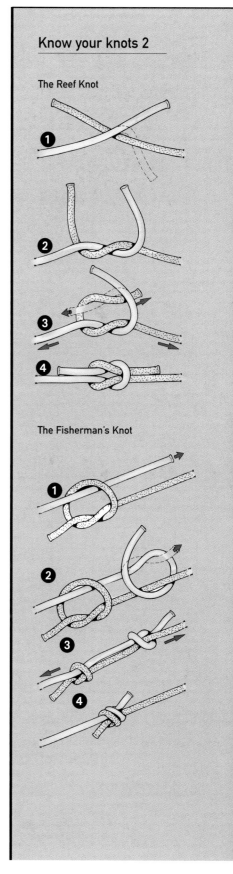

Know your knots 2

The Reef Knot

❶
❷
❸
❹

The Fisherman's Knot

❶
❷
❸
❹

FIRE

Harnessing the power of fire has enabled mankind to evolve along a different path from all other animals: with fire, humans have been able to modify their environment. Even today, in a survival situation, fire is essential. Therefore the ability to light a fire, even in difficult conditions, is an invaluable skill that needs to be learnt and cultivated.

Practical and Morale Value

Fire has many obvious practical uses. Heat sustains wellbeing and life itself in cold or wet environments. Fire can be used to cook food, to dry clothes, to purify water and sterilize medical instruments, and to signal your rescuers. Waterborne diseases are one of the greatest dangers to survival (see Water section), but boiling will kill most harmful organisms. Hot drinks provide a vital source of body heat. Cooking food not only makes it more palatable, but also destroys many harmful organisms in animal products and neutralises the toxins found in many plants.

Fire also plays an important psychological role in survival. Being able to build a fire proves to the survivor that he can control at least some elements of his situation and provide himself with the comfort of warmth and light. He will feel that he has achieved something positive by bringing back a hint of normality to his life.

To make a successful fire you need three elements: heat, oxygen, and fuel. If any element is missing your fire will not burn. However, before you even start to build any fire consider the following questions:

- Does the time you intend staying in your present location justify a fire?

- Do you really need a fire?

- Is there enough fuel nearby to sustain a fire?

- Are you in an area where fire could easily spread out of control?

Fire-starting Materials

Building a fire calls for an understanding of the dynamics involved. When any fuel is burned, part of the heat from that combustion will go on to ignite the next piece of fuel. The hotter a fire the better it will burn.

You do not need a great deal of heat for the initial ignition – a match is usually enough. However, because the first heat source is so small and lasts for only a short time, the material you apply it to must ignite very easily. This material we call tinder.

Tinder Whatever its source, tinder must fulfil certain criteria if it is to ignite readily. It must be bone dry and small in size, and must readily accept flame. Ideally the tinder should burn quickly, producing maximum heat. Included with tinder are certain combustible fuels; these may be in liquid, gel or solid form and are mostly man-made. Using ammunition or flares to start a fire can only be justified after carefully weighing the value of saving them for their original purpose. (See box for a list of tinder sources.)

'Feathered' sticks make excellent kindling.

A successful fire is best started when it is shielded from the elements with fuel added gradually.

Kindling Kindling consists of material larger in size than tinder but smaller than the main fuel to be used on the fire. Ideal candidates for kindling are small dry twigs, or shavings made from dry sticks, a process known as 'feathering'. Once your kindling takes hold, the fire should burn long enough to deal with small logs, i.e. the main fuel. Starter wood for fires needs to be dead and dry.

Fuel Your fuel should be graded and stacked ready before you start, with dry, dead material separated from green wood. A hot fire will be able to cope with green logs, as the flames will boil the sap away and dry the wood before it burns. However, green logs will not catch on a fire that is not well-established and hot.

Heaping the fuel on too quickly will kill a fire. Build your fire with care, adding more fuel only when the previous fuel is burning well. Do not stifle the fire by depriving it of the oxygen it needs – make sure it is well ventilated.

In principle, the harder the wood the longer it will burn. Try to use fuel that is close at hand, still standing, and does not require chopping. If a log is too large, drag it into the fire and let it burn through the middle. Fuel taken from the forest floor will burn if stacked above ground for a few days, or placed around the edge of the fire to dry.

- Birch burns best.
- Both oak and ash burn well and give off good heat.
- Fruit trees such as apple and cherry give off scented smoke.
- Lighter woods such as larch and pine will spit sparks.
- For a concealed fire, burn elm.

Tinder Sources

Manmade:
- Petrol, paraffin or aviation fuel.
- Oil (needs heating first).
- Cooker gel or solid fuel blocks.
- Propellant explosive from ammunition (obtainable, with care, by prying bullet/shot out of cartridge case).
- Pyrotechnics – flares, etc.
- Tampons (check with any female survivors).
- Cotton wool (check any injured survivors for useful dressings).
- Lint from twine, canvas, bandages, etc.
- Scorched or charred cloth, especially linen.
- Charred rope.
- Some photographic film.

Natural:
- Decayed or powdered dry wood and pulverised bark.
- Catface (the resinous scab found on damaged evergreen trees).
- Coconut palm frond (the fabric-like material at the base needs to be sun-dried).
- Dried Arctic cotton grass or moss.
- Termite nest material.
- Birds', rats' or mice nests.

Setting a Fire

The site for your fire must be chosen carefully, especially if you plan on building a shelter or if a strong wind is blowing. The heat should provide warmth for your shelter, but in such a way that the smoke does not envelope you (though if biting insects are a problem, a little smoke will help drive them off).

Constructing a windshield will prevent the wind from blowing out the first fledgling flames. It will also cut down the amount of fuel consumed, and reflect extra heat into your shelter.

The ground below your fire should be dry and clear of vegetation to stop the fire spreading.

If stones are available, build a circle around the fire once it is well alight. This reduces any danger of the fire setting your shelter or surroundings alight; it also defines the fire's size and fuel consumption.

If not maintained, such as overnight or while away hunting, a fire may well go out. Most fires can be relit by placing a small amount of tinder on top of the old embers and blowing. The earth below an old fire site will stay warm for many hours; this will help generate a new fire quickly.

A pit as above offers the best protection for a fire in high wind.

Keep your fire modest in size, surround it with larger timbers so that they will be dry when required.

Collect and grade your fuel, by dryness and size, before lighting the fire.

Heat Reflection

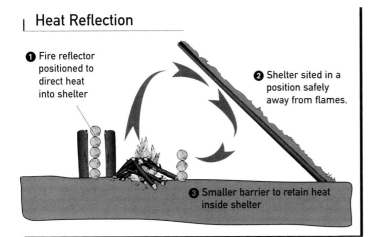

❶ Fire reflector positioned to direct heat into shelter

❷ Shelter sited in a position safely away from flames.

❸ Smaller barrier to retain heat inside shelter

Use a platform to lift your fire above wet ground.

A raised reflector both protects your fire and conserves heat.

Fire on Wet Ground To build a fire in swampy conditions the base must be raised above the water. In some cases this may mean building a platform of old logs or stones on which the fire will rest. In extreme conditions a platform can be constructed several feet above the ground. One tribe who live in tree houses amid the jungle canopy of Malaysia cook with open fires using a base of stones and baked earth spread over the bamboo floor.

Fire in the Wind If the weather is extremely windy, a fire-shield will do little to stop the flames from getting out of control or being extinguished. In such conditions the only answer is to build your fire well below ground level, by either digging a trench or finding a natural ground hollow.

Ember Pit No matter what type of open fire you make, they are all difficult to cook on. Either they will burn the meat, or you will get burnt trying to rescue your supper. Metal cans become hot and the danger of scalding is inevitable. Rather than struggling with an open fire it is a good idea to make a small ember pit for cooking. This is simply a matter of cutting out a section of turf 20cm long by 10cm wide and 10cm deep (8ins x 4ins x 4ins). Once your fire is well established, use a stick to rake glowing embers into your pit. These will supply a manageable source of heat for cooking. As the embers die down or you require more heat, simply rake in more embers.

Fire Reflectors

Once even the simplest shelter is built you will need to consider adding a fire for warmth and cooking. Place the fire where there is no danger of it burning your shelter down, and set the tinder and kindling on a base of green logs. A fire reflector will greatly increase your warmth, and can easily be made by interweaving green sticks into a small hurdle and windproofing it with daubed mud. A large rock or snow wall will serve the same purpose.

Hot bed

One way to reflect the heat from your fire is to stack large stones around the back of the fire. The advantage of this method is that the hot stones can then be taken into your shelter at night and carefully placed beneath your bed space. There they will radiate heat throughout the night hours.

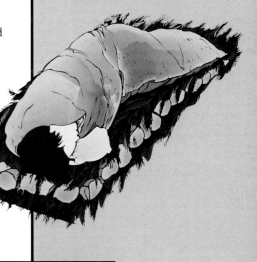

Give thought beforehand to choosing and preparing your fire site

53

Lighting your Fire

The initial heat source for a fire can be produced in any number of ways. Matches or lighters provide the easiest option, but these will not last forever. Tinder can also be ignited by sparks from a flint-and-steel set, or from an electrical source such as a car battery. Heat from the sun can also be concentrated and focused by a magnifying glass or a parabolic reflector. Most heat sources are derived from commercially produced items, but if these are not available sufficient heat to light a fire can be generated by friction.

Matches Matches are the most convenient and obvious way of initiating a flame, and it is a matter of common sense that they should be carried as a matter of course on all outdoor trips. Ordinary matches do not work when damp, however, and can be quickly extinguished if unprotected from a strong

A lighter should be reserved for lighting fires, not cigarettes. Once its fuel has run out it should still be retained for its flint.

wind. This fault can be remedied by dipping each match halfway into some molten wax. To protect the outside of the box, spray it with hair lacquer. Specially made survival matches are protected by a waterproof container, and when lit they will burn for up to 12 seconds in just about any weather conditions.

Lighters In any group of people several will probably be carrying cigarette lighters. These make an excellent survival aid, but must be used wisely and economically. Once the lighter fuel is exhausted do not just throw the lighter away – its flint will go on making sparks for a long time. A new device has also appeared on the survival market recently which con-

Survival matches will burn for longer than standard and in the worst of conditions

A burning glass will light tinder if the sun is strong enough.

Sparks from a flint-and-steel were mankind's only portable fire-starting method for many centuries.

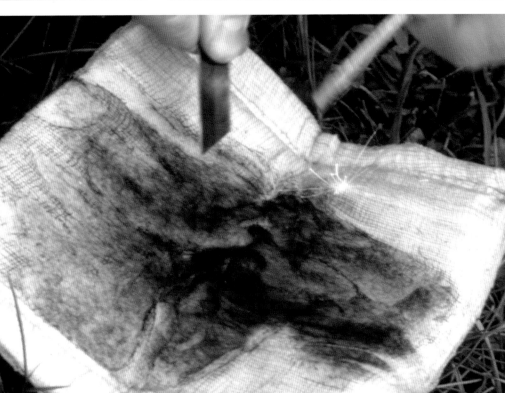

verts a standard lighter into a mini-blowtorch.

Burning Glass Using a burning glass will require strong sunlight, bu it can prove an effective way to light a fire given the right conditions. For the glass you could use a magnifying glass, or a lens from a camera, binoculars, spectacles or a compass. An ideal size would be 5cm (2ins) or more in diameter. Sunlight focused through the glass will ignite dry tinder, although you may need to fan it lightly as it smoulders.

Parabolic Reflector In hot, dry conditions with very bright sunlight it is possible to start a fire using a parabolic reflector (although in such conditions a fire may not be a necessity, and fuel may be scarce.)

Illustrations in some survival books depicting a hand torch reflector being used in this way are highly improbable – your best bet is to use a vehicle headlamp. Place your tinder in the bulb housing; a very effective reflector can be achieved by removing the headlamp glass and replacing it in reverse, i.e. concave. Positioning a magnifying glass on the top of the headlamp and aiming it directly at the sun will cause any tinder to ignite instantly. Water can be boiled in a similar manner.

Flint and Magnesium Fire Starter The specially manufactured flint is embedded into a small block of aluminium and magnesium metal which has a serrated steel striker attached. Shavings from the block can be scraped off and mixed in with any tinder. When the steel blade is struck sharply against the flint, sparks are produced which ignite the tinder. Magnesium burns in excess of 5,000° F, which is hot enough to ignite any tinder even when damp. In an emergency, scraping aluminium shavings from the frame of a crashed aircraft will produce very similar results.

Batteries If you have access to a large capacity battery from a vehicle, even if the vehicle has broken down or crashed, you may be able to start a fire by electrical means. Use a thin wire to

Car Battery Method

❶ Use a thin strand of wire rolled into a ball around which you should place dry tinder.

❷ Connect two thicker insulated wires to the battery.

❸ Connect the insulated wires to the thin wire embedded in the tinder to create a spark.

Warning: If insulated wire is not available use two split sticks to hold the wires while making the connection

One Match, One Fire

You can save on matches and lighter fuel by lighting a candle with them immediately. This candle can then be used to provide a constant flame to ignite tinder, even when it is still a little damp. Like most naked flames, the candle should be protected from the wind by a shelter. Either dig a hole into the ground or build a small stone wall around it. Place the tinder over the flame, either by piling it on top of the shelter or building a small 'wigwam'. Once the tinder has ignited, remove the candle and if you no longer need it, blow out the flame and keep it for the next fire.

Carrying Fire

One sure method of making a quick fire especially in the cold and wet is to carry embers from your previous fire. Many early hunters transported fire around in a cow or buffalo horn. This method can be still be used simply using a perforated beer or coke can as a fire carrier. The skill remains in packing the embers from last night's fire onto a bed of dry, slow burning material, and covering them with the same. The secret lies in the ability to maintain the correct amount of oxygen being fed to the embers. If they are wrapped too tightly, they will be starved of air, if too loose there is a danger that the embers will ignite the surrounding material.

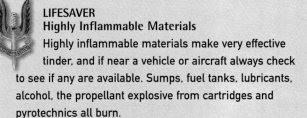

LIFESAVER
Highly Inflammable Materials
Highly inflammable materials make very effective tinder, and if near a vehicle or aircraft always check to see if any are available. Sumps, fuel tanks, lubricants, alcohol, the propellant explosive from cartridges and pyrotechnics all burn.

- Handle them all with great care.
- Metal pots or implements should never be used when mixing chemicals.
- Many such substances will give off toxic gases when they burn.
- Remember that many chemicals which simply burn when loose are highly explosive when compressed or confined.

connect the negative and positive terminals on the battery; this will short circuit the battery and cause the connecting wire to spark.

If very thin wire can be found, roll this into a ball and touch either end with both terminals; this will cause a flash bulb effect.

Chemicals Propellant explosives can be extracted from small arms ammunition or shotgun cartridges. It is best used by sprinkling it over dry tinder and applying a spark (beware – even small concentrations of such chemicals are potentially danger-

ous). Simple gunpowder – 'black powder' – is not found in modern cartridges; but it is mixed from equal amounts of potassium nitrate, sulphur and charcoal. Another mixture with a high output of heat is sugar and sodium chlorate (found in some commercial weedkillers) mixed in equal parts. This will be hot enough to light a fire even from damp tinder.

Fire Paste Fire paste is highly volatile and should be kept for emergency fire-lighting only (see Arctic Survival section). It is basically any combustible material that is held in a suitable base: aviation fuel mixed with soap is one example. A

Cane and birch torch.

small spark will normally ignite the paste, which will then burn for several minutes. As with any combustible material, the paste should be kept in an airtight container when not in use.

In a dire emergency the paste can be burnt purely as a fuel.

Fire Torch Cane has been used to make torches since prehistoric times. One end is split and separated in order to hold some form of burning material. Where the wind is not troublesome this can be even be a candle.

Birch bark rolled, split and dried also makes a good torch (see Arctic Fires).

Fire paste should be kept in an airtight container for emergencies.

Soap mixed with aviation fuel or petrol makes an emergency fire paste.

Explosive from ammunition.

Fire from Friction

Creating fire from friction may be the only method left to a sur-vivor, particularly when his consumable means of fire-making, such as matches, have run out. Many primitive peoples around the world still light their fires by friction; it is presumably the oldest method of creating a flame, and certainly dates back to our prehis-toric ancestors. Although methods vary from continent to conti-nent, the following covers the basic principles of fire by friction.

Fire Plough The fire plough method involves rapidly rub-bing a hardwood shaft against a soft wood base. Under ideal conditions both woods should be seasoned so that the mois-ture content is minimal. In an emergency this can be achieved by sun-drying green wood, although it will take several days.

The baseboard should measure around 30cm by 10cm (12ins by 4ins) and have a straight central chan-nel cut down the entire length of one side. One end of the shaft should be rounded to fit into this groove, and ground up and down the baseboard channel – adding a little sand will speed up this process. Once both the tip of the shaft and the channel have become blackened and smoke can be seen rising, the fire-plough is ready for use. Kneel and place the baseboard against the left thigh. Grip the shaft with both hands and make a sharp, stabbing, ploughing action. As you build up speed small particles of wood fibres will fall to the ground. Place a small amount of dry tinder at the base of the channel ready to catch these. Once the tin-der is smouldering, blow on it until you have fire.

Steps to Remember

1 Choose a suitable site and prepare it for the fire.

2 Gather an ample supply of fuel, grade it into categories and stack it.

3 Prepare your tinder.

4 Light the fire with small amounts of your driest fuel, and nurse it until it is burning hotly.

5 Add new material to it slowly – you do not want to smother it.

6 Check ventilation if there is any risk of carbon monox-ide poisoning.

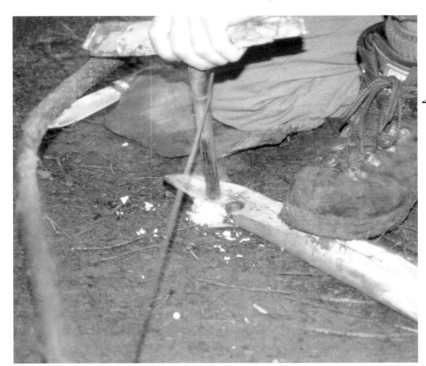

The bow and drill (see page 59)

(see page 59)

Spontaneous Combustion

It is fairly unlikely that a sur-vivor will be able to use this method, as he will seldom be carrying the right chemicals in his survival kit. However, if the right substances are available – e.g. antifreeze from a vehicle radiator, and potassium permanganate from the medical kit – it is possible to use them to start a fire.

Even when slightly diluted, anti-freeze will contain enough glycerine to start a chemical reaction with potas-sium permanganate crystals. This reaction is caused by very rapid oxidisation, and generates large quantities of heat.

1 Take a teaspoonful of potassium permanganate crystals and place them on a sheet of paper, cloth or some other inflammable material.

2 Add 2 or 3 drops of antifreeze, and roll the sheet up tightly – this is vital in order to concentrate the heat in one spot, thereby raising the temper-ature to flashpoint (for paper this is 451 degrees F).

3 After a short delay – perhaps 1 minute – the mixture should ignite and set fire to the tinder.

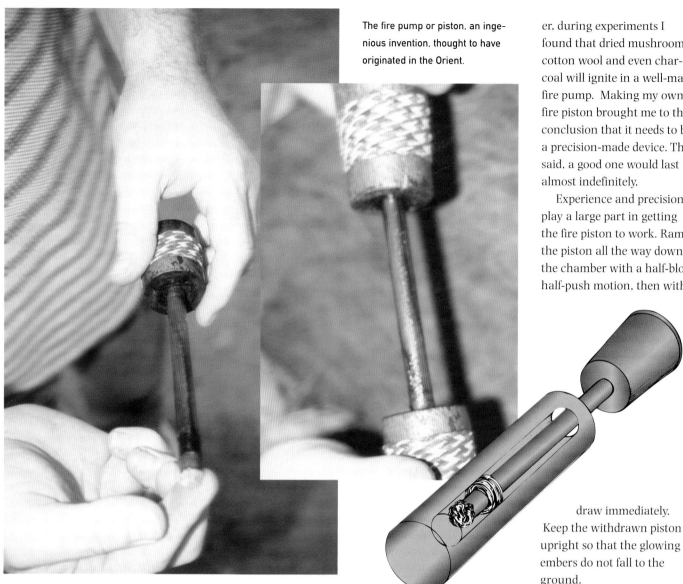

The fire pump or piston, an ingenious invention, thought to have originated in the Orient.

er, during experiments I found that dried mushroom, cotton wool and even charcoal will ignite in a well-made fire pump. Making my own fire piston brought me to the conclusion that it needs to be a precision-made device. That said, a good one would last almost indefinitely.

Experience and precision play a large part in getting the fire piston to work. Ram the piston all the way down the chamber with a half-blow, half-push motion, then with

draw immediately. Keep the withdrawn piston upright so that the glowing embers do not fall to the ground.

Fire Piston or Pump To the best of my knowledge the fire piston evolved in the Far East. It might have been invented by the Chinese or possibly the Japanese, who until recently commonly use brass cylinders of a similar type for lighting cigarettes. Whatever its origin, the fire-pump is perhaps the most innovative of all the pre-modern fire lighting devices.

It requires a body into which a 12cm (4.75in) long chamber has been reamed, similar to the barrel of a gun. A piston, with a handle to assist pressure, is inserted into the chamber. The end of the piston is cup-shaped, and into this a small amount of dry tinder is placed. The piston is then thrust rapidly into the chamber. When this is performed correctly the air molecules are forced to compress, causing spontaneous combustion and generating enough heat to convert the tinder into glowing embers.

The walls of the 'barrel' have to be straight, smooth and lightly greased. To assure an airtight fit, thread should be carefully wrapped around the piston about 2cm above the tinder cup, and this too can be lightly greased. The tinder needs to be bone dry and extremely light. The downy vest from between the layers of a banana palm stem, dried in the sunlight, is used locally in the Far East; howev-

Bow & Drill The basis of this classic method is a flat dry board of powdery wood and a hardwood stick. The principle is to make a hole in the flat board into which the hardwood stick – i.e. the drill – will fit neatly. The baseboard can be any length, but 30cm by 10cm by a minimum of 2cm thick is ideal. Cut a V-shaped notch about 2cm wide on one edge of the block.

The drill should be made from a length of medium-hard wood such as elm, willow, cedar, cypress, cottonwood or balsam fir. Make sure that the chosen piece is sound and dry, and that you are able to cut a straight length from it 20-25cm long and 2cm thick. Sharpen one end of the drill to a 45 degree point and the other end to a 60 degree point.

The baseboard should be placed on the ground and held in place by the toe of your boot. Place a small ball of tinder directly under the notch cut in the baseboard, dropping a little into the notch itself. The best tinder is dried grass mixed with small strips of cedar or birch bark. Fit the sharper end of the drill into the notch of the baseboard, and prepare to rotate it backwards and forwards. This can be done by rubbing the drill between your palms, but using a bow will speed up the drill considerably.

Make a small bow about 60cm-70cm long, and loosely string it with a length of cord or leather thong. Twist a loop in the bowstring and slip it over the drill. Pushing the bow back and forth will rotate the drill in the baseboard notch. Extra pressure can be placed on the drill by using some form of cup over the upper end to hold it in place; in my experience a near-perfect expedient is a small glass jar, as used to hold fish paste.

• Do not expect to make a fire instantly; the drill will need to 'bed' itself into the baseboard, and this can only be achieved after hours of constant drilling.

• An indication that you are close to producing hot embers will come when the drill becomes charred and smoke can be seem rising from the notch. Add a little tinder to the notch, and work the drill vigorously. Embers from the notch should fall into the tinder below. Carefully move the block away and blow gently on the pile until the tinder ignites. As with any survival skill, practice makes perfect.

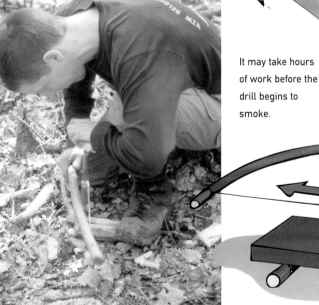

It may take hours of work before the drill begins to smoke.

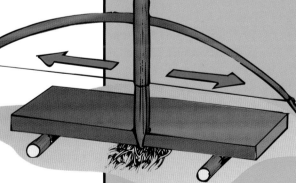

Have confidence – if it worked in the Stone Ages, it can work for you

Types of Fire

Once you have a fire, you need to make sure that it is suitable for your needs. If you are alone you will only need a small fire for warmth. Small fires need less fuel to keep them going, and can be controlled more easily.

If it is snowing or raining – and if you have the means – you should consider taking your fire inside your shelter; and the best way to do this is to improvise a stove. You can also build a fire that will cook your food while you are hunting, and warm your bed on a cold night.

Pyramid fire.

Star fire.

Star Fire This is a simple and easily controlled fire. Once the fire is established, place logs so that they can be fed inwards, increasing the flames. If less heat is required the logs can be pulled outwards. You can leave this fire for several hours while you go hunting. The flames will eventually die down, leaving the hot embers in the middle; these can be protected from wet weather by placing a large stone over the inward ends of the logs. When you return, carefully remove the warm stone and use it as a seat. To rekindle the fire simply push the logs closer together and gently fan or blow on the embers.

Lumberman's Fire A lumberman's fire is built using two long logs – the larger branches from fallen trees are ideal. The purpose is to build a normal fire between the logs until the fire has reached the point where the logs themselves will burn. If the timing is right you

Start your pyramid fire quickly by building a small stack of feathered sticks and dry twigs in the centre.

Improvised tin stove

With care, it can be used inside a shelter, with the outer metal radiating enough heat to dry wet clothing while the stove provides light. If not too large it can be carried with you, complete with hot or burning embers.

Benghazi Stove If liquid fuel is available then a simple stove can be constructed by simply filling a large can half full of sand. The fuel is added until the sand is completely saturated. It is best to burn a small amount of tinder on top of the sand; this preheats the fuel and ignites the sandy surface, which provides a good slow-burning flame. Peat or fine gravel can be used if sand is not available. A fuel candle can be produced in the same way by using a smaller can and a strip of old cloth or rope.

A rock surround will stop your fire spreading.

Fire Management

- Don't make your fire so large that you can't get near it to put a pot on.

- It is safer and better to cook using only the embers.

- If you have the means to make one, an improvised stove is more economical of fuel than an open fire, and more versatile in use.

- Keep plenty of fuel handy, and near enough to the fire to dry out before use.

- Stop your fire spreading: it's dangerous, and wasteful. Beyond a certain size you get no additional benefit from a larger blaze – and your energy expended in gathering fuel is ultimately wasted in the sky above your fire.

- If you stay in the same place for any period of time, use the same spot for your fire.

- Keep drying clothes far enough away not to fall into the fire.

should be able to cook your food on the small fire in between before rolling the logs together. You will then be able to stretch out for the night along the length of the burning logs, and have a good sleep. Separating the logs in the morning and adding a few twigs will quickly rekindle the fire for breakfast.

Pyramid Fire Building a pyramid fire is simply a matter of placing logs in a pattern to create a pyramid-shaped stack. Smaller and dryer twigs and sticks can be placed inside the fire or threaded between the layers.

This type of fire, once lit, will burn quickly and provide plenty of heat. It can also form the basis of a signal fire (see Signalling).

Improvised Stove Constructing a stove from any available metal drum is a vast improvement on a simple open fire. A stove will save fuel, as it is 50% more economical that an open fire.

WATER

Next to air, water plays the most vital part in daily survival. The human body, which consists of roughly 90% water, cannot survive without water longer than three days in a hot climate and 12 days in a cold one. In a temperate climate, carrying out a normal level of activity, the body requires a daily fluid intake of 2.5 litres (roughly 4.5 pints). This requirement fluctuates according to the humidity, air temperature and amount of physical activity undertaken. To keep the body efficient and to have a chance of survival, the minimum daily water requirements must be met. It is not only the quantity of water that is important, but also the quality. Contaminated or impure water will do the survivor more harm than good, increasing both fluid loss and the risk of serious disease.

Water loss

Water is continually lost through the normal bodily functions of urination, excretion, breathing and sweating. The amount of water lost through sweating is notably increased when in hot conditions or during physical activity. This water must be replaced. If, however, your water supply is minimal, the priority is to conserve as much water in the body as is possible (see box).

Drinkable Water Sources

Even if you practice all possible precautions, without a good supply of potable water they will only prolong your survival by a few days. It is imperative to locate or extract water from any source available while being equally cautious about filtration and purification. Waterborne diseases and parasites pose a great health risk to the survivor, but this risk needs to be balanced against that of dying of thirst.

Rain, streams and rivers provide the majority of the world's drinkable water, but it is not always easy to find.

Animals and insects will give some indication of water being present: watch grazing animals in the early dawn or at sundown, as this is when they will make their way to water. If surface water cannot be found, try looking in valley bottoms for signs of vegetation, and start digging. Water can sometimes be found high up in the mountains where storm water and mist have collected in natural cisterns. If neither surface nor sub-surface water can be located, you can acquire it from a host of sources.

Plant Sources Water is collected by a variety of plants; it is contained in living vines (see Jungle Survival) and can be extracted from cacti (see Desert Survival).

Covering foliage with a clear polythene bag is one easy way of gathering moisture – this literally pumps the water from the ground for you. Vegetation of all kinds takes water from the soil and distributes it to the leaves, where it is released as part of the respiration process. Find a suitable green plant and place the bag over the top of a piece of healthy green foliage, tying the neck around the base of the plant. Next to the plant, dig out a small hollow and press the plastic into it to form a collection point for the condensing moisture.

In a similar way the moisture contained in plant stems and leaves can be extracted. In springtime tapping into certain trees, such as the birch, will produce a drinkable sap. Make a hole in the tree one metre above ground level; the hole should be about 5cm (2ins) deep and slanting slightly upwards. Tap a peg into the hole and place your container on the ground below. You should collect 2 litres (3.5 pints) over a 24-hour period. Boil the sap to make it more palatable and prevent it going off. In a survival situation you might try other types of tree; but be aware that milky or coloured saps or juices may be poisonous.

Collecting water in a polythene bag placed over foliage.

Dew Large droplets of early morning dew can be found on most vegetation, especially grass. This is particularly helpful for those survivors who are injured and cannot move far. The droplets can be mopped up by gently laying a clean cloth over the wet grass, and wringing it out. Several pints can be collected in less than an hour, and the water is pure enough to drink without sterilization.

Collecting water from a tree.

Morning dew is a pure source of water, and can be collected by sponging with a clean cloth.

Conserving Body Fluid

- Dehydration kills quickly, but drinking contaminated water kills quicker and is more painful.

- Examine all possible water sources available to you.

- Evaluate water supplies, and discipline their use.

- Exposed skin should be covered, as this will reduce water loss.

- Cool your body to reduce your sweating. Fan yourself; in a sea survival situation, wet clothes with seawater.

- Minimise movement on hot days; work or travel by night; avoid unnecessary exertion.

- Close the mouth and breath through the nose.

- Avoid eating where possible.

- Drink when the day is at its coolest. Take small sips.

- Alcohol consumption and smoking will cause further dehydration.

Bad water kills more quickly and more painfully than thirst.

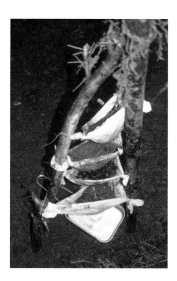

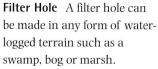

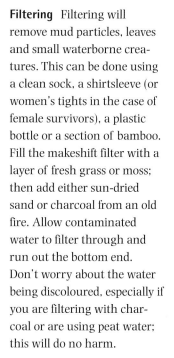

Improvised water filters (above).

Water filter pump (far left).

Filter hole (above left).

A drinking straw (left) allows you to drink from water extraction or condensation devices whose product may not be easy to pour out into a container.

Filtering Filtering will remove mud particles, leaves and small waterborne creatures. This can be done using a clean sock, a shirtsleeve (or women's tights in the case of female survivors), a plastic bottle or a section of bamboo. Fill the makeshift filter with a layer of fresh grass or moss; then add either sun-dried sand or charcoal from an old fire. Allow contaminated water to filter through and run out the bottom end. Don't worry about the water being discoloured, especially if you are filtering with charcoal or are using peat water; this will do no harm.

Filter Hole A filter hole can be made in any form of water-logged terrain such as a swamp, bog or marsh.

Clear the vegetation and dig a hole above the water line, measuring approximately 30cm (12ins) in diameter and 30cm deep. The water which seeps into the hole may be dark in colour; this of itself is of no consequence, but the water will need boiling to kill off the micro-bacteria and viruses. If you do not have the means to dig, simply remove a large stone or log and let the well underneath it fill up.

Sterilization and Distillation

Once you have filtered your water the next stage is to sterilize it. Sterilization can be achieved by boiling water vigorously for at least ten minutes. Make sure that the heat is distributed evenly – keep your water on a rolling boil.

Contained water, urine and seawater can all be made drinkable by distillation. This is a process whereby the contaminated water is converted to steam by boiling; the resulting steam is condensed and converted back into good drinking water. The process can be carried out with or without the aid of a fire, although some form of heat is required.

Another simple precaution is chemical sterilization, using e.g. chlorine-based purification tablets, potassium permanganate (see Survival Medical Pack), or iodine. Be sure to follow the instructions for use carefully.

Chemical sterilization tends to leave an unpleasant taste and odour in the water, and both the iodine and potassium will stain the water pink. Adding small pieces of charcoal to the water an hour before you want to drink it can rectify this.

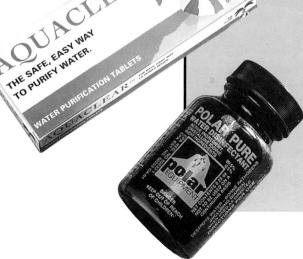

Heavy duty non-lubricated condoms will hold up to 1.5 litres of water supported in a sock or shirt sleeve. Use a bouncing action under a source of running water to stretch the condom while filling.

Sterilizing Water

• Drinking bad water causes weakening sickness, and is more dangerous than thirst.

• Filter water first, using moss and charcoal.

• Kill off micro-bacteria and viruses by adding chlorine-based purification tablets.

• If you have no purification tablets, use potassium permanganate crystals.

• If you have no chemical agents, then boil water hard for 10 minutes minimum.

Carrying Water

The survivalist should carry a supply of water even when travelling through an area where it is abundant. There is always the possibility that a lone survivor will fall or otherwise injure himself and be unable to walk. Any available container can be used, but those with a screw cap are best. Bottles, waterproof cloth, durex, animal intestine and bamboo can all be fashioned into makeshift water carriers.

Salt

Salt is next in importance to water, as it helps to regulate the fluid balance in the body. Without an adequate supply you will succumb to muscular cramps, heat exhaustion and heatstroke. The average human body requires about 10gm (0.35 oz) of salt daily to replace that lost in normal sweating. When the body is deficient in salt, the first signs are sudden weakness, muscle cramps, dizziness, nausea and a hot, dry feeling all over the body.

If these symptoms appear, rest and a pinch of salt in a mug of water are the quickest and easiest treatment.

Salt deficiency is common in arid or tropical jungle conditions, so in these environments it makes sense to ensure that you add a small amount of salt to your drinks. It would also be a wise precaution to add some salt tablets to your personal survival kit.

FOOD

Food is not an immediate factor in survival. The average adult can go 14 days without food before any serious effects start to impair physical ability, and death from starvation takes well over a month. That said, all survivors should be on the look-out for food from day one; if it grows, walks, crawls, swims or flies it is probably edible.

Animals and plants form the two sources of food available from the wild. Animals provide food rich in energy, protein and many nutrients, but the survivor will usually have to expend much time, effort and energy to catch and prepare them. The amount and type of food you will be able to eat will also depend upon your water supply.

If it is scarce, you must avoid any dry, starchy food or salty meat, since these will make you thirsty. Instead eat foods that are high in carbohydrates, such as wild plants.

PLANT FOOD

Compared to the problems of catching animals, plant food is easy to gather and is usually available in one form or another everywhere except in areas of the most extreme climatic conditions. The plant species will determine its richness in vitamins and minerals. Although some plants are very low in food value, they can still be sustaining.

In a long-term survival situation plant food on its own will not provide a fully balanced diet, and you may have to eat more than normal to fulfil your body's requirements. However, in times of need plants are a valuable resource and will keep you from starving.

Some knowledge of edible plants is required, as over half of all plant species are inedible or poisonous. Of those that are edible, only certain parts of the plant may be palatable. Whether you die of starvation or take the chance of eating a poisonous plant will be a personal decision at the time. If you choose the latter, you should at least take the precaution of doing an edibility test (see box). Although not infallible this does give some indication of the human body's reaction to the plant.

Some edible plants contain elements that are dangerous to health if they build up in the body. Therefore be wary of eating too much of the same plant, especially over long periods. A varied vegetable diet will not only be tastier but will also provide much more balanced nutrition.

The plants mentioned below are intended only as a guide. They represent only a small representative fraction of the plants which have uses as either food or medicine or both. It is recommended that you read about the plants that are native to the area where you intend to travel – learn to recognize them and know their properties, in order to keep yourself and others safe.

Some plants are easily recognised by their shape, size and fruit, while others which look innocuous can be deadly. Always carry out an edibility test.

LIFESAVER
THE EDIBILITY TEST

The edibility test is a time-consuming and thorough process. Although it may appear to be over-cautious, remember that your very survival is at stake. Plant poisons may take time before they have any effect on the body; also, plants may affect people in different ways. Make sure that you carry out plant testing before your food stocks are depleted, not after.

The edibility test may be long winded, but the time spent will prevent unpleasant illness, and may save your life.

- A plant's identity must be 100% established. If for any reason you are at all unsure whether it is edible or not, follow the simple steps below.

- Be scientific and thorough in your testing. Test only one plant and one person at a time, so that any effects can be well monitored.

- The plant edibility test will NOT work for fungi.

- Avoid collecting plants from any area which may have been contaminated, and those with milky saps (except for dandelion, goat's beard and coconut).

- Wash any plant material thoroughly before cooking, and remove any diseased or damaged parts.

- Not all the parts of any one plant may be edible. Separate the root, stem, leaves and any fruit. Treat each part individually with the same test.

- Only test plants which are plentiful in your environment. There is no point in subjecting your body to possible poisoning if there is only a handful of the plant available.

1 First test the plant for any contact poisons. Crush a leaf and rub a little of the sap onto the sensitive skin of the inner wrist. If after 15 minutes no itching, blistering or burning has occurred, continue.

2 Take a small portion of crushed plant and place it in your mouth between your gum and lower lip. Leave it for 5 minutes, testing for any unpleasant reactions.

3 If there are none, chew the plant; note whether it exhibits any disagreeable properties such as burning, extreme bitterness, or a soapy taste.

4 If it still gives no reason for suspicion, swallow down the juice but spit out the pulp. Allow 8 hours to pass to see if it has any adverse effects on the body, such as sickness, dizziness, sleepiness, stomach aches or cramps.

5 If none of these symptoms occur, eat a slightly larger amount, e.g. a teaspoonful, and wait for another 8 hours.

6 If there are still no negative results, eat a handful of the plant and wait for a further 24 hours.

7 If after this period the plant has given you no ill effects, you can assume that it is safe and can be eaten in greater quantities.

Use all your senses

- As well as the taste test described, use your eyes: brightly coloured plants may be poisonous.

- Watch to see if other animals eat the plant.

- Smell may also provide you with clues to a plant's safety – be wary of plants emitting pungent odours.

SOME EDIBLE PLANTS

Sorrel (Rumex acetosa) A perennial plant that is most usually found on grassland and also on waste ground.

It has an erect stem crowned with long flower bracts, the flowers themselves concentrated in small pink clusters. The leaves are long and taper to a point, with their lower lobes pointing downwards to the base. High in vitamin C, the young

of 2000m (6,500ft).
Habitat: Meadows, pastures, roadsides, waste ground.

Perennial. Stems, up to 30cm (12ins) long and containing a milky latex, grow from a long, fleshy tap root.

Leaves are dark green and deeply toothed; at the plant's base they form a rosette. The solitary flowers appear from March to August and are bright yellow in colour.
Availability: Leaves and roots can be used all year round.

would a root vegetable; the taste is very pleasant. The roots can also provide a good substitute for coffee, if dried and crushed.
Nutritional properties: The leaves are rich in vitamins A and C and are also a good source of iron and potassium.
Medicinal properties: The leaves have a mild diuretic effect. The juice from the root, usually extracted by boiling, makes a good tonic for the liver and the digestion.

flowers, brownish in colour, are carried closely packed together on a cylindrical spike. The ribwort plantain has narrow, pointed leaves rising out of a basal rosette. The stem is deeply grooved and the flower spike is not as long as that of the greater plantain.
Availability: All year round.
Edibility: The leaves of both plants can be eaten, although they are much more palatable when

leaves, buds and shoot tips can be eaten in salads, soups or stews. Be aware that this plant also contains high levels of oxalic acid, a poison that can build up in the body and cause organ damage.

Therefore be careful not to eat too much of this plant at one time, and avoid eating it frequently.

Dandelion (Taraxacum officinale)
Distribution: Northern Temperate regions up to a height

Edibility: The young leaves can be eaten raw in a salad, although they do have a very bitter taste; this can be remedied by soaking the leaves in cold water for a couple of hours. Older leaves can also be eaten but will need to have the tough central vein removed first; they will be more palatable if boiled. The newest shoots, picked before the stems develop, can be boiled and used like brussels sprouts. The tap roots, once cleaned, can be boiled as you

Greater Plantain (Plantago major)
Distribution: Throughout Northern Temperate regions up to 600m (2,000ft).
Habitat: Grassland, riverbanks, hedges, roadsides.

The greater plantain has large oval leaves which form a loose rosette at the base of the plant. The leaves are dark green and are rarely toothed. The smooth stem always rises above the leaves to a height of about 20-45cm (7-18ins). The very small

young, when they can even be eaten raw. Older leaves need to have their fibrous ribs removed and should then be boiled, as you would for any greens. They are, however, rather bitter and are generally best added to stews.
Nutritional properties: Unknown.
Medicinal properties: An infusion of either plant will soothe bronchial coughs. The juice expressed from the plant will help wounds to heal.

Stinging Nettle (Urtica diotica)

Distribution: Common throughout Temperate regions. Habitat: Woods, hedges, waste ground, sheltered grassy places.

A perennial plant that grows up to a height of 120cm (46ins). The stems bear heart-shaped, toothed leaves which are covered in small stinging hairs. The lesser nettle (urtica urens) is much smaller and is an annual.

Availability: Best eaten in March/April when the shoots are young.

Edibility: Young nettle shoots make a good vegetable, but they need to be boiled first as this removes the stinging properties of the juice. They make a very tasty, nutritious soup, and can be added to stews.

Nutritional properties: Young nettle shoots are rich in vitamin C, although much of this vitamin will be lost in the cooking process. Nettles are also rich in iron and other minerals. Older leaves should be avoided if possible, as they are full of uric acid crystals which can cause kidney damage. If you must eat them, boil them very thoroughly first.

Medicinal properties: Freshly pressed nettle juice is a good tonic and helps the digestion. A tea made from nettles will help to ease rheumatism, and, if left to cool and applied externally, can soothe burns, sunburn, insect bites and minor skin irritations.

Other uses: The fibres from older nettles have been used in the past to make yarn for clothing and twine.

Eat only the young tips of the fern.

Tap Roots

The most natural-seeming parts of a plant to eat are the young leaves and shoots. However, valuable carbohydrate can be obtained by cleaning and cooking the fleshy tap root or rhyzome of some plants, notably dandelion, bracken, goat's beard, flowering rush, arrowhead and many more.

The Youngest leaves of most plants are the most edible.

Bracken
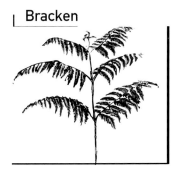

Hazel

Silverweed

**Bracken
(Pteridium Aquilinum)**
Distribution: Throughout the world, except the extreme south and north.
Habitat: Heaths, moors, woods.

A perennial which can grow up to 8ft (2.4m) in the right conditions, but is usually only about 2-3ft (0.6-0.9m) in height. The stem is erect and tree-like, with a velvety feel to it at the base. It carries large pinnate fronds, usually three on each stem. The young fronds are coiled inwards but soon unfold, and can be seen to have three prongs. The rootstock or rhizome is long, thick and succulent, and creeps horizontally beneath the soil.

Be careful not to confuse this plant with the male fern which can be found growing alongside bracken. The male fern tends to have only one frond.
Availability: All year round.
Edibility: The young fronds can be cooked as vegetables, like asparagus, although you will need to scrape the hairs off first. They also need to be boiled for about 30 minutes as they tend to be very bitter otherwise. The starchy rhizome can be cleaned and roasted; the inner portion can then be eaten.
Medicinal properties: None, although the rhizome's astringent qualities may make it useful for healing wounds.
Other uses: Bracken makes good bedding material, and also can be used to thatch the roof of a shelter. When burnt, bracken ash contains high proportions of potash. When the ash is mixed with a little water or fat it can be used as a soap substitute.

Daisy (Bellis perennis)
Distribution: Common throughout Temperate regions.
Habitat: Grasslands and meadows.

Small perennial plant. Leaves are arranged in a basal rosette; erect stems produce white, many-petalled flowers from early summer to late autumn.
Availability: Spring to late summer.
Edibility: The leaves from the basal rosette can be added to salads raw or added to soups, although they have quite an acrid, pungent taste. The young flower buds can be treated in the same way.
Medicinal properties: Made as a tea, an infusion of daisies will help combat catarrh, rheumatism, arthritis, liver and kidney problems, and diarrhoea. It is also a good blood purifier.

**Bramble, Blackberry
(Rubus fruticosus)**
Distribution: Common in northern Temperate regions below 450m (1,500ft).
Habitat: Woods, heath, scrub, wasteland, hedges.

A perennial deciduous shrub with long, arching, thorny stems forming intertwining bushes. The leaves are mid green, pinnate, with five to seven toothed leaflets. The flowers are pale pink and may be seen on the bush at the same times as the fruits. When ripe the latter are black in colour and consist of many segments.

Bramble

Cloudberry

Billberry

Sorrel

Availability: Early spring to early autumn.
Edibility: The ripe berries are the most obvious food of the bramble and can be eaten raw or added to salads.

A refreshing drink can also be made from them. Blackberry leaves also make an excellent tea. For this, the leaves must either be very fresh, or will need to be slowly dried and crushed.
Nutritional properties: High in vitamin C.
Medicinal properties:
The leaves of the blackberry are very astringent, so a tea made from them is effective in treating diarrhoea and gum problems.

Hawthorn (May)
(Crataegus monogyna)
Distribution: Europe, North Africa, Western Asia.

Clover

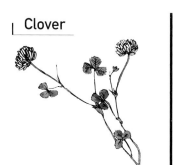

Habitat: Woods, hedges, scrubland.

Small tree or shrub which can reach a height of 9m (30ft). It has light-coloured bark and is covered in thin thorns. In spring it produces plentiful white blossom, which from July to October bear small red fruit, 1cm (0.4in) in diameter with a small stone in the centre.
Availability: Spring, autumn.
Edibility: The young buds can be eaten raw, and young leaves may be added to stews. The fruit can also be eaten, and – contrary to popular belief – are not bitter.
Medicinal properties: A tea made from either the flowers or the fruits will soothe sore throats, and also help to ease diarrhoea.
Other uses: Hawthorn is an extremely hard wood and

Wild Rose

makes one of the best fuels, as it burns very hot.

Rowan (Sorbus aucuparia)
Distribution: Throughout the Temperate regions. Habitat: Montains, hillsides, hedgerows and woodland.

This delicate-looking deciduous tree can also be found in places that have been, or still are, inhabited by humans. It grows up to 20m (65ft) high, with pinnate leaves and a smooth, grey bark.
Availability: The white flowers appear in May to June, and are followed by bunches of red berry-like fruits in July to September.
Edibility: The fruits are edible; although not poisonous raw, they are extremely bitter. To counteract this the berries should be briefly boiled and then the water discarded.

Plant Infusions

A 'tea' or infusion made from many natural occuring plants will have mild but beneficial medicinal properties.

- Silverweed
- Coltsfoot
- Greater Plantain
- Ribwort Plantain
- Stinging Nettle
- Daisy
- Blackberry
- Hawthorn
- Clover

Hawthorn

Daisy

Colt's Foot

Medicinal properties: The fruits contain high proportions of vitamin C. An infusion of the dried flowers and fruit can help to combat constipation, and rheumatic pains. The juice of the fresh fruit has the same effect.

Goat's Beard (Tragopogon pratensis)

A dandelion-like annual or perennial plant which may be found on grassland and waste ground throughout the Temperate regions. It has a tall stem containing a white sap. The leaves, which grow up the stem, start by semi-clasping the stem and then tapering to a sharp point. Both stem and leaves have distinctive white veins. The flower heads are large and solitary, having yellow petals which close at mid-day.

Edibility: Before flowering, the young plant and buds can be eaten like asparagus. Most of the young plant, including the root, can also be chopped up for use in salads, soups or stews. Once the plant is more mature the root can still be used, although it should be blanched, peeled and boiled first.

Wild Rose (Rosa canina)

Wild roses are common throughout Temperate regions and can be found in hedges, woodland and scrub. Deciduous in nature, the green or brown stems have an arching habit and are covered in many hooked thorns. The leaves are pinnate. The pale pink flowers are usually solitary and have no scent. The fruit, appearing in autumn, is red, shiny and smooth, and contains many seeds.

Edibility: The fruits or hips can be boiled up to make a syrup, or added to soups. However, before they are used the seeds and hairs must be removed, as these are an irritant.

Medicinal properites: Rose hips are full of vitamin C, and provide a very useful tonic against exhaustion and colds. For this, boil the finely chopped fruit for ten minutes. This drink is also effective against constipation.

Clovers (Trifolium pratense and Trifolium repens)

Both red and white clovers can be found commonly on grassland throughout the Temperate regions. They are perennial plants with distinctive three-lobed leaves. The white clover differs from the red not only by the colour of its flowers but also by the fact that it possesses a long, creeping rootstock, the means by which it spreads. The flowers of the white clover are also scented.

Edibility: The most edible part of both types of the clover plant is the leaves, before the plant flowers. They can either be cooked on their own, like spinach, or they can be added to soups, stews, sauces and salads. The flowers can be dried and used as a tea substitute.

Crab Apples (Malus sylvestris)

The wild apple, like cultivated varieties, is deciduous. It can be found in woods, hedges and scrubland. The height can range from a scrubby bush to a tree 11m (36ft) tall. The bark is greyish brown and rough, the leaves oval in shape. White-pink flowers appear in spring and are arranged in clusters on the end of twigs. The fruits which follow are round, greenish-yellow, and usually over 2cm (0.8in) in diameter.

Edibility: Wild apples are extremely acidic and sour to the taste. They are best cooked with other fruits if a bad case of diarrhoea is to be avoided.

Hazel (Corylus avellana)

The hazel tree is a common sight in woods and hedges throughout Temperate regions.

It does not usually grow very tall, and often appears more like a shrub than a tree. The bark is smooth and red-brown in colour, and the leaves are almost round in shape. The most visible flowers are the male catkins which appear in spring; they are followed in autumn by the familiar fruit, the hazel nuts.

Edibility: The nut is pleasant to eat on its own and also highly nutritious, being rich in oils and vitamins.

The oil can also be crushed out of the nut to provide a cooking oil.

Coltsfoot (Tussilago farfara)

Another plant common throughout Temperate regions, appearing on waste ground, banks, scree and dunes. The remarkable feature of this perennial plant is that the yellow flowers and their purple stems appear in March/April, ahead of the leaves which come forth in May. The leaves are large, polygonal in shape and have a whitish look to their underside.

Edibility: The young leaves are edible, either eaten raw in a salad or cooked in soups and vegetable dishes.

The same applies to the young shoots and flowers. Coltsfoot has a rather aromatic flavour which is quite pleasant once one has got used to it.

Medicinal properties: An infusion of coltsfoot leaves, either fresh or dried, will help to soothe coughs and will calm the stomach if digestive problems occur. Small cuts and wounds can also be helped to heal by placing a bruised coltsfoot leaf on them.

Water Chestnut (Trapa natans)

Widespread in Eurasia, the water chestnut is a

free-floating plant found in quiet water. It has arrow-shaped leaves which float on the surface in a rosette, and also possesses sub-aquatic leaves which are long and feathery. It produces small, white flowers but does not possess a root.

Edibility: The nuts themselves are to be found beneath the water and are hard, greyish in colour and two-horned.

These may be eaten raw, cooked with other vegetables, or roasted.

Bulrush (Typha spp.) Widespread plant found in shallow, fresh water and marshes. It can grow up to 4.5m (15ft) tall, and is distinguished by its large, long, dark brown flower head. It has long, narrow leaves which are grey in colour.

Edibility: The edible parts are the rootstock, young shoots, leaves and pollen. The rootstock and young shoots can be eaten raw, but the leaves taste best when boiled. Pollen can be used to make damper bread. Bulrushes are also a useful building materials for shelters, baskets, bedding, etc.

Flowering Rush (Butomus umbellatus) Common in Eurasia, this shallow-water plant grows up to 1.5m (5ft) tall and has long leaves rising from the base. It produces loosely-clustered pink flowers with three petals.

Edibility: The edible part of the plant is the rootstock, found below ground. This

should be peeled and boiled before being eaten.

Silverweed (Potentilla anserina) A small creeping plant commonly found on wet ground in Temperate regions.

It gets its name from the silvery-green colour of its soft, sharply-serrated leaves, which are arranged alternately on a central leaf stalk. The flowers resemble those of buttercup – yellow with five petals.

Edibility: The small creeping rootstock may be eaten, although many will need to be collected to make a meal.

Luckily, silverweed usually appears in abundance. Although the roots can be eaten raw they are extremely astringent, and will taste better cooked.

Medicinal properties: An infusion of either the leaves or the plant will help in cases of diarrhoea, sore throat and stomach cramps. If applied externally it will soothe and heal wounds and haemorrhoids.

Arrowheads (Sagittaria spp.) This aquatic plant is widespread throughout many regions of the world. It can grow up to 0.9m (3ft) tall, and is distinguished by its large, glossy, arrow-shaped leaves which stand boldly above the water. Submerged leaves have a ribbon-like look to them. The flower stem rises from the root and carries small flowers composed of three white petals each.

Edibility: The edible part is

Bulrushes (above).
Arrowheads (right).

the root tubers, which are the size of walnuts and grow just beneath the mud. They can be eaten raw but are much better when cooked.

Nutritional properties: The roots are a source of vitamin C.

Reeds (Phragmites communis) Fresh-water aquatic plant, commonly found throughout the world on river banks.

A stout grass which can grow up to 3m (10ft) high, it has a creeping rootstock and grey-green leaves. The flowers, carried on the tall stems, are purple-brown in colour.

Edibility: The root, which is high in sugar content, can be cooked. The stem, if crushed, will yield a sugary gum which can be used for sweetening.

PREPARATION

All plants and leaves should be washed in fresh water before consumption. While some of them can be eaten raw, it is generally safer to cook all food. Add plants and berries to other dishes, such as stews and soups. Not only will the addition enhance the taste of the food, but it will also add to the general nutritional values of your cooking.

Roots and tubers can be boiled, but they are much better baked or roasted. Wash or scrape first.

Wild grasses grow in many parts of the world, even as far north as the Arctic circle.

Sunflower seeds (above) and poppy seeds (right) can be eaten and also used to produce oil.

Seeds

All edible cereals are derived from wild grasses that produce heavy seed yields. A wide variety of grasses can be found in most regions, from the coldest tundra to all but the hottest desert. Although laborious to collect, the seeds will provide a basic food. They are best removed by simply gripping the seed head and pulling backwards so that the seeds fall into your hand. They can be collected in any improvised container, such as a hat or spare shirt. Once you have collected enough, rub the grain between your hands to loosen the chaff, and separate by throwing the whole lot into the wind, which will blow away the lighter chaff.

The seeds can then be ground into flour using a flat surface and round smooth stone. This flour can be mixed with either nuts or fruit, and baked into bread or biscuits.

Oil-Producing Plants

Sunflowers, poppies, olives and walnuts all produce oil which is both edible and can be used as fuel for lamps.

The poppy is one of the easiest flowers to recognized growing in the wild, and is almost always found in abundance. It favours recently broken ground. In moderation the seeds can be eaten raw with no ill effects, but they are best used to produce oil.

The seeds or fruit of any oil-producing plant need to be harvested and wrapped in cloth to make 'cheeses' (flat, round cakes); these are stacked on top of one another, and pressed. If using seeds, they are best cracked first on a smooth stone before being pressed. In a pure survival situation pressing presents a problem and some form of leverage needs to be implemented. A simple press can be made if a vehicle jack is available.

The residual 'cake' is also edible, and is best rolled into biscuits and fried. Olives can be wrapped in a clean cloth and left out in the sun. The oil exudes into the cloth, which can then be wrung out. At the end of the process the cloth can be used for lamp wicks.

Nuts

Nuts are an extremely valuable food source and can be found in most countries and climates except for the Polar regions. Nuts are extremely nutritious, providing high levels of protein, fats and vitamins. Tropical nuts include coconuts, brazil nuts and cashews, whereas trees in temperate areas produce hazelnuts,

The Brazil nut
is contained
within its hard shell which itself is
contained in a large, fibrous husk.

Fruits such as figs are found from
the temperate to marginal desert
regions. Others such as lychees
and the Cape gooseberry are
more tropical.

Wild chillies can be incred-
ibly hot and should be
treated with caution.

PREPARATION

Leaves, stems and buds are best boiled until they are tender. Keep replacing the water if your plant material has a bitter taste – this will reduce it.

Grains and Seeds can usually be eaten raw, but most will taste better after being parched. Parching is usually done in a metal container, but can be done on a hot, flat stone on top of a Yukon Stove if no other container is available. Heat the grains or seeds slowly until they are well scorched.

Nuts are in most cases perfectly edible raw, but some, such as acorns, can be very bitter. These are best boiled for two hours and then soaked in fresh water for three or four days. All nuts can be ground up into a paste, which can either be added to soups or stews, made into a gruel, or dried into a 'flour' to make unleavened 'bread'. Sweet chestnuts (not to be confused with poisonous horse chestnuts or 'conkers') taste delicious whether roasted, baked, steamed or raw.

Fruit Berries and soft fruits provide a welcome change to a survivor's diet. Both are best eaten raw as they contain many valuable vitamins which may be lost when cooked. Those fruits with thicker or tougher skins can be boiled, baked or roasted.

walnuts, beechnuts, acorns, almonds, sweet chestnuts and pine nuts.

If you have a plentiful source of nuts, gather as many as possible and store them in a cool dry place. The nut will remain edible for several months if left in the shell. Nuts are quite easily carried and make an excellent portable food store.

Fruits

Fruits, like nuts, are found in all climatic regions except for the most extreme. Fruits can be extremely high in vitamins and sugars, and often occur in plentiful amounts. Do not gorge yourself on wild fruits, however, as this may well cause severe diarrhoea and sickness. What you can't eat at once, collect and dry. Make sure that you dry them thoroughly, however; otherwise they will become coated with harmful moulds and mildew. For the same reason, only pick and eat fruit that are healthy and not overly ripe.

Clamping Many root vegetables can be preserved through the winter by 'clamping'. A thick layer (20cm/ 8ins) of dry straw or bracken is used as a base onto which the tubers are placed in a pyramid. Cover the pile with more straw or bracken; and allow it to settle for two days before covering the whole pile with dry earth. It is a good idea to allow some strands of straw to protrude through the earth so that your 'clamp' may breathe.

FUNGI

Fungi provide a nutricious and palatable wild food source, and they often occur in areas where other food resources are scarce. Only two to three per cent of fungi species are poisonous to human beings; and yet opinion is divided on advising their use as a source of survival food. The major problem arises from the fact that THERE IS NO EDIBILITY TEST FOR FUNGI.

This is due to the delay between poisoning and symptoms appearing, and also the exceptionally toxic properties of some species. Even species not considered poisonous can cause some extreme reactions in susceptible individuals who may have an allergy to them. Just because one person can eat a certain species quite safely does not mean that every member of a survival party can.

- Even though only a small percentage of fungi are poisonous to humans, some are extremely deadly – even if only a tiny portion is consumed.

- After eating a poisonous species of fungus the symptoms may not present themselves until ten to 40 hours later. By this time they will be serious enough to warrant hospitalisation. In the worst cases, without hospitalisation the casualty will die. Even with proper medical care irreversible damage may be caused to certain organs.

- Less poisonous species, although not fatal under normal circumstances, may cause poisoning serious enough to threaten the life of an already weakened person in a survival situation.

Identification

There is only one safe way to identify fungi, and that is by visual means. Make sure that you can positively identify certain species beyond doubt. Learn fungi identification by studying pictures from a good guidebook and comparing them to specimens found in the wild. Keep in mind that even reference books may disagree from time to time on whether a particular species is edible or poisonous. A decision to eat fungi must be based on sound knowledge and first-hand experience of identifying edible species, and where no alternative food source is available in the locality. If you are not able to do this, it is safer to leave fungi well alone.

Field Mushroom (Agaricus campestris) The Field Mushroom is similar in appearance to the Horse Mushroom except that it is not so large. It is found mainly in the summer on meadows and lawns, especially after rain.

The cap is white, convex, up to 12cm (4.75in) in diameter and sometimes covered in thin, smooth scales. The gills are free from the stem and densely packed together. The colour of the gills ranges from pinkish-red when young to black-brown later on. The stem grows to a height of 8cm (3ins) and is white and smooth. The flesh has a pleasant taste and smell. It can be fried or cooked in soups and stews.

Warning: The Field Mushroom looks extremely similar to the deadly Death Cap and Destroying Angel, especially when young, so be sure of your identification.

Bay-Capped Bolete (Boletus badius) The Bay-Capped Bolete has a convex cap, chestnut to dark red-brown in colour. The stem is a lighter colour, straight, thick and cylindrical, growing up to 8cm (3ins). It has olive-brown spores. It is found in deciduous and coniferous woods, and is extremely common. When cut or bruised the flesh turns blue. It can be fried, cooked on its own as a vegetable, or added to stews and soups. It can also be dried and stored for later use.

Cep or Penny Bun (Boletus edulis) The Cep is found in all types of woodland. It has a brown, convex cap 5-20cm (2-8ins) in diameter, which is thick and fleshy. It has a thick, cylindrical stem, which is usually white but can also be tinged with a pale brown and have a whitish network of veins. It has olive-brown spores. The cep is one of the few species that can be eaten raw; however, like the Bay-Capped Bolete, it can also be fried, added to soups and stews, or eaten as a vegetable on its own.

Warning: Do not eat any similar-looking mushroom with pink or red spores.

Sponge Cap (Boletus testaceao-scabrum) (Leccinum versipelle) Usually found growing with birch trees, this large mushroom often occurs in substantial numbers. It has a large convex cap, up to 15cm (6ins) in diameter and yellow-brown to orange-brown in colour. It has a thick stem, growing from 7-15cm (2.75-6ins) tall. The stem is white to grey and covered in dark woolly scales. The mushroom has brown spores. The flesh is firm when young but softer later, and can be coloured anything from white to pale pink to greenish-blue depending on age. The Sponge Cap is not recommended for soups, and is best fried or dried.

Buff Meadow Cup (Camarophyllus pratensis) This is to be found in open aspects, such as woodland clearings or open grasslands and meadows. It has a convex buff-coloured cap, which later becomes more flattened in shape, often with a slight dip or a centrally raised arch. The gills are the same colour as the cap, thick and loosely arranged. The stem is slightly paler than the cap, 3-8cm (1-3ins) tall, and widens at the top into the cap. It has white spores. This mushroom can be either fried or stewed.

Horn of Plenty (Craterellus cornucopioides) This is easily recognized by its funnel-shaped fruit body, very dark brown in colour and rough and crinkled. It grows up to 10cm (4ins) in diameter and has a short, hollow stem. The Horn of Plenty is usually found in deciduous woodland amongst rotting leaves. The flesh is thin and spicy, and is best when mixed with others in soups and stews. It can also be fried.

Chanterelle (Cantharellus cibarius) Like the Horn of Plenty, this mushroom is also funnel-shaped, but is orange-yellow in colour and smells of apricots. In younger specimens, before the funnel forms, the cap is convex or flat. It has a short, pale stem and cream/pale red spores. It is to be found in woodland, especially under birches, although it also grows in coniferous woodland. The flesh is peppery to taste and is fairly indigestible unless it is chopped small and thorough-

ly cooked. This mushroom is not very good for drying.

Beef Steak Fungus (Fistulina hepatica) This leathery fungus grows on trees, usually oaks. It is rough in texture, and is red on the top with a paler pink underside. It has red flesh and a red juice. Older fungi tend to be bitter, so collect younger ones if available. Even then, the fungus will need to be soaked before being stewed.

Parasol Mushroom (Macro-lepiota procera) This mushroom occurs in deciduous woodlands and clearings. It has a large, brownish cap which is at first globular, but later becomes convex, and finally flat. Its diameter can be anything up to 25cm (10ins). The gills are white or cream,

densely arranged and free from the stem. The stem grows from 15-30cm (6-12ins) high and is quite thin and pale brown in colour, with irregular dark brown bands around it. It has white spores. The flesh of the Parasol tastes nutty, like almonds or brazil nuts. The best method of cooking this mushroom is to discard the stem and fry the cap.

The closely related Shaggy Parasol (Macro-lepiota rhacodes) looks similar to the Parasol, but is smaller and has a shaggy-looking stem instead of the transverse brown markings. It is edible in the same way.

Common Puff Ball (Lycoperdon perlatum) The fruit body of the Common Puff Ball is very round to pear-

The Danger of Fungi

• Only a small percentage of fungi are poisonous to humans, but these are extremely deadly.

• Death can occur even if only a tiny portion is consumed.

• NEVER try testing fungi for edibility.

• Even less poisonous species, not usually fatal, may cause life-threatening sickness and weakness in a survival situation.

The Field Mushroom

Bay-Capped Bolette

Buff Meadow Cap

Oyster Fungus

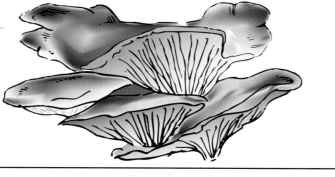

Parasol Mushroom

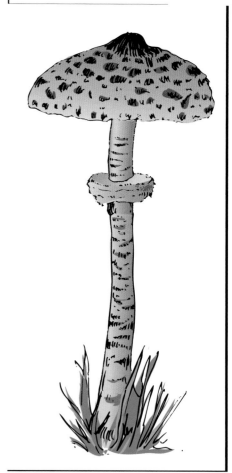

Chanterelle

Beef Steak Fungus

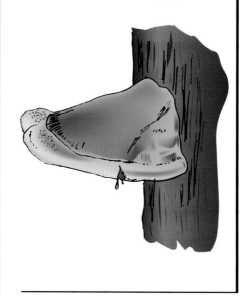

Common Puff Ball

Common Morell

The Giant Puff Ball

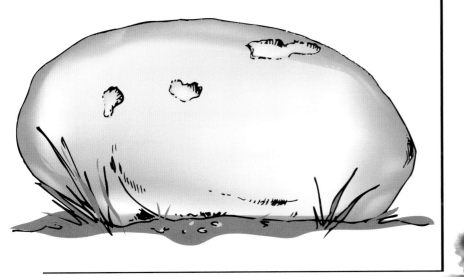

You must be 100% sure you know what you are eating – 99% sure could be fatal.

WARNING

Full and confident recognition is the only safe way of being sure whether a fungus is poisonous or not. There are no other safe methods available. If you find yourself forced to eat fungi, the following guidelines will give some measure of safety:

• Avoid old specimens of fungi, or any that are diseased, have insect infestations, or have been partly eaten by insects or maggots.

• Avoid very young specimens, especially those that are still in the 'button' stage. At this point many fungi have not yet developed their identifying features – these only appear as the fungus approaches maturity.

shaped and is supported on a short, fat stem. The whole mushroom grows to about 5-8cm (2-3ins) in height and 4-7cm (1.5-2.75ins) in diameter. The fat cap is greyish white when young, later maturing to a yellow-brown colour, covered in small 'warts'. It has olive-brown spores. The flesh of this fungus should be eaten when it is still young and white, and is best fried.

Warning: Other related species may look similar but are inedible.

Giant Puff Ball (Calvatia gigantea)

One of the largest fungi on earth, this mushroom looks like a giant football, up to 60cm (24ins) in diameter. It has smooth white skin and pure white flesh. It is found in woods and grassy places. It is delicious to eat and also has medicinal uses: the spores can stop bleeding from wounds and are also antiseptic.

Common Morel (Morchella esculenta)

The Common Morel is often found where the soil has been disturbed, especially in grassy areas. The fruiting body is globular, yellow-brown and honey-combed in appearance. It can grow up to 20cm (9ins) tall. The stem is white or cream, cylindrical, and breaks easily. It has colourless to very pale yellow spores. The Common Morel has a white, waxy flesh which is very spicy-smelling. To cook, it is best to chop the flesh into small pieces first. It can also be dried.

Warning: The Common Morel must not be mistaken for the False Morel, which is poisonous.

Oyster Fungus (Pleurotus ostreatus)

The Oyster fungus can be found growing on the bark of dead or living deciduous trees. It has a shell-shaped cap, flattish and usually brown in colour on the top. The gills are white but later turn more yellowish. The stem is very short, and hairy at the bottom. The Oyster produces large amounts of purplish spores. Collect only young fungi, as older ones tend to be tough. The flesh is soft and has a pleasant taste and smell. It can be fried or added to stews.

Common Blewit (Lepista personata)

Found in open grassland, this variety usually grows in rings. It has a convex cap which later becomes flattened, buff in colour and about 6-12cm (2.5-4.75ins) in diameter. The gills are densely arranged and are white to pinkish-buff in colour. The stem is short, thick, and of a blue-lilac colour. This mushroom tends to appear in late autumn/early winter when most other varieties have disappeared.

It is best fried or stewed, but does not go well in soups.

Warning: Some individuals tend to have an allergy to the Common Blewit, so test with a small piece first.

POISONOUS FUNGI

Most poisoning by fungi is caused by species of one family – the amanitas, many of which are toxic to a fatal degree even in small quantities. The amanita family includes the Death Cap, the Destroying Angel, Fly Agaric and Panther Cap.

The amanitas share many common characteristics, such as possessing a cup or volva at the base of the stem; white gills; a smell of potato or radish; and fragments on the cap. Any mushroom possessing these characteristics should be avoided. Amanitas grow on their own and are only found in woodland – never in fields or open grassland. It is recommended that this family should be studied with the aid of a good guidebook for identification purposes.

Death Cap (Amanita phalloides)

Young specimens are egg-shaped but later the cap develops convexity, and in maturity becomes flattened. The colour of the cap is pale yellow to olive-green with light lines leading from the centre to the edges. The stem is paler and possesses a volva at the base. The gills and flesh are white.

This fungus is found in woodland and is usually associated with oak trees. The flesh of young specimens possesses a sweet smell and a pleasant taste, but later the smell becomes less agreeable. This is one of the most poisonous of fungi and is fatal after consumption of even a small piece. The symptoms develop from one to three days after consumption; these include vomiting, sweating, excessive thirst, diarrhoea and convulsions.

Often the casualty will seem to make a brief recovery, but death soon follows, from acute liver failure. There is no known antidote for Death Cap poisoning.

Destroying Angel (Amanita virosa)

This fungus shares a similar shape with the Death Cap, but its cap and stem tend to be pure white. The stem is more slender, shaggy, and tends to be slightly curved, but it still has the distinctive large volva at its base. The gills are white. The Destroying Angel is found in woodland, especially coniferous. It prefers mossy ground and will not be present in grassland. The flesh is white and soft and, like the Death Cap, has a sickly sweet smell when young. Older flesh has a less agreeable 'laboratory' type of odour. The symptoms and severity of poisoning are the same as for the Death Cap.

Panther Cap (Amanita pantherina)

The Panther Cap is at first convex in shape but then flattens out and becomes cushion-like. The colour of the cap is a dull brown, and it is covered with white flecks. It has white gills and a white, smooth stem with a volva at the base which consists of two to three concentric rings. It is found in woodlands, particularly under beech. The white flesh often smells of raw potatoes.

Fly Agaric (Amanita muscaria)

The Fly Agaric is easily recognized by its bright red cap covered with white spots – the original 'fairy mushroom'. This member of the amanita family tends to grow under pine or beech trees. Symptoms of Fly Agaric poisoning include vomiting and diarrhoea, dizziness, hallucinations and convulsions, followed by a coma-like sleep. Despite the seriousness of the symptoms, the victim usually recovers.

Devil's Boletus (Boletus satanas)

This fungus is similar in appearance to the edible boletus edulis, but can be distinguished by certain differences. In younger specimens the cap is greyish-white and red at the edges, but more

mature specimens have an ochre hue. The pores are blood red. The stem is coloured yellowish-orange above and purple below. Although poisonous, it is not usually fatal. Symptoms of poisoning include severe vomiting.

Inocybe patouillardii

This fungus may be confused with an edible agaricus by a beginner. The cap is white in the younger specimen before turns yellowish. The cap is often split at the edges. This mushroom stains red when bruised. Symptoms of poisoning include dizziness, sweating, blindness and a lowered temperature. In very severe cases the victim may become delirious and die.

Paxilus involutus

This species is found in birch woodlands and is very common. It has a funnel-shaped, yellow-brown cap with a rolled rim, and yellow-brown gills. It may easily be confused with the Chanterelle, and is very toxic.

WARNING

• Before picking any fungus, first examine it for any sign of a volva or cup at its base. Picking a mushroom first may destroy such evidence by damaging the volva or leaving it in the ground. Any fungus possessing a cup or volva at its base should not be picked or used in any way.

• Similarly, avoid any fungus with a ring of scales on the base of the stem, or if its cap is covered with small white patches or fragments.

• Fungi with red on the underside of the cap, or which produce red spores, should also be avoided.

• Leave any fungi that have white gills, or any gilled mushrooms that have a milky-looking juice.

• Any fungus should be boiled before being eaten, and the water should be discarded. This is because some poisons are destroyed by cooking. However, there are also other poisons, such as those found in the deadly Amanitas, which are NOT neutralised by cooking.

Destroying Angel

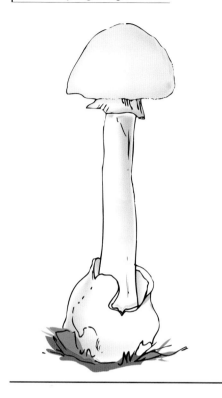

Panther Cap

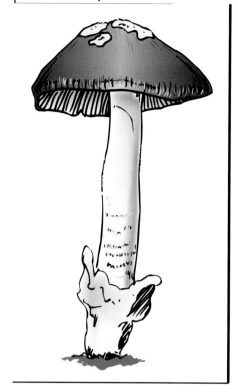

Fly Agaric

Inocybe Patouillardii

Delayed Action Death

- After eating poisonous fungi symptoms may not appear until between 10 and 40 hours later.
- By this time effects will be serious enough to need hospital treatment.

Paxillus Involutus

- In the worst cases, casualties will die without hospitalisation.
- Even with full medical care irreversible organ damage may occur.
- In survival situations, hospital care will never be available.

Devil's Boletus

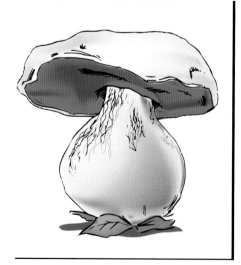

ANIMAL FOOD

Mammals, birds, fish, reptiles, crustaceans and insects are all sources of animal food that can be found in the wild. Animal foods of any type will provide a higher food value than that obtained from plants; however, far more energy-sapping effort will be needed to catch an animal than to gather plants. Hunting and trapping all require time, skill, and good information. It is vital, therefore, that the result matches the cost of the methods employed. You must not expend more energy in catching the food than that derived from the food value caught.

Hunting Hints

The process of catching an animal is called hunting; this can be achieved by either trapping or pursuit. The first requires constructing some a form of trap best suited to catch your animal; pursuit means to stalk or ambush an animal and kill it by direct means, i.e. stabbing, clubbing or shooting.

Traps can be constructed to catch just about any size of animal from a mouse to an elephant. If pursuing your prey or waiting in ambush you will need a weapon; this can range from a rock to a gun. A firearm will provide the best chance of successful hunting, with snares coming a close second. The construction and efficient use of primitive types of hunting weapon require a great deal of skill and practice.

Unless you are an expert, hunting with anything less precise than a rifle will probably produce little success; but lying in ambush will increase your chances.

- To be able to ambush your prey you will need to know where it lives and when it moves. Look for an animal trail, especially one that leads to water. Most animals will use these trails between their feeding and bedding grounds and their water source either in the early morning or in the late evening; so pick one as your time of ambush.

- Animals have more acute senses than humans, and are always on the alert for danger. Be patient; observe all potential prey; camouflage both your appearance and scent – daub mud over your face and hands. Keep a low, silent profile and use smooth, careful movement downwind while the animals are feeding. Find a good place to hide, and position yourself there well before any prospect of animal movement.

Balanced Pole snare.

Monkeys are a staple to many people and should be regarded as such in a survival situation.

Author's Note

It is my firm belief that there is no justification for hunting any animal for sport. Only within the context of this book do I advocate hunting, and then only as a matter of human survival under the laws governing nature – in as much that the strong and intelligent of any species will survive by preying on the less fit. Even in this situation the hunter must act responsibly, and not let any animal suffer unecessarily. (All the dead animals pictured in this book were purchased dead from local country markets.)

- Snares and nets work well when set around an area where an animal has been cleaned or butchered. The entrails will act as a very effective bait.

- Care must be taken when returning to a trap or a snare, as any wounded animal may be dangerous.

- A sharp whistle can stop rabbits and hares if startled into running. You may even be able to attract them to you if you make a high-pitched kissing sound with your lips on the back of your hand – this simulates a squeal.

- Birds should be watched to see if their movement will reveal a nest site containing nutritious eggs or young. These should never be overlooked as a food source.

- As a last resort, the survivor must consider eating anything that walks, flies, swims, crawls, creeps, jumps or wriggles.

- Where possible, try to use all of a carcass – do not discard anything without careful thought. Skins can be made into clothing; bones can be fashioned into arrowheads, fish hooks or needles; sinews and gut make good bow strings or sewing thongs.

Snares

Snares and traps are a far better alternative to hunting and ambushes, as they require less physical effort and time spent waiting. A well-made and correctly sited and set snare or trap will be effective 24 hours a day, without the need for constant vigilance. This method guarantees a 'cost-effective' meal in terms of the effort/benefit equation of survival. Start out by snaring small game; they are easier to trap, transport and prepare.

Always set several snares, but keep some distance between them; an animal caught in one snare will create enough noise to alert others to the possibility of danger. Make sure that all snares are checked on a daily basis – the caught animal may be your next meal, but there is no reason to let it suffer unnecessarily. If you are successful with any of your snares, collect the animal, kill it if necessary, and reset the snares for the next day.

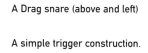

A Drag snare (above and left)

A simple trigger construction.

Drag Snare If properly positioned the simple drag snare is a most effective way of catching a meal. Ideally the snare should be placed along a fresh run, in such a way that the animal's head will be caught. Tie the noose to a stake which has been driven firmly into the ground; or, if it is suspended above the run, secure it to a strong branch. To set the noose, position it so that its bottom edge is about 10cm (4ins – the width of the average hand) above the floor of the run; and adjust the noose until it is about the size of two clenched fists. If possi-

ble, encourage the rabbit or other animal into the trap by piling up dead twigs and branches on either side of the path leading up to the snare. However, do not make the mistake of using green twigs – the animal may consider these to be a distractingly tasty snack.

Balanced Pole Snare The simple drag snare can be modified to make it even more efficient. A balanced pole snare will not only catch your prey, but will also lift it clear of the ground – out of reach of any other hungry preda-

Whore trap

Squirrel snare

Snaring

The use of snares is discussed here purely in the context of survival; snaring animals is against the law in some countries, and is disapproved of in many others.

Making a Snare

The easiest type of snare, both to make and to use, is the drag snare, which kills by strangulation. A noose can be fashioned of any strong wire, nylon cord, hide strips, or even a wire saw (see Survival Kit). The best material to use is brass snare wire. You will need about 80cm (30ins) of wire for each snare. Make a 1cm (1/2in) loop in one end, passing the other end through the loop to make your noose. The pliability of the brass wire makes for a quick, smooth strangulation, which will lock in place as the animal struggles. Before setting it make sure that the wire is free of kinks and that the noose runs freely. Snares are best rubbed with animal excreta to remove the brightness of the metal and the human scent which your hands will leave on the wire.

Setting a snare.

tors or scavengers. This requires a suitable length of pole secured at its mid-point across the trunk of a nearby tree in such a way that the lighter end of the pole can be pivoted downwards directly above the animal run. Fix a snare firmly to that end of the pole. At the opposite end of the pole fasten a heavy rock to act as a counterweight. This counterweight should be heavy enough to lift your catch clear once the snare is activated.

Make a trigger by cutting interlocking notches in two pegs, which hold them together against straight line tension (i.e. when you try to pull them apart along the axis of the pegs) but which slip apart easily when disturbed sideways. Hammer one peg firmly into the ground at the side of the animal run. Attach your snare to the

other, free peg; and also tie a line from this free peg to the light end of the pivot pole. Swing the light end of the pole down and hook the trigger halves together; check that they work smoothly. Check that you have set the noose at the correct height above the run and that the wire loop can move freely.

Spring Branch Snare A similar effect an be achieved by substituting a springy, bent-over branch from a nearby tree, or a bent-over sapling, for your pole and counterweight. Again, hold it bent down under tension by tying it to your notched trigger pegs and tying the snare to the free peg. If you intend using this method you are advised to check the spring strength of the branch beforehand, and adjust your trigger setting accordingly.

Hoop Spring Snare A hoop spring snare can be used where trees are scarce and you are forced to rely on small saplings. Using two saplings – either growing naturally close together, or cut down and firmly planted in the ground where you need them – bend them into an arch. The two tips are locked together by a notch which in turn is held in place by a vertical bait bar. (A rock can be attached to the bait bar if necessary, to supply the downwards tension to lock the notch.) A number of snares are attached to the saplings and positioned in such a way that the animal must pass its head through a loop in order to get at the bait. Movement on the bait bar will trigger the trap and snatch tight the snares.

Whore Trap The whore trap relies on forcing the animal's head into a baited 'V'. A willow stick, sharpened at each end, is bent into a hoop and forced into the ground. The snare is fixed to the end of a bent-over sapling, or the end of a balanced pole snare. A bait stick is positioned so that the snare peg, which fits through the hoop, can rest on it. Two large logs or a series of stones form a barrier either side, forcing the animal to place its head through the snare before it can eat the bait. As the bait is taken the snare is activated. Of all the snare traps shown this is by far the most reliable.

Purse Net A simple purse net, if you have one, is another efficient way of catching small game. If you do not have one, make a gill net (see Fishing). The net can be used in several effective ways. First find a burrow showing signs of recent use, and stake the net over a fresh entrance. Block all of the other burrow holes except for one. In this hole either light a fire and blow smoke, or simply pour in water. Either method will make any occupants of the burrow panic, forcing them into the net.

Long Netting This is a simple and effective way of catching several rabbits at once. You will require a long net, which is placed between the burrows and the grazing ground. It is erected rolled up and balanced on several sticks; a cord is attached which allows the net to be drawn out. It is best

Figure Four Trap

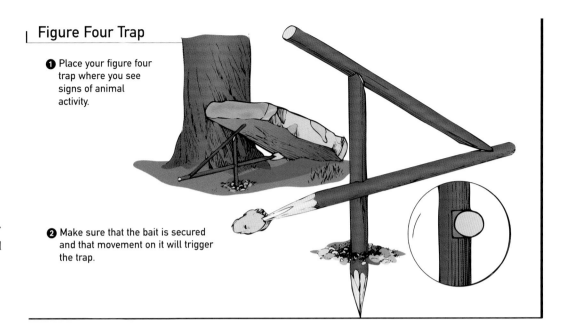

❶ Place your figure four trap where you see signs of animal activity.

❷ Make sure that the bait is secured and that movement on it will trigger the trap.

used after dark when the rabbits are feeding. Stretch out your net, and then get behind the rabbits and make a lot of noise. The rabbits' first reaction is to bolt for their burrow.

Figure Four Trigger This type of trigger has the advantage of being easy to make, light to carry around with you, and capable of supporting any combination of useful traps. It is constructed from three lengths of thick branch, notched in such a way that they form a figure four. This trigger is firmly fixed in the ground where it will support a deadfall log or flat rock, or alternatively a drop net. Whichever method you choose, once the trigger is disturbed the trap will activate. The Figure Four Trigger is the ideal trap to use while travelling.

Squirrel Snares Once you have identified the presence of squirrels in an area it is

fairly simple to catch one. The most effective way is to induce the squirrel to climb down a pole which is purposely positioned. Look for signs at the base of a tree to make sure squirrels are resident – pine cones husks, nut shells and bits of old mushroom are a good indicator. Fit three or four snares evenly spaced to a suitable pole about 4-5m (13-16ft) long. Place this against the tree, wedging it into a fork just below the foliage line. Any squirrels climbing the pole to

their tree will run into the snares and be caught. A struggling squirrel will often attract others, who will come to investigate and then ensnare themselves.

Tin Can Trap One way to catch small animals is to dig a hole large enough to sink your billycan and half fill it with water. This is best done along the animal run, concealing the open top with grass. Most Arctic rodents feed on grass seed or moss, making them an attractive source of clean food.

Bird and Fish Catcher

In isolated regions where man is rarely seen, most birds will remain perched and unafraid. Use a long gaff with a snare attached to hook your dinner.

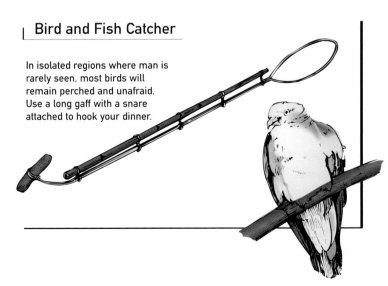

Birds

All birds and birds' eggs are edible. Their taste depends on their habitat: those which live or feed at sea will be less palatable than those that feed on the land. The flesh from sea birds is nutritious but barely digestible, though this can be improved by thorough cooking it.

The normal indication of bird presence is simply to see them flying overhead, but many also leave sign near their nesting or feeding areas. Although it is difficult to identify a particular bird species by its track, you can still get a rough idea of the type of bird. By using the following simple guide lines you should be able to tell the difference between perching birds, swimming birds and wading birds:

- Perching birds (e.g. sparrows & crows) leave tracks with a long first toe (the gripping toe) behind three front toes.
- Swimming birds (e.g. ducks) leave webbed footprints.
- Wading birds have long slender toes spread wide apart. You will find their tracks in mud.

Bird Snares Birds can be caught in any number of ways, from throwing a stone to hitting them with a long stick. One of the simplest ways is to snare them. First find a perch that is well used by birds – this can easily be identified by the large amount of droppings either on the branch or on the ground below. The snares can then be hung above this branch. Once a bird has put

Birds are easily trapped by rigging collapsable perches.

its head through a loop it will not withdraw but will try to escape by flying forward, and thus become trapped.

Another method is by using the baited perch. If you have sufficient wire – at least 2m (6.5ft), make a snare loop at either end and fold them over a branch. Next form a square-ended perch with the trailing end onto which the birds are enticed to land. When a bird rests on the perch it will dislodge the whole snare, trapping the bird's neck at the same time. In most cases both bird and trap will fall to the ground.

Baited Bird Hook A simple baited hook (an open safety pin is ideal) can be used to catch larger birds such as seagulls, wild ducks and

The Simplest Rodent Trap

- Find an established run used by small animals.
- Dig a hole and sink a tin can below ground level.
- Half-fill the can with water.
- Conceal the hole with grass.

The trap in the photograph has caught a mouse.

Floating trap – snares attached to a log or other floating object – should be camouflaged with foliage.

Bird's eggs are a rich source of nutrition.

geese. These birds are greedy and swallow their food quickly. Make sure the line is well secured, and that you check all of your snares each day.

Bottle Trap Floating traps can be used to capture waterfowl while on the water. If you do not have a bottle use a small log instead. Half fill the bottle with water, and tie two or three snares to the neck so that they sit about 5cm (2ins) above the water. A little foliage will make the trap more attractive to any curious bird.

Unless the water is shallow and safe enough for you to wade in and retrieve the trap, secure it to the bank with a line so that you can pull in any catch.

Eggs Any survivor should keep an eye out for birds' nests; eggs offer high nutritional value, are convenient and safe, even if the embryo has developed inside. They can be boiled, baked or fried. Hard-boiled eggs can be carried as a food reserve, and if submerged in clean water will keep for several weeks. A thin coat of fat or grease around a fresh egg will keep it edible for a month or more. A survival diet of bird's eggs and boiled nettles will sustain life for a long time.

Never remove all the eggs from a nest; by leaving one or two you will encourage the bird to lay more. Mark those you leave, to ensure that you are removing only the fresh eggs.

Preparation of Birds

Before cooking, birds need to be prepared by plucking and cleaning. Most birds can be plucked more easily either immediately after death, or after being plunged into boiling water. The exceptions to the latter are waterfowl, which are easier to pluck dry. Do not throw away clean feathers as these can serve many purposes, from insulation in bedding or clothing to making flights for arrows. Although it is possible to skin a bird, removing its feathers at the same time, remember that the skin will provide extra food value.

Once the bird has been plucked, cut off the head and feet and make an incision into the lower stomach below the breastbone. Use this hole to draw out the bird's innards and neck bone. (The heart, kidneys, liver and neck bone will form the basis of a good stew.) Wash the bird thoroughly, both inside and out, with fresh water. Small birds, once gutted and cleaned, can be enclosed in clay and baked on an open fire; the feathers and skin will pull away with the clay.

Carrion eaters – e.g. vultures, buzzards and carrion crows – are likely to be carriers of disease and parasites. They are still edible, but need to be boiled first for at least 20 minutes before you continue with any other form of cooking. Boiling will not only kill any parasites and bacteria present, but will also serve to make stringy meat more tender.

Scissors Trap

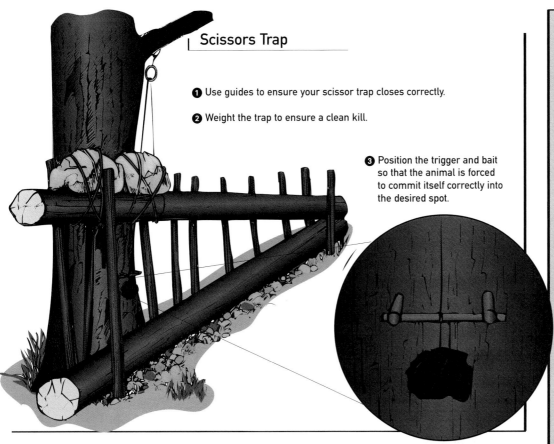

1 Use guides to ensure your scissor trap closes correctly.

2 Weight the trap to ensure a clean kill.

3 Position the trigger and bait so that the animal is forced to commit itself correctly into the desired spot.

Deadfall Traps

The best traps to use for larger game are those which work on the deadfall principle – i.e. by triggering a heavy weight to fall on the animal when it disturbs the bait. Bear in mind, however, that deadfall traps require a lot of time and energy spent in their construction. Points to be considered by the survivor include, what sort of weight can he handle safely while setting up the trap? Are the materials at hand capable of supporting the deadfall weight, i.e. is the supporting cord for the trigger strong enough? It must also be remembered that large traps are dangerous not only to the intended prey, but also to the survivor and any other person who may be in the area. Conversely, the energy put into building a large deadfall trap must be justified by the confirmed presence in the area of the intended prey.

Deadfall and spears

Traps for Larger Game

Scissors Trap A simple scissors trap features one log raised above another in a V-shape. The falling log is held in position by a trigger, and the direction of its fall is guided by stakes. It is essential that both trigger and retaining cord are strong enough to support the deadfall, yet upon activation will release quickly and smoothly. The falling log can be weighted to improve kill efficiency. One of the best trigger release systems is where two pegs or modified branches support a toggle attached to the release line. The toggle itself should be baited to avoid the risk of the cord being chewed by the animal, and placed in a position where the animal must expose its neck in order to get at the bait.

Deadfall and Spears A variation on the scissors trap is to cross the animal trail with a trip line, which when activated will drop either a log or weighted spears. *Note:* Many survival books illustrate this trap with the deadfall or weighted spears falling or swinging across the line of the path. Situating the fall to activate along the line of the animal trail will produce much better results.

Baited Pit Constructing a trap by digging a hole takes a lot of energy, although there are times when the ground is soft and the surrounding area

is habitat to the ideal catch. The jungle is just such an environment, and wild boar and pig the game.

Providing you have the means, you need to dig the pit at least 1m square by 1.5m deep (3.25ft square and 5ft deep). Placing sharpened bamboo stakes in the bottom may help disable the animal, but they are unlikely to kill it. Covering the pit so that it matches in with the natural surroundings is vital. Likewise, the support for the concealing cover needs to be firm enough so that it gives way only when the animal is 'centre stage' – this can be achieved by cutting part way through the supporting branches. Always approach an activated pit with care: injured animals can leave a nasty infected bite. Make sure your prey is dead by stabbing it with a spear before attempting to remove it from the pit.

Bait The use of bait will increase your chances of catching a meal, be it an animal or fish, but what you use as bait is important. The idea of baiting is to attract the animal by offering an easy meal, and to optimise the efficiency of the trap or snare. In the first instance the bait must be acceptable to the animal; there is little point in using a worm if the wet ground is covered with them. Conversely, strange-looking bait may make the animal wary. Almost all animals and birds are attracted to blood, brightly coloured berries, and salt.

Deep, baited, camouflaged hole with spikes to disable falling animals.

Hunting with a Weapon

Man has established his supremacy over all other animals through his ability to make weapons. As man's weapons technology improved so did the number and size of animal he could hunt. The slingshot, spear and bow allowed the hunter to kill from a distance, and thus avoid being injured or killed by his intended large prey. With the invention of firearms man was left with no enemies other than his fellow man.

The ability to make a weapon gives man the opportunity to control other animals in his environment, for the purposes of both food and self-defence. Most improvised weapons, whether hand-held or projectile, require the addition of a cutting or piercing blade or edge. These can be fashioned from a wide variety of materials. Stone can be chipped to form an edge, and flint is particularly good for making weapons. Wood can be shaved with a knife into a point and hardened by charring slightly over a fire. Some woods, like bamboo, are naturally hard and only need trimming to a point. You can use man-made materials such as metal and glass to produce a good cutting edge.

AR-7 Survival Rifle Though it is rare nowadays to find a rifle packed in a survival kit, they do exist, and in certain environments prove most useful for hunting. Most survival weapons are of small calibre, since the relatively devastating ammunition used on the battlefield is unnecessary for hunting. The popular AR-7 survival rifle fires a .22 Long bullet. The AR-7 conforms to the needs of a survival situation, since it packs down for carriage into its own hollow stock, is lightweight, and will even float in water. Its 20-round magazine should, if used with sensible economy, supply sufficient meat to last several months.

The weapon is semi-automatic, which means it will fire a round each time you pull the trigger, i.e. you are not required to cock the weapon each time. For this reason, be careful not to let your trigger finger 'run' – aim for one round, one

kill. Try to shoot an animal that will provide a good amount of meat, such as a fox, wild pig or capybara. Rabbits and birds can be caught by snare and are a waste of ammunition. Conversely, if you hunt game that is too large, such as a moose or bear, you will only wound it – which is wasteful of ammunition, cruel, and often extremely dangerous.

Assembling the AR-7 is simple:

- **Open the rear of the stock, and empty out the parts.**
- **Slot in the trigger housing and bolt action assembly.**
- **Match up the barrel and body notches and secure with the screw collar.**
- **Check all parts are hand-tight; then fit the magazine.**

Zeroing Under survival conditions your ammunition will be limited, perhaps to one full magazine (20 rounds).

If the rifle is inaccurate, even by a small degree, you could miss with every shot. You are therefore advised to test the rifle by firing three rounds at a large target.

From a distance of 50m (55 yards), fire at the same fixed point each time. Estimate an imaginary point at the centre of your three bullet holes, and measure the distance and angle from your fixed point. If the centre of your group is left 5cm (2ins) and slightly high, then you need to aim off to the right by the same distance and slightly low. Aiming off is better than trying to adjust your sights, as you will need to confirm any adjustment by firing more ammunition. Always

aim at the centre shoulder area of your animal.

Bow and Arrow Providing you can locate the correct materials it is possible to make a good hunting bow in a fairly short time. The most important part of the process is to select your stave – the part that forms the arc of the bow. Select carefully, choosing a strong, healthy section of wood without side shoots. The best and most traditional wood to use is yew, but oak, birch and hickory are all suitable. The wood should be long enough to make a bow stave about 130cm (50ins) in length.

Flex your stave several times to find out which side bends naturally. Mark this side, and taper off the last 50cm (18-20ins) at both

Making a Bow

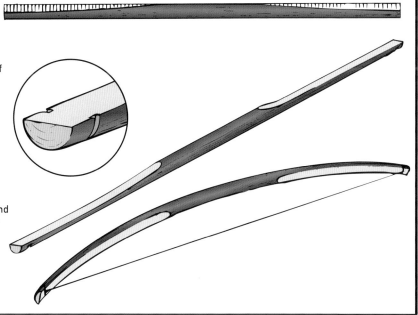

1 Select a hardwood staff about 1.3m in length that is free of knots and limbs. Chamfer a third of the length at each end.

2 Notch both ends to receive the bow string.

3 String the bow by securing one end and forming a slip-over loop on the other.

Target Practice

To become accurate takes practice, and arrows take a long time to make. It therefore makes sense to practice shooting at a target that neither allows your arrows to get lost if you miss, nor breaks them if you hit.

Balala Light

'Balala light' is an African term for hunting with a light. A powerful torch is attached to a helmet or hat and aligned with the eyesight. When game are near the light is switched on, illuminating both the animal and the gun sights. The animal is temporary frozen by the bright light, and is easily killed.

ends. Traditional English bow makers always tapered their bows to a round section and made the ends as even as possible – this was to stop the bow twisting when it was drawn. The bow stave should be slowly dried over a fire for about two or three days. Notch the ends to receive the bowstring.

To string the bow use whatever cord you have to hand, as long as it is very strong; parachute cord or oiled rawhide thong will do. Another alternative is to use cleaned animal intestines dried and twisted together to form a string. Tie the string on to one end of the bow only. Make a loop in the other end so that it can be slipped over the other end when the bow is flexed. The bow should only be strung like this when you intend to use it; at all other times it should be left untensioned.

Arrow flights.

Arrow shafts Arrows are made from straight, strong wood about 65cm (25ins) long and 1cm (0.4in) in diameter.

Most types of wood will do, but choose birch saplings if you can find them. Clean any bark off the arrow and straighten it as much as you can – a good method is to gently chew the arrow between the teeth. Remember – a straighter arrow will fly further and hit with greater force. Balance the arrow on your finger at its halfway point. Insert your flight in the lighter end and the arrowhead at the heavier. At the flight end cut a notch about 6mm (0.25in) deep to take the bowstring – check the width against your string material.

Arrow flights Arrows need flights – 'feathers' – in order to keep them on course when shot. They can be fitted with double or treble flights, and these can in practice be made from actual feathers or plastic, polythene or cardboard. The flights should be 10cm long and 5cm wide (4ins by 2inches). In a survival situation a one-piece double flight is best used.

Using a knife or other thin blade, carefully make a split about 15cm (6ins) long into the flight end of the arrow shaft. Insert a double flight into this – i.e. a single piece which protrudes equally on either side of the shaft. If the arrow splits completely, bind the split ends together tightly with light cotton, fish line or very fine snare wire.

Arrowheads A variety of arrowheads can be made using different materials, but all are attached in a similar manner to the flights: carefully split the shaft, insert the head, and bind the split shaft tightly. If you can find

nothing to act as a arrowhead, harden the tip of the shaft by turning it slowly in a fire. Once hardened, any charred material should be removed and the tip sharpened to a point.

Blow Pipe Although most people think of the blowpipe as a weapon used by jungle tribes, it is possible to construct a very effective modern-day variation which can be used for hunting small game such as birds and rabbits. Most of the materials required can be found in any modern vehicle or aircraft. For example, the body of the blowpipe can be constructed by simply cutting out a length of fuel pipe. Choose a section that is straight and at least 1.5m (5ft) in length; if this is not possible, try joining two or three shorter sections together . More air will be forced down the pipe if a mouthpiece is fitted at one end; this can be cut from card or plastic and held in place with ducting tape.

Metal darts between 10 and 15cm (4-6ins) long are constructed from stiff wire. Heat one end in a fire until it is glowing red, then flatten it to form a point by beating. Allow it to cool or dip it in water. The flight can be made from any soft, pliable material, e.g. seat foam or polystyrene. Use a short section of pipe which has the same diameter as your blowpipe to stamp out your flights; this

An arrow shaft, approximately the length of your arm.

will ensure an airtight fit, while allowing the dart to be blown easily through the blowpipe. Shooting with your blowpipe needs no explanation, other than to say that your accuracy will become second nature after a little practice. The example illustrated here has a range of 25m (80ft), and is capable of killing a rabbit.

Slingshot The slingshot is a very simple weapon, easy both to make and, with practice, to use. Take two equal lengths of cord or leather about 35cm (14ins) long, and attach one end of each to a small, shallow pouch of fabric or leather which will hold a walnut-sized pebble. Tie a loop in the opposite end of one cord, and a knot at the end of the other.

Place the loop over the index finger of your dominant hand, and trap the knot between index finger and thumb.

Place your ammunition securely in the centre of your pouch – ideally this could be a small, smooth pebble. Bring the sling above your head in one quick swinging motion to gain momentum. Let go of the knot to release the stone. You do not need to swing the sling more than a couple of times. Try using a flicking action to improve accuracy.

Throwing Stick Throwing sticks have been used by country folk for many years, especially during late summer when the rabbits trapped in the

WARNING

Blowpipes are extremely dangerous weapons. Their construction here is illustrated for use in a survival situation only.

Improvised arrowheads

Hand/eye co-ordination comes with practice – persevere with patience.

Throwing stick

Winding up to throw a bolas.

Practice throwing at a tree.

corn where forced out by the harvesters. Used properly it is a most effective means of knocking down and stunning a running animal. It is best to cut several 50cm (20in) lengths of heavy fist-sized sticks for throwing. Hurl them overhand or by side-throw, using a flicking motion on release to make the stick spin through the air. Advance on the animal the moment it is down, and club it to prevent any undue suffering.

Club The club is probably rivalled only by the picked-up stone as the oldest known weapon. In its basic form it will extend the range of your arms and deliver a more powerful hit than your fist. Clubs can be made from either wood, stone or metal, and can be weighted or formed into a 'mace'. Construction of any club should be designed around its planned use and the ability of the user. Making a club will protect the survivor against some larger animals,

such as wild dogs; and will also serve to ensure a clean kill of any animal caught but struggling in a trap.

Bolas The bolas is a very effective weapon for bringing down large, long-legged animals such as deer, wild sheep or ostrich. It is simply made, comprising three lengths of strong cord knotted together at one end and weighted with stones at the other ends. The stones should be of even weight and no larger than a duck egg.

Practise on a nearby tree by swinging all three lines in unison, in a arc above your head. When you let go of the knotted end the lines will separate and wrap around your target. You must be ready to spear your game the moment it is down, as the bolas will not immobilise it for long.

Catapult If you have the means to make a catapult under survival conditions it will prove to be a highly effective

hunting weapon. All you need is a strong, forked twig and a length of elastic (you might even consider putting some into your survival kit). A good source is the rubber taken from a vehicle's inner tube. Avoid clothing elastic, as this is generally too weak for the purpose. Construction is simply a matter of tying the ends of the elastic to the forks of your Y-shaped twig and the other ends to a good-sized projectile pouch – tie them tightly, and make sure the pouch is centred.

If you have a good length of elastic available, experiment with using an arrow instead of a stone. Once this method has been perfected you will find that it is both more accurate and more deadly.

Spears Spears are useful for protecting yourself against an attack by a wild animal, but they are of less use for hunting. To make an efficient throwing spear and achieve consistent accuracy demands

The Bolas

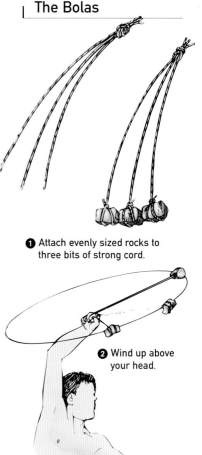

❶ Attach evenly sized rocks to three bits of strong cord.

❷ Wind up above your head.

❸ The stones will separate as you throw them at your prey.

skills of a high order. A thrown spear is less accurate and projects less killing power than an arrow. For hunting a spear can really only be used against cornered prey, although fishing spears are of more value.

To make a spear, choose a strong staff about 180cm (70ins) long and sharpen the end. If you have the materials and the time, experiment with making and using spearheads of other materials, such as flint, or metal or glass from a vehicle or aircraft.

Spears

❶ Spears with multiple barbed heads are best for fishing.

❷ Split the shaft to attach a metal or stone head.

Animals to Hunt: Tracks

Whether or not you actually see a prey animal, you will often be obliged to try to identify and locate it by studying and following its footprints or tracks. Efficient tracking is a highly sophisticated skill, and acquiring it in a survival situation will present a considerable challenge to most people from a modern urban background.

One animal's track can look like that of a completely different animal depending on the surface into which it is imprinted. Sand, mud and snow will alter the image of an animal's footprint. You will rarely find a perfect print with the elements against you, i.e. snow thaws and rain will wash away mud, resulting in a distorted shape. Even if you overcome these difficulties and are convinced that you are trailing one type of animal, it could still turn out to be another. There is always a chance that a young animal could leave a print similar to that of a smaller creature. Likewise, the different tracks made by fore feet and hind feet can trick you into thinking you are following the tracks of a different animal.

With all this against you, you need to have a clear idea of what to look for in the first place. Your conclusion should not be based purely on the print, but also on your surroundings. You should be considering what type of surface the track has been made in; the time of day or night; the weather conditions which may have affected the print; and, most important of all, the probable game in your particular surroundings. Also remember to look for any other clues near the track.

As an example of similar tracks, consider a rabbit and a squirrel. The rabbit will push off with its hind feet and land on its fore feet, which touch the ground one after the other. The hind feet then touch the ground landing in front of the fore feet. This

A catapult can be used effectively with arrows as ammunition.

Tracks

• Study your environment at length, and use your common sense. What animals are likely to leave tracks here? Where are they going, and why?

• How is the surface – sand, mud, etc. – affecting the tracks?

• Is the weather affecting the tracks?

• Is this a full-grown small animal, or a young larger animal?

• Can you tell the front from the rear prints?

• If so, do the tracks tell you anything about the speed of movement?

• Are there any other tell-tale signs – droppings, or chewed vegetation?

Rabbits can be found on all continents and in all conditions, making them an excellent food source.

Rabbit Rabbits deserve a special mention; they are a great source of wild food, and are found on every continent living in all conditions, from Arctic to desert. They are easily recognizable, and being a social animal are always found in large numbers. They usually stay in one territory all their lives, where they live in burrows, often with more than one entrance. They are most prevalent in open grassy areas and open woodlands, especially where the soil is dry and sandy. Burrow sites are made in banks and slopes with light tree or shrub cover.

The tracks that rabbits regularly use are called runs. These are easily seen between the burrow entrances and, if in present use, will have rabbit droppings on them – small, dark, round 'currants'. When you set a snare make sure that it is a little distance from the burrow entrance itself – animals are far more wary when emerging from underground than at most other times, and a snare set too close to the entrance may well be seen by the rabbit and avoided. Take care not to disturb the ground or foliage around the run when setting the snare, and conceal your scent by rubbing the snare and your hands with animal droppings.

Rabbits can be caught or killed in a number of ways, including purse and long netting and snares. A live rabbit is best killed by holding its hind legs in your left hand and its neck in your right. Stretch and twist the neck sharply until the neckbone breaks; death will be instantaneous.

Deer Deer can be found from the lower Arctic to the lower reaches of the jungle. They walk on two toes, leaving a definitive track. They live in open country and woods. Many have branched antlers, which they drop after the October rut – the mating time for deer and other hoofed animals. Red deer start off as spotted calves; during the summer their coats change to a red/brown colour. Their diet consists of grass, fruit, heather and tree bark; it is also not unknown for them to raid crops. Throughout the winter they separate into two herds, one female and one male, joining together into one large herd after the winter. During the rut the stags will be heard roaring.

Elk and Moose These are large deer, their coats ranging

leaves a print of the larger hind feet, followed by the print of the smaller front feet. The squirrel has a similar type of movement, with the hind feet landing in front of the fore feet, leaving the same type of print. Being so similar it would be very difficult to decipher which footprints had been left by which animal – if it were not for one simple clue. A squirrel's trail starts and ends at a tree.

A series of tracks made by an animal will give you a trail. This gives you an idea of the speed at which an animal was moving. The greater the gap between the groups of tracks the faster the movement. A walking animal moves its right fore foot first, followed by the left hind foot. Then the left fore foot is moved, followed by the right hind foot, and so on. A trail made by a walking badger will show that the hind foot has landed on the track of the fore foot. This is called 'being in register', and is what happens when an animal has been walking or trotting – it moves its legs in a definite order. If an animal has been galloping, the tracks will not be in register.

from grey/brown to black in colour. They live mainly solitary lives, but can live in small groups. Their habitat is open forest, especially close to water (they are very good swimmers). Marshlands make an ideal setting for them in the summer, although they often move to drier ground in the winter months. Their diet includes leaves, young shoots, water plants, grass and moss.

Wild Goat These have horns with a simple, gentle curve which can grow up to 1m (3.25ft) long. They tend to have a shaggy coat in the winter months, and live in small herds on open hillsides. They are found in the uplands of North and South America, Europe and Asia. Their diet includes grass, leaves, lichen and moss.

Wild Boar The adult wild boar has a dense, dark-coloured coat, although youngsters are striped. They have a long snout and the male has large tusks, which can grow up to around 30cm (12ins) long. The male lives a solitary life except in the rut. They live in deciduous woodlands and marshes of North America and Europe, and in the tropical forests of South America and Asia. Their diet includes roots, bulbs and fallen fruit. Some tropical boar can be very dangerous; despite their size they are able to attack humans, being fast, heavy and aggressive. Wild boar are heavily infested with worm.

Fox The fox's coat varies from sandy to a dark chestnut colour. The red fox has a bushy tail, usually with a distinctive white tip. Their preferred habitat is woodland, although they are very adaptable and will live in built-up areas. They are usually nocturnal, and are active all year round. Their natural diet includes young deer, small mammals, birds, poultry, grass and fruit. Foxes can sometimes be seen going to ground just before the sun comes up. They normally live in a single-entrance burrow, making them easy to catch if you dig them out.
Warning: Many foxes carry rabies.

Rodents Rodents belonging to the subspecies known as myomorpha make up about a quarter of all mammals. The best known of these animals are the various types of rats and mice. They have adapted themselves to surviving in almost any location except for Antarctica and the colder regions of the Arctic. Their diet usually consists of seeds and other vegetation; but certain species have become omnivorous, and will often eat any food left out by humans.

The problem for the survivor is that rodents are the carriers of many diseases – leptospirosis, rabies, ratbite fever, murine typhus, bubonic plague, hantavirus and spirochetal jaundice, etc. Through their urine, droppings and hair food can easily become

© 1995 Softkey International Inc.

Wild goat.

© 1995 Softkey International Inc.

Rackoon.

contaminated, and at the very least will pose a threat of bacterial food poisoning. Despite this, the animals are edible. This makes them a ready source of food, and one which mankind has often turned to, especially in times of famine.

Trapping vs. Hunting

• Hunting demands practised skills – silent movement, concealment, reading the natural environment, predicting animal behaviour. Survivors from urban backgrounds rarely have them. All potential prey animals do.

• Trapping demands the ability to visualise basic mechanical cause-and-effect, to fashion simple materials, and to study the surroundings. These are skills which even urban adults can master well enough to deceive most animals.

• Hunting means movement, sometimes over long distances. This expends the survivor's energy. If he is unsuccessful, it is not replaced.

• Making and setting traps and snares demands little strength, and less movement across country – therefore less energy loss.

• The hunter normally has to focus on a single prey. If that prey escapes him, his time and energy have been wasted.

• The trapper can set many snares, all of which are potentially working for him simultaneously and for 24 hours every day. They are dramatically more productive by the equation of cost against possible rewards.

Hamster In the West these have become popular pets, known for their docile nature. However, in their native environment in the Middle East, Russia, China and some areas of Europe they are often considered a pest, as they can cause serious damage to crops. They live in chambered burrows which can be found 20-30cm (8-12ins) below the surface of the ground. Being a naturally solitary animal, the hamster will defend its territory aggressively against any other hamster, and will even fight during mating. The female has a very weak maternal instinct and it is not unknown for her to abandon or even eat her young. The normal diet mainly consists of seeds, leaves, roots and fruit.

Norway Rat The Norway or Common Rat actually originated in eastern Asia, making its way into Europe at some time during the Middle Ages. This rat can be distinguished from others of its species by its blunter nose, smaller ears and shorter tail. It is a very adaptable animal, capable of living either in the wild or urban habitats, but its preferred environment is a wet or damp one. In towns it can therefore often be found living in cellars or in the sewer systems, whereas in its natural state it will live along river banks or beaches. The Norway rat is a burrowing animal; its burrows, usually in river banks, will often be up to half a metre (18ins) deep and will have several entrances and chambers. Small family groups, organised by a system of hierarchy, inhabit these chambers. These rats tend to have small territories and, as long as there is enough food, will stay within their boundaries. They are creatures of habit and will follow the same foraging trail each time they go to seek out food.

Jerboas Jerboas are desert-living rodents, able to cope with the high temperatures and aridity of their native regions of North Africa and Asia. Their bodies are small, with disproportionately large hind legs and feet enabling them to jump great heights and long distances. Their fore feet are smaller, with strong claws so that they can dig out their burrows at the edges of sand dunes. They have long, tufted tails which act as a balancing aid when they jump and also as a support when they stand upright. Jerboas have very broad heads and large eyes, which, in the nocturnal species of North Africa, help them to see in the dark; during the day they remain in their burrows with the entrances blocked to prevent any unnecessary evaporation of water. Their sense of hearing is extremely acute, allowing them to communicate even when scattered over a vast area. Like most desert living animals, jerboas receive all their water requirements from the food they eat.

Rodents are widespread but may carry disease.

The Preparation of Animals

Skinning and dressing an animal carcass will be much easier if it is done as soon after death as possible. First the carcass should be bled. Smaller and medium-sized animals can be hung upside down from a frame, with the ropes attached around the hocks. The throat should be cut and the blood collected in a container below. Do not throw away this blood; it contains many valuable vitamins, minerals and salt, and once it has been boiled thoroughly it can be used as a food source. It is ideal for thickening and adding flavour to soup.

Note: If you catch an extremely large animal such as a moose or bear, which is impossible to haul up for butchering, you should consider moving your camp to the beast rather than trying to carry it back piecemeal.

Preparing Rabbits Rabbits and small members of the cat family can provide a survivor with a relatively easy-to-catch source of meat. However, rabbits lack the fats and vitamins needed to sustain a survivor's health. Be aware that although a rabbit-rich diet may be easy and tasty, it can also lead to severe malnutrition over a period of time.

When skinning a rabbit, first make a cut behind the

head and make sure that it is large enough to insert two fingers. Peel the skin back and cut off the head and lower limbs. To gut the carcass, cut a line down the belly and open out the body. Most of the innards should fall out when you give the carcass a sharp shake, but make sure that any remaining pieces are scraped out with a knife and washed away with fresh water.

Preparing Rodents Rats and

Preparing a Rabbit

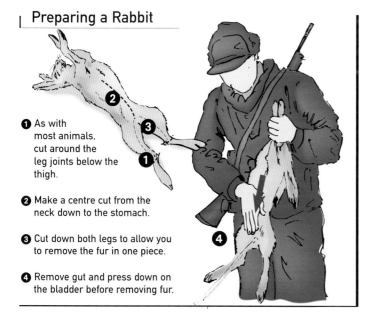

❶ As with most animals, cut around the leg joints below the thigh.

❷ Make a centre cut from the neck down to the stomach.

❸ Cut down both legs to allow you to remove the fur in one piece.

❹ Remove gut and press down on the bladder before removing fur.

CANNIBALISM

Although it may be thought controversial, this survival book would not be complete without brief reference to cannibalism. For the majority of people in developed and undeveloped countries alike it is a subject which is simply closed, with the choice of starvation being ultimately preferable. Yet in some long-term situations, where rescuers have failed to locate parties of survivors and those survivors have been unable to 'walk out', cannibalism has taken place – and repeatedly, over significant periods.

Out of these extreme situations two governing factors have emerged: time, and prevailing weather conditions. Those who have eaten human flesh have not done so until death from starvation has been imminent. It would also seem that their ability to collect food from the wild has been impaired due mainly to immobility, and cold weather conditions. These same weather conditions have also preserved the bodies of the dead in a condition which rendered the prospect of cannibalism less repugnant, i.e. they have been frozen.

Those who have eaten human flesh and have later been rescued alive have suffered humiliation and remorse once reunited with civilization, not so much at the hands of others as from their inner selves. It could be argued that this revulsion at their own remembered behaviour is countered by the fact that they are at least alive to feel it – but this is apparently an argument that does little to ease the conscience.

Butchering a rabbit is easy. Remember to keep the fur in one piece, and utilise the inedible parts for future bait.

Wild fowl can either be plucked or skinned, but the latter method will loose a lot of the food value.

mice are not only edible; they are delicious when stewed with dandelion leaves or other kinds of vegetable. Skin, gut and wash them in the usual way; but boil them for about ten minutes before any other form of cooking, to destroy any parasites or bacteria they may be harbouring.

Preparing Hedgehog, Porcupines etc. Animals that have a protective coat of spines or a thick shell are best rolled in a thick layer of clay and cooked in the embers of an open fire. Make sure that these animals, especially large ones, are cooked all the way through; any sign of blood when you open it means it is not cooked

properly. Crack and remove the clay; the spiny skin will pull off with it to reveal the flesh below. Eat only those parts you are familiar with, keeping the rest for use as bait.

Preparing Insects To humans, insects are not the most appetizing food source; yet any survivor would be foolish to overlook their potential. They are the most plentiful life form on earth, and pound for pound provide twice the amount of protein as the best steak. The tribal peoples of undeveloped regions continue to harvest this bounty with enthusiasm. This reticence to eat insects on the part of modern urban man is understandable, but

resistance is primarily based on aesthetic disgust at the thought of eating a live, wriggling, pollution-filled creepy-crawly – and the well-informed survivor will not have to face this ordeal.

Insects live both above and below ground; in either case their nests are easily found. Rotting logs provide homes for grubs, termites and beetles. Large flat stones make good nesting sites for a whole host of different species. Remember that insect larvae are also edible and highly nutritious.
Warning: A few insects are best left alone. These include any which are brightly-coloured or hairy, and those that carry disease such as

ticks, flies, and mosquitoes. Be aware that some adult insects will bite, and those with hard-shell bodies can harbour parasites.

Almost all insects are found in abundance, so their small individual size is of little consequence – the mass will provide enough protein. The appearance of insects is also of little importance other than providing the means to recognize its suitability for eating. The secret of dealing with insects lies in how they are prepared.

This is best done by collecting as many as possible – a minimum of several cupped handfuls. These should be placed in a metal container which has been preheated over a hot fire (a lid of some sort will stop the more active species from crawling out).

It will take several minutes for them to cook, and it is best to turn and shake the container in order to toss the insects and prevent them from burning. Once all the insects are inert, leave them to dry further beside the fire. A good test is to pick an insect from the container and crush it between your fingers; the whole body should disintegrate to a dark brown dust. Next, grind the cooked insects using a stick as a pestle. When this is done pour the powder into a container of warm water; this will separate the wings, legs and any body crustaceans, which will float on the surface where they can be removed. The remaining liquid is little more than a tasteless protein soup, to which edible plant parts can be added to make a nourishing meal.

Insects to Avoid

The following should not be considered as potential food under any circumstances:

• Those with bright colours – all over, or in spots, stripes or patterns. These are usually so coloured to warn animal predators of their poisonous nature.

Clay Cooking

❶ Wrap spiky animals such as hedgehogs in a thick layer of clay.

❷ Make sure it is cooked through before eating.

❸ Crack open the clay covering and the spines and skin will be easily removed

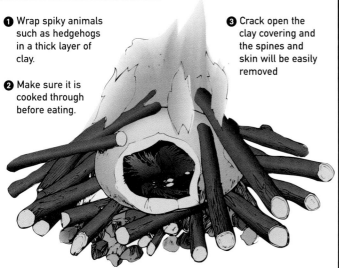

Worms are plentiful, and once dried they can be turned into a nourishing protein soup.

• Creatures with a hairy skin – again, these may be poisonous, or have stinging contact defence hairs.

• Ticks, flies, lice and mosquitoes, all of which carry disease.

• Those hard-shell insects which may carry parasites.

Properly prepared insects can be nourishing.

Butchering Larger Animals

Once your deer, pig, wolf, etc. has 'bled out', the carcass can be skinned:

❶ Make the first cut around the knee and elbow joints. Carefully make a full circular cut around the genital organs. Then, starting at each knee, cut the skin down to the abdomen, forming a V-shaped cut.

❷ Continue cutting down the front of the animal, stopping at its neck. Be careful not to pierce the abdominal wall beneath, as this will spoil the skin. To protect the abdominal wall from the knife, place your hand behind the cut, inside the carcass.

❸ Make two more cuts from the front elbow joints into towards the belly.

❹ Return to the hind legs and peel back the skin; a cutting and pulling action is best. Continue until the skin has been completely removed.

❺ Cut open the abdominal membrane – without piercing the stomach or other organs – down to the chest bone. Use wooden skewers to pin back the flaps. Much of the gut will fall from the stomach and drop onto the ground.

❻ Check that you have removed all internal organs, starting with the windpipe and moving upwards. To clear the entire mass, use a knife to make a deep circular sweep around the genital organs; avoid cutting the bladder.

❼ After inspection for any signs of disease, keep back the parts of the offal which will be useful (e.g. the kidneys, liver, heart, and the fat surrounding the intestines). Use the rest of the innards for bait, or to make sewing gut. Also keep back the meaty parts of the skull; the brain, eyes and tongue are all edible.

❽ Once you have cleaned and prepared the meat the skin can be cleaned and dried in order to preserve it.

Author's Note: This beast was shot as part of a planned and controlled cull in order to maintain the quality of its herd.

FISHING

Of all the aquatic foods, fish are the easiest to catch and offer the most obvious form of nourishment. Even with the crudest of fishing equipment, as long as you have knowledge and patience you will be able to catch enough fish for your needs. As with most things, catching fish is a skill and requires practice, and it is unlikely that you will catch much on your first attempt. With growing experience, patience, and the ability to vary your methods according to the situation, you will find a fishing technique which will achieve the results you want.

There are not many general rules that apply to fishing, as they can be caught by a variety of methods – hooks, nets, traps, snares, spears, stunning, poison, and even by simply using bare hands to grab them. All species differ in their feeding habits; however, it is generally accepted that most fish will take bait at dawn and dusk – look for the signs of feeding at those hours. Big fish are hard to catch as they are heavy and full of fight; if you do not have the correct fishing kit in your survival pack, then improvise. If you see large fish close to the surface try using a spear or bow and arrow, stalking your fish with extreme care in order to get close enough.

When and Where to Fish

In hot weather fish will tend to seek cooler water, either in deeper river pools or under shade; these are the places in which to cast for fish. The outer bank of a river bend also holds deeper water and this may be a good place to fish, especially if water levels are running low. Deep lakes are also good bets in hot weather. Fish tend to shelter below underwater rocks and logs or undercut riverbanks.

In cooler weather, or at dawn and dusk, fish tend to prefer shallower water or can be found around the edges of a lake or pond. Fish need a certain amount of warmth and will seek out warmer water. They also tend to feed better in shallow water. Fish will always lie in the water facing the oncoming current. This enables them to spot any food coming towards them, and also ensures a better flow of water over their gills. Knowing this, you will have better success if you let your natural bait move downstream towards likely shelter spots at a natural pace, so that they can see it and hopefully accept it as a normal piece of food.

Fish also like to be where the water is well aerated, such as at the bottom of a small waterfall. When using natural bait, cast it into the cascading water and let it move naturally down and across the pool, or for a little distance downstream if in moving water. Then, very smoothly and quietly, bring the line in and cast again as before. The best pole to use for this type of fishing is a

Sometimes fish are so plentiful that it is a simple matter of stunning them with rocks or sticks.

Look for Fish:

In warm weather:
• In deep pools and lakes

• Under shade, and undercut banks

• On the outside of bends In cool weather, and at dawn and dusk:

• In shallows

• Round the edges of ponds and lakes

In any weather:

• Under white water

slender, flexible one, as this enables the line to be pulled gently out of the water instead of being dragged back through it. This type of pole also makes casting and recovery a lot less effort for the angler. If you are fishing for carp, catfish or eels you need to be aware that they feed on the muddy beds of slow-moving rivers and ponds. With this in mind, bait will need to be cast on the bottom and then moved very slowly.

Bait Your first choice for bait should be food that is normal to the fish's diet. Before you start to fish on a stretch of water, study it and the surrounding shore for morsels normal to the fish. Look for insects, worms, shrimps, minnow or shellfish. If none of this natural bait is available you will have to substitute an alternative, such as small scraps of meat or artificial substitutes.

Fish are often attracted by the struggles of live bait. Try using a grasshopper or a beetle and see if it is taken by a fish. If it is, take another insect and carefully impale it on the hook without killing it. This should attract another bite from the fish, which this time will end up being caught. Minnows can also be used as bait in this manner, but under the water. The hook should pass through the body under the backbone and to the rear of the minnow. A float will be needed to keep the bait off the bottom of the water.

Lures and Hooks A lure is some form of artificial bait. It is designed to look like an insect or a small fish in order to fool the fish into thinking that what it sees is its natural food. A convincing appearance alone is not enough; the angler must also be able to manipulate the lure in order to mimic the movements of live bait struggling in the water.

Lures can be improvised from many sources of material. They can even be made from a tuft of hair (from your own head if necessary), feathers, a scrap of brightly coloured cloth, or a fish fin with a piece of flesh attached. In fact, anything will do as long as it looks like an insect of some description. The lure should be constructed around the hook so that this is hidden.

Your basic survival fishing kit should contain a good supply of variously sized hooks. Good fishing hooks can also be improvised from a wide variety of materials and items – thorns, safety pins, wire, etc. Always make sure that your hook is the correct size for the fish you are trying to catch; and that, once you get a bite, the hook will stay attached to the line.

Fishing Hints

Fish tend to be very wary, and will swim away and hide at the first sign of anything they perceive not to be in their normal pattern of events. They are able to detect even the slightest vibration in the water, and are even aware of heavy footfalls on the bank. Therefore it is vital that when you approach the edge of the water you do so slowly and gently to keep any ground vibration to a minimum. Keep as low as you can, as quiet as you can, and move as little as possible. Never let your shadow fall onto the water.

Put your bait into the water slightly upstream from the location of the fish, and allow it to drift downstream with the current until it has passed you. If by that time no fish has taken the bait, gently recover it and try again. If no fish take the bait after a few tries, change your fishing pitch – but remember to make your move slowly and quietly. If you still are having no luck, try again at the opposite end of the day, or even after dark if the water is clear and shallow.

Attracting Fish Attracting fish to a feeding ground is a good way to ensure a bite. Many anglers throw ground bait into the water to lure fish into what they perceive to be a good feeding ground. If you have plenty of bait it is recommended that you do the same. An alternative method when fishing in a pond, pool or lake is to tie a piece of unwanted offal or carrion to a branch overhanging the water. This will attract blowflies to lay their eggs in the meat. After a

Attracting fish with carrion.

Fish Hooks

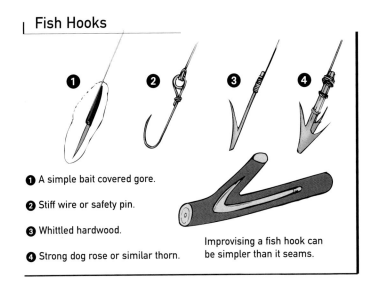

❶ A simple bait covered gore.

❷ Stiff wire or safety pin.

❸ Whittled hardwood.

❹ Strong dog rose or similar thorn.

Improvising a fish hook can be simpler than it seams.

Night Line

1 A float will indicate when you have a bite.

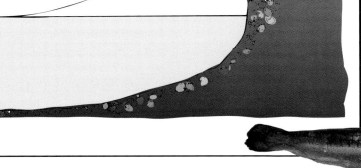

2 The addition of a weight will allows you to determine what depth your bait is.

few days maggots will appear, and will fall into the water at a steady rate, thus attracting the fish. If you then place one on your hook you should soon catch something; better still, use a large net.

Night Line Fishing A night line consists of a line with one or more hooks which is left in the water all night. The hooks (preferably gorge hooks) should be baited with something that cannot easily be lifted off by eels, such as a small fish or a small piece of meat. The line should then be fastened firmly to a rock or a stake on the bank or an overhanging branch. The line should be checked every morning for a catch; if here is one, remove it and replace the

bait. The line can have a single hook, or several stretched on a line across the river. The depth of the hook can be adjusted with weights to catch variety of fish under most conditions.

Fish Traps Fish traps can be used in both fresh and sea water. The type of trap required will be dependent on the water in which you are fishing and the size of the fish. Traps can be made to be portable or permanent.

The most common form of fish trap is the portable basket type, built with a cone-shaped entrance. They can be constructed from hazel or willow sticks, reeds or bamboo, or improvised from man-made discarded containers such as

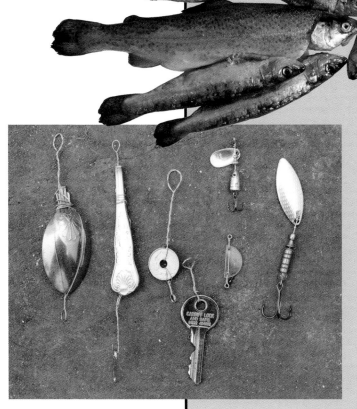

Commercial and improvised lures.

Fish Pen

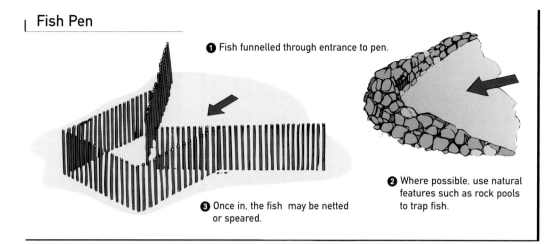

❶ Fish funnelled through entrance to pen.

❷ Where possible, use natural features such as rock pools to trap fish.

❸ Once in, the fish may be netted or speared.

Water can be channelled into natural features to trap fish.

a plastic bottle. This shape makes it easy for the fish to get in and almost impossible to escape. Once constructed, the pot should be baited and placed facing upstream in a river or a rock pool.

Permanent Traps An on-site trap can be made by piling stones or driving wooden stakes into the riverbed to form a pen. It may be necessary to form the trap in such a way that fish will be funnelled through the entrance into a secure compound. The siting of the trap is critical, but where possible full advantage should be taken of natural features which will enhance your catch and save time and energy. It may be possible to herd fish by wading into the water starting 100 metres upstream and walking towards the trap. Trapped fish can be speared with a sharp stick.

Fish and Wild Fowl Snares

Snaring fish is not as easy as snaring small game, but it works on similar principles and can be achieved with time, care and observation. Take a normal animal snare and attach it to the end of a stick, which should be at least 200cm (80ins) long. Tie an extension on to the end of the snare wire so that you can close the noose at will. (see page 87.)

Fishing Nets It may even be

possible for the survivor to make and use his own fishing net – a gill net – as long as he has enough line (a possible

source for this would be a parachute rigging line). First decide how long the net has to be, and then tie the top line of the net between two saplings or stakes the right distance apart. Tie another line below this to define the width of the net. Any nylon lines that are available should have their inner cores stripped out. Take a piece of this inner core and double it. Tie it to the upper of the two lines using an overhand loop. The two ends, which should be 30% longer than the required width of the net, should then be allowed to hang down loose. It is now just a matter of repetitive knotting; but you probably have lots of time on your hands. Depending on your location, the materials available and your ability to manage it, make your net as large as possible.

Providing a stream is not too wide nets can be erected right across it; if it is, then the stream can often be dammed to make it narrower. Support the net by stretching a line across and secure the bottom edge in the water with heavy stones. In a larger body of water, such as a river, nets should be set just above or below an eddy.

Wherever they are set, it should always be in a stretch of quiet water. On a lake shore the net should be set at right angles to the bank, preferably off a small headland.

Minnow Traps Small fish

Portable Fish trap

❶ Portable fish traps should be woven according to the size of fish you are trying to catch.

❷ Place in the water with the mouth facing upstream.

Making a Fish Net

1 Place your top line between two trees and hitch a double length of cord every 3cm.

2 Cross tie the hanging strands with a simple granny knot to form a diamond pattern.

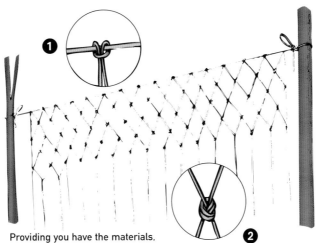

Providing you have the materials, making a fish net is always a good idea. Not only can it be used for catching fish and game, it is also handy when gathering plants.

such as minnows can be found in most water, especially where it is shallow, such as at the edge of a river or a lake. A normal net will be too large, but several fine-meshed nets can be constructed from a pair of women's tights. Cut a length off the tights, knotting one end if it is not the toe piece; splay the open end around a ring of stiff wire, and secure this to a forked branch. A well-perforated tin can attached in the same way will serve the same task. Do not disregard the food value of very small fish; dried and roasted in quantity, they make good eating.

Eel Traps A simple eel trap can be made from a suitable box. On each side of the box, near the top, make a couple of small holes. Inside the box lay some ripe meat as bait. Weight the box and put it into the water, checking it every two or three days. (To do this, take the box out of the water

first and part-empty it before opening it to see what you have caught. Eels are proverbially slippery, and it is almost impossible to hold on to them long enough to lift them out of the water.)

Spearing Spearing fish can be difficult, especially in the hours of daylight, but with practice it is possible. The fish will need to be fairly plentiful if you use a single-point spear, and you are advised to use a three-pronged head or trident for greater efficiency. The spear should be stabbed into the water at the fish, not thrown; and the stab should be aimed directly downwards. Spearing in this way reduces refraction in the water, and thus the risk of misjudging the angle; and will also pin any speared fish to the streambed. The best position for this method is

standing directly over a fish run. Make sure the spear is strong enough to withstand the thrashing of a large fish. Always chase after a badly-wounded fish, as they will not go far.

In much the same way, fish can be shot using a bow and arrow. Use long arrows which will be visible above the surface and will restrict the movement of any wounded fish trying to escape.

Tickling Trout Trout are extremely nervous fish which are to be found only in clear, moving water. They prefer to conceal themselves beneath some sort of cover such as undercut banks, rocks and logs, or even in water rat holes. When they are in this cover it is possible to catch one by hand, something which would be impossible in open water.

Tickling a Trout

When you get near what looks like a good spot for trout, lie on the bank and dip your hand in the water to bring it to water temperature. Begin at the downstream end of any possible cover, working upstream, gently and carefully feeling for fish. If fish are present you will encounter the tail first. This should be gently stroked a few times before moving the strokes up the body towards the gills. Once your hand is under the gills, flick the fish quickly out of the water and on to the bank.

There are three main factors to tickling trout successfully:

- Knowing where the fish can be found. Carefully study the water, and discover where they hide.

- Be relaxed. Most people will flinch at the first contact will a slimy fish – prepare yourself mentally not to react. Move slowly and gently, and touch it lightly.

- Be warned that trout are very slippery fish to handle – roll your body back on to the bank as you flick the fish out of the water.

Take time to study their habitat before trying to catch fish.

Killing or Stunning with Poison Poisons, usually derived from plant sources, are used by some native peoples to catch fish. Fish are quickly affected by poison being introduced into the water, normally rising to the surface quite soon. The speed at which the poison works will depend on the water temperature. Around 21 degrees C (70 degrees F) or warmer is ideal.

One of the most common poisons is rotenone, a substance found in tropical plants that stuns or kills cold-blooded animals while leaving the flesh safe to eat. The following plants can be used to stun or kill fish:

- Derris eliptica is the main source of commercially produced rotenone, which is a natural pesticide. The roots from this large order of tropical shrubs and woody vines are ground and mixed with water, which is then thrown into the river. Where possible the mixture is best left overnight to strengthen.
- Anamirta cocculus is a woody vine which grows in southern Asia and on islands in the South Pacific. Crush the bean-shaped seeds and throw them in the water.
- Croton tiglium is a shrub or small tree that grows in waste areas on islands of the South Pacific and which produces seeds capsules.

Crush the seeds and throw them into the water.
- Barringtonia is a large tree that grows near the sea in Malaysia and other tropical regions. It produces a fleshy one-seeded fruit that can often be found rotting on the ground. Both the seeds and the bark of this tree can be used as fish poison by crushing and throwing into the water.
- On the coastline, burning coral or seashells can produce lime. The white dust residue can be thrown into the water.

Crustaceans Crustaceans include crabs, lobsters, crayfish, shrimp and prawns. All are edible, and can be found in fresh and salt water around the world. Most are best caught at night, using a light such as a torch held near the surface of the water. Mussels, limpets, clams and periwinkles can also be eaten, as can scallops, sea urchins and starfish.

To clean a crustacean, throw away the intestines and gills – the rest of the meat, including that inside the shell and claws, can be eaten. Warning: All crustaceans must be thoroughly cooked as soon as they are caught, as they do not keep. If you delay in eating any crustacean or you fail to cook it properly, then you run the risk of the worst type of food poisoning.

Frogs make good eating, but must be skinned before eating – the skin can be poisonous.

Crustaceans all make good eating, but must be thoroughly cooked and eaten immediately after catching.

Frogs Small amphibians such as newts and frogs can also provide a good meal. They are to be found around fresh water, usually revealing their presence by croaking. However, any croaking will stop as you approach, so have plenty of patience and keep still until they are fooled into thinking that you have gone away again. During the mating season (February/March) catching frogs becomes quite easy. All you need to do is to splash the back of your hand gently against the surface water and frogs will jump onto it. It is possible to catch several in as many minutes.

Preparing Fish, Snakes and Amphibians Once you have caught a fish you will need to bleed it immediately. To gut the fish, slit open its stomach from the lower jaw to the tail and scrape out the innards. Wash the area thoroughly to flush out any remaining pieces. Fish can be cooked with their scales on, but if you have the time they make more pleasant eating with their scales removed. To do this, scrape downwards with a knife from the tail to the head. Fish such as catfish and sturgeon, which do not have any scales, can be skinned instead.

Smaller fish, e.g. those less than 3 inches long, do not need gutting, but some will still need scaling or skinning. The head should also be cut off unless you are going to cook the fish on a spit. Raw fish may contain parasites, and should only be eaten cold if the means to cook are outside your capabilities. This should very seldom be the case if you have a fire; fish can be cooked in a wide variety of ways – spit-roasted, baked, boiled or fried. Fish heads, tails and intestines all make good bait.

Gutting and cleaning fish before cooking: slit open the stomach (top), scrape out the inside (middle), and clean thoroughly in fresh water.

Spear Fishing

• Stand directly above a 'run' used by fish

• Use a strong, three-pointed spear

• Don't throw it – stab directly downwards

• Chase any wounded fish

Snakes and Reptiles Skin a snake by cutting off its head and slitting its body skin from the severed end downwards for about 20cm (8 inches). Peel back the skin to the length of the cut; grip the flesh and continue pulling the skin downward until within a few centimeters of the tail; then cut off the remainder. If the snake body looks bloated or lumpy, split it open and remove the innards. Cut the body flesh into small sections and cook – roasting or boiling is best.

Lizards, frogs and turtles are good to eat. Before cooking, take off the head and skin; this is particularly important in the case of frogs, as their skins may contain a poison. Turtles will need to be boiled first to remove the shell. The turtle meat can then be sliced up and used to make a tasty soup with vegetables.

Molluscs Shellfish make an excellent base for a soup to which vegetables can be added. In addition, they can be boiled, steamed or baked in their shells.

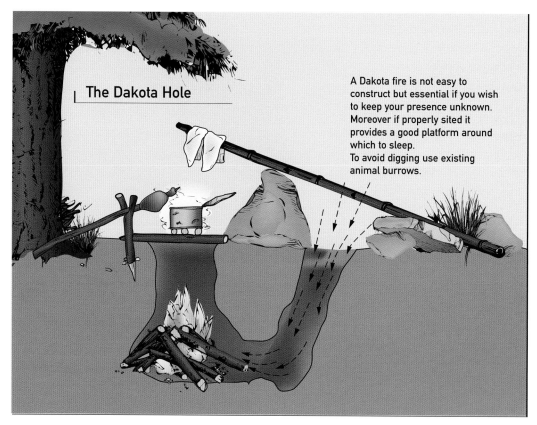

The Dakota Hole

A Dakota fire is not easy to construct but essential if you wish to keep your presence unknown. Moreover if properly sited it provides a good platform around which to sleep.
To avoid digging use existing animal burrows.

Methods of Cooking

The proper preparation and cooking of food will make it safer to eat as well as more appetising and digestible.

If possible you must try to have one hot meal a day. Most foods, whether animal or plant, require some form of preparation, whether washing, cleaning, scaling, plucking or skinning. How you cook the food also makes a difference, and will eliminate wastage. In the event of a food surplus the survivor is advised to prolong its edible life by preserving.

Roasting Stick Initial roasting should be done over a high heat, which will crust the outside of the meat and seal the juices in. This is followed by slowly turning the meat over a more placid flame. The dripping juices will cause the flames to flare and burn the meat; prevent this by placing a tray below the roast. These juices can be used to baste the roast, and improve its flavour. Larger animals (those larger than a domestic cat) should be cut into small pieces before roasting. These can be roasted by simply pushing the meat onto a stick and holding it over or near hot embers. If you do not want to sit and hold the stick you could construct an arm or a crane.

Automatic Spit With a little ingenuity you can prevent food from burning by constructing a spit which is turned by the wind. This not only cooks the food evenly, but saves the time which is otherwise wasted while watching to make sure the food does not burn. A normal crane is fitted with a wire line (cord will burn through) on which the meat is hung.

A roasting stick.

Adding a flat slab of bark about the size of your open hand will allow the wind to twist the meat; a natural counter-action will turn it back the other way.

Boiling Tough meat will need to be boiled to tenderize it, even if you intend to finish it off by some other cooking method. Any nutritional value leached out of the meat through the cooking process will also be retained in the water, which makes boiling a very efficient cooking method as long as you retain and use the water. One thing to remember, however, is that the higher in altitude you go, the longer it will take for water to reach boiling point due to the reduction in air pressure. Above 4000m (12,000ft)

cooking raw food by boiling becomes almost impossible and should not be attempted.

Water can be boiled even if you have no metal container – you just have to look for alternatives. Suitable containers, which will not burn while the water is boiling, include half a green coconut; or a short length of bamboo, cut just below each of two joints; or a suitable large shell. A large single banana leaf, or a waterproof container made from a piece of folded birch bark, will also hold water while it is boiled as long as the fire is kept low and the leaf or bark kept moist. Use thorns to pin the folded corner points.

Baking Baking is a less intense form of cooking than

Attaching a 'flag' above your Billy can will cause the breeze to gently turn it, thus cooking your food evenly.

roasting, and the heat is more constant. To be baked food must be enclosed, either in an oven, or in a wrapping of leaves or clay in a pit under the fire, or in any closed container. Baking is best done with glowing coals rather than flame.

Steaming Steaming food can be done without having a container. It is best for foods which do not need much cooking, such as tender greens. The other advantage of steaming is that it retains more of the nutrients in the food than any other method of cooking. To use this method, first dig a pit and place in it a layer of heated stones. Cover the stones with leaves and put the food to be cooked on top of the leaves. Use more leaves to cover over the food, and push a stick down into the food space. Finally, pack a top layer of earth over the leaves and around the stick. Withdrawing the stick will leave a little hole that leads down to the food space.

When water is poured down this hole it will hit the hot rocks and turn to steam, slowly but effectively cooking your food.

Cleaning Fish

• As soon as you land a fish, kill it by hitting the head with a stone or club.

• Slit the stomach from jaw to tail.

• Scrape out the innards.

• Wash out the body cavity thoroughly.

• Hold the tail and scrape off the scales, moving down towards the head.

• Unless you are going to cook on a spit, cut off the head.

• Don't eat fish raw – cook by spit-roasting, baking in embers, or frying.

• Keep head, tail and guts for bait.

Crustaceans

• All crabs, crayfish, shrimps, prawns, etc, start to spoil the moment they are caught.

• Cook them at once, by dropping them alive into boiling water.

• Only thorough cooking destroys any organisms they may contain.

• Throw away the innards and the gills.

• The meat inside the shell and claws is edible.

• Failure to cook quickly enough, or thoroughly, invites serious food poisoning.

The Hangi

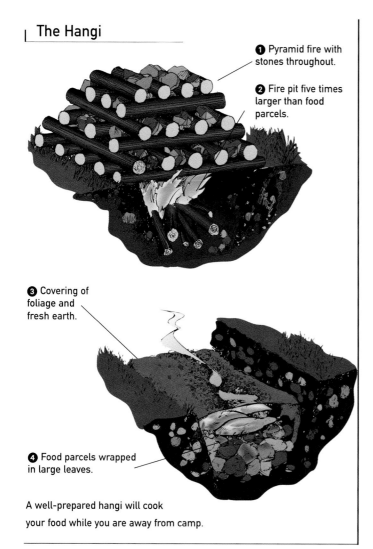

1 Pyramid fire with stones throughout.

2 Fire pit five times larger than food parcels.

3 Covering of foliage and fresh earth.

4 Food parcels wrapped in large leaves.

A well-prepared hangi will cook your food while you are away from camp.

Hangi The hangi is a cooking method which originally came from Polynesia. It is slow and safe, especially if you need to be away from camp, or if you have no utensils to cook your food in. First, dig a pit five times the size of the food parcel it must accommodate. Lay your tinder and kindling in the middle of the pit. Make a pyramid fire above the hole, placing each layer of logs at right angles to the last layer. Build this up to a height of about six layers, with fist-sized stones and rocks placed between the layers. (Do not use soft, porous or flaking stones such as limestone, as these may explode when exposed to heat.) Once the fire is established it will burn its way through the log pyramid and the hot stones will fall into the pit.

Rake the hot embers to the side of the pit exposing the hot stones. The food should be wrapped in large, clean leaves (make sure that they are not poisonous) and placed on the stones. Meat and any other food which needs the most cooking should be placed at the hottest point of the pit, that is, the centre. Softer foods such as vegetables should be placed nearer the edges. Once all the food has been packed into the hangi, cover the pit with a roof of foliage and seal it pit with the earth spoil, to keep the heat in and prevent animals from foraging. The food may take three to four hours to cook in this way, but the advantage is that it will not become overcooked even if left for up to eight hours.

Improvised Haybox Another method of slow-cooking food is to construct an improvised haybox. This will prove especially valuable where firewood is scarce, and allows for a meal to cook safely while you are is out foraging or attending to more pressing matters. Another benefit of the haybox is that it cooks food well and cannot overcook or burn it.

A box or container is lined with a thick layer of insulating material; if no such container is available then a polythene bag will do. As the name implies, hay was used as the insulating material but more modern insulating materials such as polystyrene or crumpled newspaper can also be used. The other requirement is a can which will act as a cooking pot, preferably one with a well-fitting lid. Heat you meal over a fire until it starts to boil, then seal the cooking pot with a tight-fitting lid. Place it at the centre of your haybox and surround it with well-packed insulating material. Leave for approximately five hours before opening. It is advisable (although not necessary) to bring the pot back to the boil over an open fire before eating.

Flesh Food Preservation

Food-gathering may not always be successful: there will be times when game will be difficult to find or catch, or when the weather will make food collection difficult. The survivor must not rely on the assumption that a regular supply of wild food will always be available. In these circumstances, knowing how to preserve and store foods is a valid survival skill. Preserved food will not only back up fresh supplies but may also be carried with you if you plan to move on.

The aim of food preservation is to prevent the deterioration of the food and so prevent wastage. A cold climate makes food preservation relatively easy, as the food can be quickly frozen. To do this, cut it into small strips or pieces and lay it out on the ground around the shelter. Make sure that scavengers do not steal it while it is freezing. Frozen food should also be stored at least 6ft above ground level, out of the reach of other hungry animals.

Meat can be dried either in the sun and wind or else over a fire. The aim of drying is to drive as much of the moisture content from the meat as possible. This not only concentrates its nutritional value, but will also preserve it longer from decomposition and moulds. A piece of dried meat should contain only about 5% of its pre-dried content of moisture. Meat should be

Air-dried meat.

cut into long, thin strips and placed to dry on a platform safe from scavengers but open to the sun and wind. The process may take up to two weeks, and during this time the strips need to be kept dry from any rain and free from flies.

In warm or damp weather when meat deteriorates rapidly, smoking over a low fire can save it from spoiling for some time. Care must be taken to keep the meat from getting too hot. Cutting it across the grain into thin strips and either drying it in the wind or smokng it will produce 'jerky', which was one of the staple foods of the pioneers. Fish should be flattened by removing the backbone, and skewered in that position for smoking; thin willow branches with the bark removed make good skewers. Willow, alder, cottonwood, birch, and dwarf birch make the best smoking woods, and are found throughout the Arctic and sub-Arctic regions. Pitch woods such as fir and pine should not be used.

A small version of a North American tepee with a platform constructed in the middle makes an excellent smokehouse. By tying meat to the upper ends of the poles and closing the smoke flaps a good concentration of smoke is obtained. Try to create a fire with little flame which produces quantities of smoke. The meat will be ready when it is brittle.

Plants, leaves and fruits can also be dried by the methods described. To dry fruits successfully, cut them into thin slices first. Mushrooms also dry well, but may need to be soaked in water before use.

Berries are best preserved by being turned into jam or jelly.

Salt Brine Salt is difficult to find in the wild, but if you are near the coast it is well worth your while simply boiling sea water until it evaporates. Salt can be used in the preservation of either wet or dry food.

In cool climates, joint your game into usable pieces, rub with salt and allow to hang in the fresh air; repeat the salt-rubbing process for several days. If a container is available, make a strong slurry of salt and water (natural sea water is not strong enough for preservation); submerge your meat completely in this, and cover.

Store the container in a cool, shaded spot.

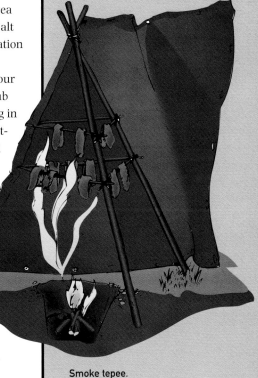

Smoke tepee.

Preserve food whenever you can – your supply of fresh food could run out at any time.

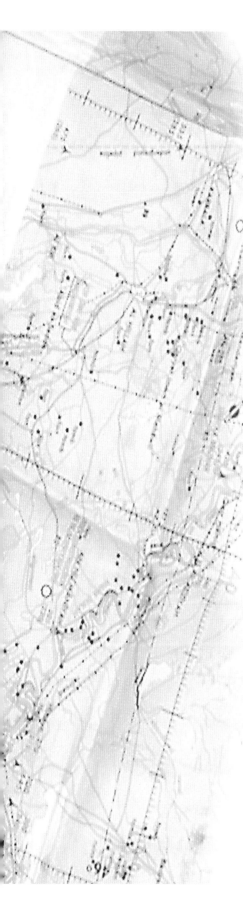

NAVIGATION

There are several ways one can navigate and define direction. Using the sun, moon and stars is the oldest, while a map and compass is the most traditional. However, the introduction of the satellite Global Positioning System (GPS) in the 1980s has totally redefined navigational methods, to the point where most shipping and aircraft have become reliant upon it. To the survivor any method of navigation is acceptable providing it is accurate, but a sound knowledge of how to use a map and compass will always prove a bonus. Other basic navigational skills, not dependent on map, compass or GPS, can also be learnt and are extremely useful in survival situations.

Maps A map is a sheet of paper on which an aerial view of the area it represents is drawn. The detail included on the map will vary, depending on who did the survey, what use the map is intended for, and the scale.

Most maps have one thing in common: almost all have a grid overlay dividing the map into squares which are either lettered, numbered or both. Most maps also contain a legend explaining the scale, distance and symbolised features.

Different maps are made to suit different purposes. Aircraft operators and strategic planners normally use maps with a scale of 1/250,000; these provide only generalised information and show only principal features. Maps used by the military for route

selection are normally to a scale of 1/50,000; these show detailed features and relief. This book uses a 1/50,000 scale map to illustrate the meaning of elevation, contour intervals, conventional signs, the grid sys-

tem, and information on magnetic variation.

Compasses A compass is a precision instrument which allows the user to identify North and thus the other cardinal points. Used in conjunction with a map, it allows for navigation over the surface of the planet. There are many shapes and sizes of compass, but all work on the principle of a magnetised needle continually pointing North. Always remember that any compass works on the magnetic attraction situated close to the North Pole; local power supplies or heavy metal objects can pull the needle from its correct course. Most compass manufacturers dampen the movement of the

needle by filling the compass housing with a liquid. This sometimes produces a bubble, but providing that this is not large it should not affect the operation of the compass. This book uses a 'Silva'-type compass to illustrate the various uses, and its relationship to a map.

Conventional Signs Every map has a panel of conventional signs which indicate a variety of objects such as roads, railways, rivers, cliffs, buildings, etc. In a survival situation identifying a man-made object on a map which covers your area can lead you

Whenever you stop to rest, it is a good opportunity to check your map.

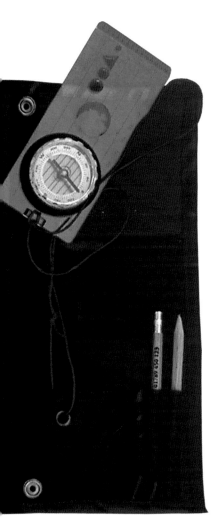

Protecting your maps and compass will ensure their lon-term usefulness.

One of the many pocket-size compasses on the market.

Map Scale

Maps to a scale of 1/50,000 show all roads, tracks, paths, rivers, streams, lakes and most man-made eatures. In addition they indicate ground relief using contour lines, and areas of forest. The numbered grid divides the map into 1000m (1,093 yard) squares that convert into longitude and latitude bearings.

Finding Your Way

• Given a rough idea of your position relative to inhabited areas, you can find and follow an approximate direction across country even if you are a lifelong city-dweller.

• Map, compass, and basic knowledge of their use are very valuable; but even without them you need not be 'lost'.

• You may have the means to make yourself a simple compass.

• Even if not, the sun by day and the stars by night will always show you the direction of North.

LIFESAVER
The Compass
This compass is constructed with a clear plastic base and a compass housing which contains the magnetic needle. The base of the compass has a magnifying glass and is etched with a variety of scales and a number of romers – scales to accurately divide a grid square into tenths to help calculate grid references. The rim of the compass housing can be rotated, and is marked with segments showing degrees, mills or both, while printed on the base is an arrow and orienteering lines. The 'bearing' gives the direction to a certain point. It can be defined as the number of degrees in an angle measured clockwise from a fixed northern gridline ('easting'). The bearing for North is always 0/360 (the number of degrees in a circle) or 0/6400 (the number of mills in a full circle).

tour values, which are given to the nearest metre, are marked so that they read facing uphill. Remember, however, that while the heights are in metres, the contour lines are 50 feet apart.

Setting a Map by Inspection If you possess a map that you know to represent the local area, you will be able to orientate yourself. Look for an obvious and permanent landmark, for example a river, road or mountain. Identify the feature on the map, and then simply align

the map to the landmark. The map is now 'set' to conform to the surrounding features. If you do not have a compass, make a note of a distant feature at one of the cardinal points – North, East, West or South.

Setting a Map by Compass You can set any scale map and align it with the surrounding terrain by simply using a compass. Choose a North-South grid line on the map, and lay a flat edge of the compass along it with the direction arrow pointing towards North (top of the map). Then, holding the map

to safety. A complete study should be done of any map in your possession to establish not only your position, but also what else is in the area. Even if it is barren of any human structures it may guide you to a more habitable place of food and shelter.

Contours Contours are used to represent different elevations – e.g. valleys, hills and mountains – on a flat surface such as a paper map. They are intended to give a perspective view of shape and elevation. Each contour line follows the same height around the hills, into the re-entrants, and over the spurs. On the 1/50,000 Ordnance Survey map the contour lines are 50 feet apart. Therefore, if the lines are close together it follows that the land is rising very quickly, and if far apart, that the slope is gentle. Con-

Reading Contours

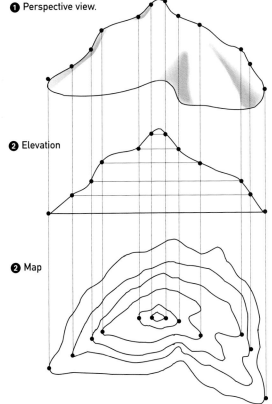

❶ Perspective view.

❷ Elevation

❷ Map

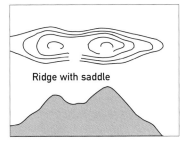

Ridge with saddle

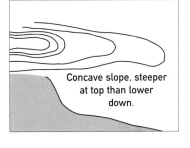

Concave slope, steeper at top than lower down.

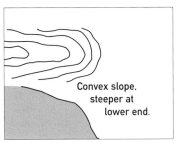

Convex slope, steeper at lower end.

and compass together, turn both until the compass needle points North. The map is now set to conform to the surrounding features.

Finding a Grid Reference

Almost all maps are covered with light horizontal and vertical lines, each marked with a two-digit number. These are called grid lines – on a 1/50,000 map they are blue and spaced 1km (0.62 miles) apart. The vertical lines are called 'eastings': these are always given first when quoting a grid reference. The horizontal lines are called 'northings'; these are given after the eastings. The numbers straddling the left grid line of the easting and the centre bottom of the northing defines each grid square – an example is illustrated.

As each grid square measures 1000m by 1000m – which is quite a large area – it is desirable to reduce this by calculating a six-figure grid reference. This is done by mentally dividing the square into tenths – e.g. half way up or across a square would be '5'. This reference is then added after the relevant easting or northing figure. To gauge the tenths accurately use the romer on the compass, or a protractor as illustrated.

Taking a Compass Bearing from the Map

Once you have established where you are, and where you wish to go, you can work out your route. Plot the most logical route to your objective, taking into account the distance, terrain and any obstacles. Divide your route up into 'legs', if possible finishing each leg close to a prominent feature, e.g. a bend in a river or the corner of a forest area. If using a 1/50,000 scale map the ideal distance for each leg should not be longer than the length of your compass base.

First take a bearing from where you are (call this point A) to the feature at the end of your first leg (call this point B). Place one edge of the compass along the line joining A to B, making sure that the direction-of-travel arrow is pointing in the way you want to go. Hold the compass plate firmly in position and rotate the compass dial so that the lines engraved in the dial base are parallel to the North-South grid lines on the map.

Finally, read off the bearing next to the line-of-march arrow on the compass housing. To walk on this bearing, simply keep the magnetic arrow pointing North over the etched arrow in the base, and follow the line-of-march arrow as illustrated. Repeat this process for each leg.

Magnetic Variation

When we talk about 'North', bear in mind that there are three Norths. True North is not generally used in navigation; it is the fixed location of the North Pole. Grid North is more familiar – it is the North indicated by the gridlines on a map. Magnetic North is where the needle on the compass always points due to the strong magnetic attraction generated by the Earth's magnetic field. However, the direction of magnetic North may vary by a small fraction from year to year due to changes in this magnetic field. This difference can be calculated using the information shown on the map, i.e. the date it was printed and the degree of

Magnetic Variation: Don't Panic!

Some people put a lot of emphasis on adding or subtracting the magnetic variation, but for survival purposes you can virtually forget about it. By simply shortening the legs of your selected route and choosing a prominent feature to march towards or from, you reduce the risk of magnetic variation error. Some will criticize me for saying this; but I have never bothered to work out the magnetic variation when walking – and I have walked across more desert, jungle and Arctic tundra than most. That said, it is advisable to adjust the variation when plotting long routes across barren land, or when travelling by vehicle.

Grid Reference

A compass with a built in romer makes it easy to subdivide a grid square and produce a more accurate six figure reference.

The example shown is 175298

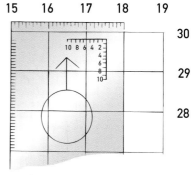

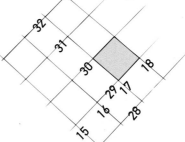

Contour lines close together mean steep slopes.

Check your map whenever you reach a prominent feature.

ty can be avoided if you consult the map every time you meet a prominent feature. Careful study of the map should provide you with a mental picture of the ground relief, which will in turn warn you of any obstacles such as rivers or marshland.

There is a tendency during conditions of fog or poor visibility to wander downhill when you are contouring. Every 100m or so take a few steps uphill to compensate for this. Don't forget that you will move slower in poor visibility.

Global Positioning System (GPS) Developed by the United States Department of Defense, the GPS system consists of 24 military satellites which orbit the Earth, continually giving out the time and their position. Receiver units on Earth pick up this information and convert it into readable information. Designed primarily for the military, the system now guides most of the world's shipping, aircraft (and

'smart' missiles).

Many outdoor workers and enthusiasts also carry small hand-held units, no larger than a mobile phone. The GPS unit is able to receive and assimilate information from several satellites, converting it into a recognizable position and altitude at any point on the Earth's surface. Receiving units commercially available to civiians vary, as does their accuracy. A deliberate error, called Selective Availability (SA), was built into the system. This 'dithers' the signals so that only a Coarse Acquisition (CA) can be obtained,

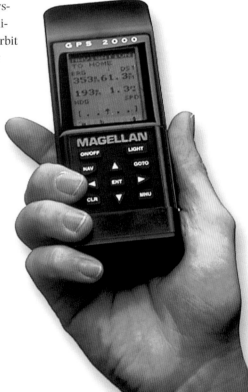

Hand-held GPS unit.

variation. This variation is then either added or subtracted to Grid North to get a more accurate bearing. Put simply:

'Mag to Grid, get rid' – i.e. subtract the variation from your compass bearing before applying it to the map.

'Grid to Mag, add' – i.e. add the variation to your map bearing before applying it to your compass.

Keeping on Course Three factors will determine which route you take: the weather, the time of day, and the terrain between you and your final destination.

In good visibility, select features that are both prominent on your map and visible to the eye. Once you have taken a bearing, choose a feature along the line of march and head towards it. This saves you constantly looking at your compass. A back bearing will help keep you on course if the terrain pushes you off track, i.e. you are forced to contour or avoid some obstacle (see box). Success in reaching your final goal depends upon having confidence in your route selection, and not becoming a slave to your compass. Mistakes in poor visibili-

therefore reducing accuracy to about 40m (130 feet). The SA can be overridden for military use by a 'P' code, and this gives an accuracy of about 10m (33 feet). P-code receivers are very costly and are not normally available for civilian use. All users of GPS systems, however, can experience P-code type accuracy during times of heavy military activity, when the SA is switched off.

How it Works The GPS receiver unit searches for and then locks on to any satellite signals in the sky above. The more signals you receive, the greater the accuracy, but a minimum of four is sufficient. The information received is then collated into a usable form – for example, a grid reference, height above sea level, or a longitude and latitude. Individual requirements for use either on land or at sea can be programmed into the unit. By measuring your position in relation to a number of known objects, i.e. the satellites, the receiver is able to calculate your position. This is called satellite ranging. It is also able to update your position, speed and track while you are on the move; and can pinpoint future waypoints, thereby taking away the need for recognizable landmarks.

Making a Sketch Map All aircraft and most vehicles which venture away from civilization carry maps, and these should be located first. If nothing is found then consid-

GPS

❶ Hand held unit locks on to any satelite in its range.

❷ At least four satelites need to be available. The more contacts, the more accurate will be the information returned.

❸ Satelites return signal to GPS unit.

❹ The unit translates the signal into information required; grid reference; height above sea level etc.

eration should be given to drawing a sketch map.

The sketch map will help you to plan any travel, indicate to others the route taken, and provide an easy reference to navigation.

A sketch map is best drawn similar in orientation to that of a normal map, i.e. with North at the top centre of your sketch. Choose a high vantage point to observe the surrounding countryside, and fill in the detail working outwards from the centre. Divide your map using a distance grid ruled along the top and down the left side. Next draw in all prominent features – mountains, rivers, forests, marshes, etc – using the grid as an estimate of distance. If

no coloured pens are available, black and white line drawings are fine; information can be qualified by the addition of notes. Mark camp sites and routes as you travel.

Electronic Compass Electronic compasses have been around for a number of years, but until recently they have not behaved well and were fairly unreliable. However, a newer improved generation has started to appear which provide something between a magnetic compass and GPS. Partly developed through military technology, the electronic compass has a num-

Back Bearing

If you become disorientated there is a simple way to pinpoint your position and keep yourself on course. This is called a back bearing; as the name implies, it is the oposite to a forward (normal) bearing. For example, if a bearing is 260°, and you subtract half a circle – 180° – you get a back bearing of 80°. If the original bearing is less than 180° you simply add 180°; e.g. if your bearing is 60°, plus 180° gives you a back bearing of 240°.

This has several uses. If you leave a prominent feature and move across rough terrain which forces you off your line of march, you can always double-check by converting your bearing to a back bearing and re- fixing on the feature behind you.

By converting the bearing of two landmarks that you can identify on the map, it is possible to establish yourcorrect position. Take a bearing to the first landmark; e.g. say this is 280°. If you wish, calculate the magnetic variation, which we will say is 5°, and subtract. This leaves us with a revised bearing of 275°. Since this is greater than 180°, a back bearing can be achieved by subtraction of that number, i.e. giving us 95°.

This bearing is applied to the compass dial and the edge of the base is set against the landmark shown on the map. Pivot the whole compass until the orienteering lines in the base of the housing are running parallel to the eastings. This should allow you to draw a line from the feature at an angle of 95°.

Repeat the whole procedure for your second landmark, and draw another line. Your position is indicated where the two lines cross.

ber of features well suited to the survival situation. These include course memory, night vision back-light, automatic route reverse, stored bearings, and a clock which gives time and distance.

Electronic compasses are simple to operate, and are extremely handy during the hours of darkness. Power is a consideration, as the unit runs on batteries; however, the battery life is around 200 hours and most are fitted with automatic shut-down.

Improvised Compass By magnetising a small, straight piece of metal such as a needle, pin or razor blade, and suspending it so that it can swing freely, it is possible to make a simple compass. The piece of metal can be magnetised by stroking it in one direction with one pole of a magnet. Magnets can be found in any radio set, installed as part of the speaker. The pointer will then need to be suspended, a task that is often made difficult by stiff or twisted thread – any thread that will not allow the pointer to move freely will frustrate your purpose. With a small object such as a needle or razor blade this can be overcome by floating it on water.

To do this, improvise by sticking the pointer through a small piece of cork, or by balancing it on three matchsticks or a small twig. Warning: Remember that the container which holds the water must not be made of metal, as this may affect the mag-

Stick and Stone

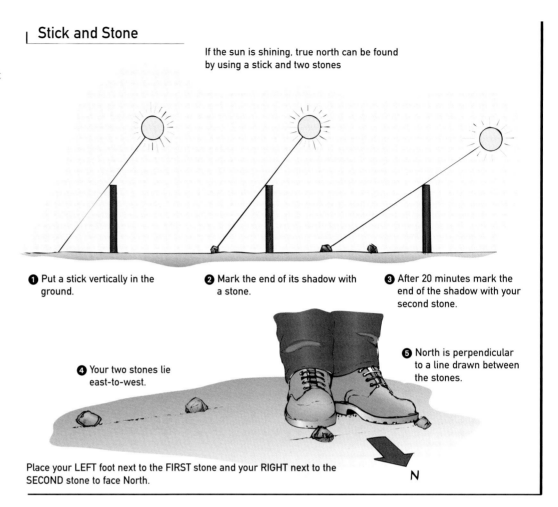

If the sun is shining, true north can be found by using a stick and two stones

1. Put a stick vertically in the ground.
2. Mark the end of its shadow with a stone.
3. After 20 minutes mark the end of the shadow with your second stone.
4. Your two stones lie east-to-west.
5. North is perpendicular to a line drawn between the stones.

Place your LEFT foot next to the FIRST stone and your RIGHT next to the SECOND stone to face North.

N

The 'stick and stone' method of determining North in practice.

netic field and cause the pointer to give a false reading. Also, remember that after a time the magnetising effect on the pointer will wear off and will have to be repeated.

Steel pointers can also be magnetised with electricity. For this you will need a battery that is capable of producing more than 6 volts, and a good length of insulated copper wire. Suitable wire may be found in the coils inside radios and generators, as well as in any electrical equipment in most kinds of vehicles. To magnetise the pointer, first wrap the wire around it as many times as you can. Take the ends of the wire, strip them of any insulation, and attach to the battery for 15-30 minutes. Make sure that the wire wrapped around the pointer is long enough, otherwise it will get too hot. In the event of this happening, disconnect the wires from the battery and allow them to cool down before starting again. Once the pointer has been magnetised (you may have to repeat the process several times before this is achieved), the end indicating North will be that nearer to the negative battery terminal (remember: N stands for both Negative and North).

Finding Direction Without a Compass

Compasses and GPS systems may be the easiest and most convenient methods of finding a direction, but survival starts in the most unusual places, and the odds are you will be without either. Luckily the most important aspect of survival navigation is direction, and this can be established through a number of time-honoured methods by using a bit of intelligence.

Stick and Stone Method

The accuracy of this method depends on using level ground and marking the shadow with some degree of accuracy. A North/South indicator can be produced if a line is drawn at right angles to your East/West line; any other direction is simply a calculation from these cardinal points.

- On a sunny day, find or cut a stick about one metre (39ins) long, and push it upright into some level ground.
- The stick will cast a shadow. Using a small stone, mark the end of the shadow as accurately as possible.
- After 15 to 20 minutes the shadow will have moved. Using a second stone, mark the tip of the new shadow.
- On the earth, draw a straight line running through the positions of both stones. This is your East/West line.
- Put your left foot close to the first stone, and your right foot close to the second. You are now facing North.

Using a Watch Using an analogue watch face allows us to find direction. In the Northern Hemisphere this is achieved by the following method. Check that your watch is accurately set to local time, reset for any local summer time which may have been added.

- Point the hour hand at the sun.
- Using a thin twig, cast a shadow along the hour hand through the central pivot.
- Bisect the angle between the hour hand and the 12 o'clock position.
- This line will be pointing due South, North being furthest from the sun.

The same procedure applies in the Southern Hemisphere, having once again made sure that your watch is set to local time:

- Point the number 12 at the sun.
- Using a thin twig, cast a shadow to achieve more accuracy.
- Bisect the angle between the hour hand and the 12 o'clock position.
- The end of this line nearest to the sun indicates North.

Shadow the sun along the hour hand and through the central pivot to determine direction in the northern hemisphere. Shadow the sun along the 12'o'clock position and the central pivot in the southern hemisphere.

Navigation by Night

Navigation by the stars has been practised for thousands of years, and is still employed in map making. Learning about the stars is beneficial in itself, but this knowledge comes into its own in survival navigation. Bright stars that seem to be grouped together in a pattern are called constellations. The shapes of these constellations and their relationships to each other do not alter. Because of the Earth's rotation, the whole of the night sky appears to revolve around one central point; and using this knowledge can help you to find directions.

The North Star In the Northern Hemisphere a faint star called Polaris, the Pole or North Star, marks the central point. Because of its position it always appears to remain in the same place – above the North Pole.

As long as Polaris can be seen the direction of True North can be found. To find Polaris, first locate the constellation variously known as 'The Great Bear', 'The Plough' or 'The Big Dipper'. A line through the two stars furthest from the 'handle' always points towards Polaris. Take the distance between the two stars and then follow the line straight for about six times the distance. At this point you will see the Pole Star. If you are unsure which way to look or wish to confirm that you have found Polaris, look for another constellation called Cassiopeia. The five stars which make up this constellation are patterned in the shape of a slightly flattened 'W'. Cassiopeia is positioned almost opposite the Plough, and Polaris can be found midway between them. As long as the sky is clear the Plough, Cassiopeia and Polaris remain visible all night when seen from any country north of 40 degrees N latitude.

The Southern Hemisphere The Southern Hemisphere does not have a version of Polaris conveniently marking the direction of South. Instead you will need to locate the constellation of the Southern Cross, made up of four main stars with a fainter fifth one just off the centre point of the cross. Take a line through the longer of the cross's arms and extend it for four and a half times its length. If you have the right line, it should pass through a group of four very faint stars shortly after the Cross. This will take you to the point where you will find South. To make navigation easier, find a landmark directly below this point to indicate South in a terrestrial plane.

Star Movement Method Clear skies cannot always be guaranteed, but if there is only partial obstruction by cloud and you are still able to see individual constellations, navigation by the stars can still be employed. The Star Movement Method is based on knowing how the stars wheel around the sky. Depending on which way they are moving, you should be able to get a rough indication of the direction you are facing. To do this you will need two fixed reference points, such as two sticks set in the ground like the sights of a gun. These should be aimed at any prominent star.

If the star appears to be:

- **Looping flatly towards the right, you are facing approximately South.**
- **Looping flatly towards the left, you are facing approximately North.**
- **Rising, you are facing approximately East.**
- **Descending, you are facing approximately West.**

You can also use your eye as the second fixed reference point, as long as your head is steadied against some solid object first. With this method, it is best to use a series of glances to observe the star. Fixed staring will produce an optical illusion of either the star wandering about, or not moving at all.

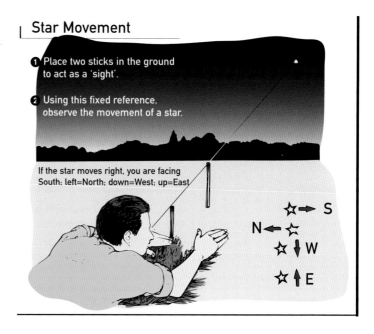

1 Place two sticks in the ground to act as a 'sight'.

2 Using this fixed reference, observe the movement of a star.

If the star moves right, you are facing South; left=North; down=West; up=East

☆→ S
N←☆
☆↓ W
☆↑ E

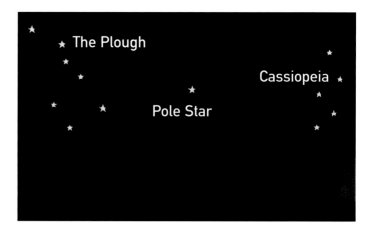

The Plough

Cassiopeia

Pole Star

The Moon

The movement of the moon also follows a set pattern and can aid navigation. There are two methods which can be used:

The Quarter Moons Both waxing and waning quarter moons can be used. Draw a line through the horns down to the horizon. The point where it touches gives a rough indication of South, if you are in the Northern Hemisphere, and North if you are in the Southern Hemisphere. Although not very accurate this will at least provide you with a rough guide while travelling at night.

The Moon and Time Make sure that your watch is correct and set to local time. The phases of the moon pass through certain directions at certain times; so by using a watch in conjunction with the table below you should be able to get a good idea of the direction you are travelling in.

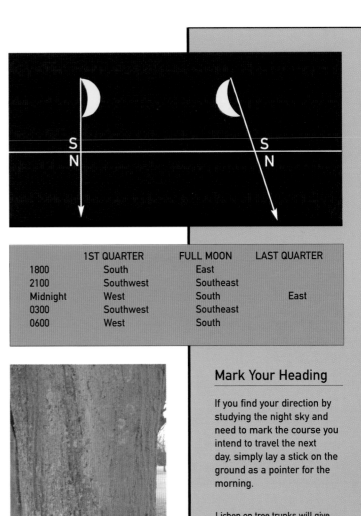

	1ST QUARTER	FULL MOON	LAST QUARTER
1800	South	East	
2100	Southwest	Southeast	
Midnight	West	South	East
0300	Southwest	Southeast	
0600	West	South	

Vegetation Tips to Navigation

Vegetation can help you to find your direction. It will not be very accurate, but at least you will have a general idea of which way you are heading.

Trees and shrubs which are perennial tend to produce more foliage on the side most exposed to the sun, that is the side nearest to the Equator. This is especially true of conifers. The more slender types of trees such as willows, poplars and alders have a tendency to lean towards the sun. However, strong prevailing winds may also cause a greater amount of foliage to grow on the leeward side. Use your common sense and observation to discern whether wind or sun has had greater effect. The moss plant family prefer the damp and the shade and so tend to grow on the side of a tree or rock that is least exposed to the sun – i.e. they tend to grow on aspects that face towards the Poles rather than the Equator.

Prevailing Winds

Prevailing winds may not blow all the time, especially in the interiors of large land masses. Sometimes local winds will hold sway. For a wind to be prevailing, it must remain constant for a few days at a time. In the desert, where vegetation is sparse, prevailing winds can still provide an indication of direction. This is because they will dictate the shape of the sand dunes. As long as you know which way the prevailing wind blows, working it out by observation if necessary, the shape of the dunes will give you a rudimentary idea of direction. Winds around coastal areas and mountains are also apt to have their own patterns.

During the morning they tend to blow offshore and in the evening they change direction and blow onshore.

Mark Your Heading

If you find your direction by studying the night sky and need to mark the course you intend to travel the next day, simply lay a stick on the ground as a pointer for the morning.

Lichen on tree trunks will give you a clue to direction.

Prevailing winds affect the shape of sand dunes in the desert and provide directioal clues.

SURVIVAL TRAVEL

The choice of whether to travel or to stay put is one of the great dilemmas any survivor must face. Without communications it is difficult to assess whether there will even be a rescue attempt, let alone how successful searchers may be in locating you. The factors governing any decision should be based on where you are, your chances of survival if you stay there, where you intend moving to, and the related hazards in getting there.

A realistic judgement of your physical, mental and material resources - your ability to travel and to reach a given point accurately - must also be made.

Once you have determined the need to travel you must prepare. Before you start, it is important to check the weather and work out a travel routine based on the type of terrain and conditions you will be passing through.

The pace should be steady and unrushed, with a break of five to ten minutes at least every hour. Use this break productively, not just to rest but also to evaluate your progress so far and to consider the next part of your route. This is also the time for minor repairs and adjustments to clothing and kit. Make sure that you do not go beyond your physical limits - and take into consideration that your feet will be doing most of the work while you are travelling. It wise to take care of them; prevention is much better than cure. At the end of every day's march remove all footwear and wash your feet; also wash and clean your socks, stockings or footrags, and boots or shoes. Make a fire and dry the footwear overnight; that way it will be clean and dry for you to put on again the next morning.

Horseshoe Bandoleer This is one of the easiest packs to make, and can be carried quite comfortably over one shoulder. To construct it you will need a square-shaped piece of material, such as a blanket. This should be laid flat upon the ground and the items to be carried placed along one edge - and padded, if necessary. The items should then be rolled within the material towards the opposite edge to form a sausage shape. The two open ends need to be tied securely, and more ties added along the length to prevent the contents shifting. The two ends can then be joined with another piece of soft material, and the pack is slung round the body.

Square Pack For this pack you will need some sort of rope or cordage. Hopefully this is already available, otherwise you may need to make some from what ever materials you have about you. Once you have this, you will be able to construct a square or wishbone frame from sticks or bamboo.

❶ Wrap your kit in a blanket or tarpaulin and carry it over your shoulder.

❷ Alternatively, if the materials are available, make a pack to carry your kit on your back.

Route Selection

If you can, choose to follow a trail along a ridge rather than a route that takes you through a valley. Valley routess generally present more obstacles, such as thick undergrowth and possible river/stream crossings. Other hazards include swamps or marshy ground, which are at the best hard going and at worst, dangerous to navigate.

If you have alternative routes, it is always best to detour around such areas.

Ridges also tend to provide better visibility, which will make it easier to keep your bearings. A ridge may be orientated in the direction you are travelling; more often than not, however, it is likely that the direction of the ridge will head off on a totally different bearing to the one you wish to follow. Even so, it may still be worth following the ridge for a short while, keeping an eye out for a suitable alternative route to take.

Contouring offers a useful half-way measure between ridge and valley floor. A trail that follows such a contour may take a longer route than a ridge top, but it will mean that less climbing has to be done. Without a detailed map your route selection is best made based on careful observation of the terrain.

Travel Equipment

Some means of carrying food, water and equipment will be necessary. With a bit of ingenuity a rucksack or pack can be made from almost any material, whether it be canvas, clothing, plant fibres, animal skins, wood, bamboo or rope. The construction does not have to be complicated – in fact the simplest methods are not only the easiest to employ during a survival situation, but also work extremely well.

The military are trained to travel distances on foot often with heavy loads (above and right). Carefull route selection will determine the speed and success of the trek.

The Seasons

Apart from the need and the means to travel, a survivor must also take into account the season and the weather.

Depending on the terrain, spring can be a mixed blessing for survival travellers. For example, in the Arctic the snow will start to thaw into slush, turning the frozen tundra into an impassable bog. Spring travel through the desert or jungle will be cooler by comparison to the summer heat. There should be signs of new plant life with young roots, many of which can be eaten. Likewise, the birds will start to lay eggs and young animals will start to appear.

Summer is kinder to the survivor; the days are longer and the sun warmer, food will be readily available, and shelter easier to construct. Autumn is the survivor's most promising time, as there is a host of fresh fruit, nuts, plants and fungi; but this bounty should be harvested if you have reason to expect that you may remain unrescued for any extended period. Winter is the worst possible time to find yourself in a survival situation: cold, shortage of food sources and the most difficult travel conditions all pose the greatest possible challenge.

Weather

In most survival situations long term weather factors for any terrain are governed by the seasons. The immediate weather is of importance, however, as it figures in decisions about travel, shelter-building and protective clothing. Any weather conditions to which exposure is liable to cause frostbite or heatstroke are good reasons for postponing current activity.

Although we cannot change the weather, we can to a certain extent predict its approach by observing the sky and cloud formations. A clear sky with high cloud will indicate a clear and sunny day; dark sky with low cloud normally indicates rain; it is simply a matter of gauging the degree between the two. Do this by looking towards the direction of travel. Try to estimate the height of cloud, colour of sky and wind direction. With a little practice you will be able to anticipate the weather conditions for several hours ahead.

Fog can be dangerous: it is disorienting, and hides dangers such as cliff edges. Where possible in these conditions, stay where you are until visibility improves. If you have to keep going then consider roping the members of the party together. In this way you can be assured that no one will get lost and it may also save someone from a nasty fall.

Travel through deep snow is slow and exhausting.

Weather conditions can change rapidly from being fine to being life-threatening, especially in mountainous regions.

Wind gusts, especially in exposed places such as high ridge lines, can be powerful enough to knock adults off their feet. If there is any danger of this, get all party members to crawl on hands and knees and keep them close together. Again, it may be necessary to rope everyone together.

Hailstones can be up to an inch in diameter, and can fall with sufficient force to cause serious injury and damage. In the rare event of being caught out in a hailstorm, make sure you find shelter or at least cover your head.

Lightning It is wise to take precautions against lighting, although it is very rare for an electrical storm to occur without some advance warning, e.g. the appearance of thunderclouds in the distance followed by flashes of lightning and rumbles of thunder as the clouds approach. Be aware that lightning striking the ground normally seeks the easiest point of contact, which is usually the highest point in the area. If caught out in a lighting storm it is much safer to stay out in the open, even if in driving rain. Sit down, preferably on your rucksack, and minimise your contact points with the ground, drawing your knees up and placing your hands in your lap.

If caught out in a lightning storm the priority is to get low, and reduce your points of contact with the ground.

LIFESAVER
Obstacles
Where survival travel is concerned, obstacles can be divided into two types: natural features, and living creatures. Natural obstacles obviously include e.g. rivers, swamps and mountains; while wolves, bears, elephant, rhino, crocodiles and alligators are but a few of the dangerous animals a survivor may face.

Dig In

Fatalities involving the weather often involve some human carelessness or ignorance; both can be avoided. If the worst happens and you do find yourself and your party trapped on a hill or mountain in bad weather, find, construct or dig some form of shelter; keep together; and wait it out.

In bad weather stay in a group and wait it out.

River Crossing Techniques

Sometimes when a survivor is confronted by a major water-course there is little option other than to cross it.

The width of the river, its depth and water speed all pose problems, as does the type of riverbed.

Mud and silt can be extremely dangerous, to the point where you become permanently stuck or - worse - sucked below the surface. Few riverbeds are flat, and most have hidden depths into which anyone crossing may fall.

Strong currents can dash the strongest of swimmers into rocky outcrops, or plunge them into falling rapids. All these obstacles must be taken into account before attempting to ford any river.

Never cross on a river bend, as the speed of the current and the depth of the water will increase from the inside of the bend to the outside. Instead, choose a wide stretch where the water is flowing slower, and where one can carefully wade across. Avoid any temptation to jump from stone to stone, as these are often slippery and a fall could result in a sprain or a fracture; at the least you may drop vital equipment. When wading across, use as many aids to safety as are available.

If you flounder or slip in the water and find yourself floating downstream, it is important not to panic. Float feet first with the current, fending off any obstacles, until you feel the river bed beneath you and are able to stand, or until you reach the safety of the bank.

Depending on the weather conditions you are advised to remove your socks and trousers before wading any river; this will allow you some increase in comfort and warmth when you dress after reaching the opposite bank. When crossing a river alone use a stout stick to provide extra stability in the water and to test ahed of you for depth, potholes and underwater obstacles.

If a rope or line is at hand and you are with a companion, make sure that the person crossing is safely secured to the bank. A survival party of three or more should follow the procedure illustrated here, which will ensure that the person crossing is always secured by at least two others.

If the water is too deep for wading and you have to swim across, make buoyancy aids. Your rucksack secured in an air-tight survival bag will make an excellent floatation aid. Injured survivors should be assisted by the party linking arms around each others' shoulders, with the weakest swimmer in the middle. If necessary, place the casualty on top of a secured bouyancy aid such as several rucksacks lashed together. Move across the river with the strongest member on the upstream side, against the flow of the current; move slowly and support each other if one should stumble or fall. Take care when entering and leaving the stream, especially if the banks are steep; hold onto the bank, and help the weakest person out first.

3-Man River Crossing

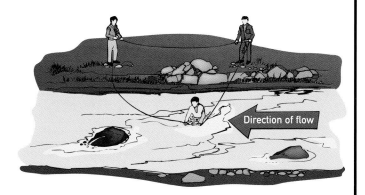

1 Make your rope into a loop. The first man can cross, inside the loop for extra safety, supported by the other two.

2 The second man can cross the river supported from both banks of the river.

2 The third man can then be helped across by the first two.

5 If crossing a river, or travelling through water, without a rope, then , even in shallow water it is wise to use a buoyancy aid or travelling stick to aid your progress.

Rafts

Rivers and their immediate surroundings contain many resources useful to the survivor. In addition to food and water, you will also find materials with which you can build a simple raft. Forget any ideas about constructing a canoe - it takes skill and a great deal of time, and requires special resources such as resin for waterproofing. However, making a raft is within everyone's capabilities. Rafts can be built with anything that has a degree of buoyancy - you do not necessarily need the luxury of old oil drums, or even timber; empty bottles tied up inside a polythene bag will serve you well. If using wood, choose a light wood such as bamboo if available.

Once your raft has been constructed, ensure that all your supplies and equipment are firmly secured to it in case the raft tips over. Do not attach too much weight to your person - if you fall in it may prevent you from staying afloat. To steer your craft in order to avoid any river obstacles such as rocks or rapids, use a long punting pole. Leave time at the end of each day to locate a riverbank campsite. Mosquitoes and other biting insects are liable to be a hazard close to water, so locate your camp on higher ground if possible. A higher location will also prevent problems if the river level rises quickly. This can happen without warning in a rainforest, even if there has been no rain in your locality, as rain may have fallen in the upper reaches. When you set up camp for the night, take great care that you have secured your raft, even taking it out of the water if possible. Check the raft for serviceability every morning and repair as required.

Constructing a Raft A raft is basically anything that floats with enough buoyancy to support a human being. The secret behind any good raft is its strength and durability over water; it does not have to keep your feet dry. The materials for making a raft can vary from brushwood and logs to polythene sacks and ponchos. Their construction needs little imagination and several ideas are illustrated here. Keep in mind that it is trapped air which makes a raft float.

Floatation Aids

Foliage wrapped in tarpaulin will make an efficient floatation aid.

A Poncho Raft

❶ Make a cross of two lengths of wood, place them with some foliage on the poncho/tarpaulin.

The Simplest Raft

Cut two lengths of good sized timber and lash them together to make an 'armchair'.

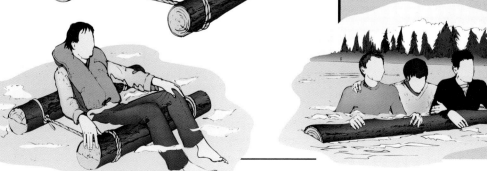

River Tips

- Plan your route to avoid having to cross water if possible. Cross only if absolutely necessary.

- Always look for the safest crossing place. Choose the widest and shallowest stretch, and avoid bends.

- Unless in a life-threatening situation, never attempt to cross a river in flood.

- If alone, use a buoyancy aid.

- Use a safety line if available.

❷ Wrap into a package and secure with cord.

❸ Double wrap the pack with another square of material to make a long-lasting floatation aid.

129

Mountain travel

Mountains, especially the lower slopes, offer the survivor or escapee many possibilities of shelter, food and water. Their drawbacks are that travelling may be more difficult, and the survivor may be at more risk of injury. Remember that surviving above the snow line will be very hard and even dangerous, so avoid climbing this high if you can. There are three basic rules to remember when travelling through mountains:

❶ Avoid any loose rock when climbing, and always make sure that you have three points of contact.

❷ Always make sure that it is possible to climb back down again if you need to.

❸ Stay out of snow fields, glaciers and overhanging snow.

Climbing with Rope

If you have a rope use it for both climbing and descending, it will make your travel through mountains far safer.

Climbing without Rope

If you have no rope always maintain three points of contact when climbing. Do not over stretch yourself. Face away from the rock when descending.

Movement in the dark

There may be times when a survivor needs to move during the hours of darkness. For instance, in the Arctic winter there may be little option; but desert travel is best undertaken at night. In other situations it may be expedient to move by night to avoid the enemy, or to get a seriously injured survivor to immediate medical attention. If, for whatever reason, moving in darkness is the only option in your situation, you need to consider how to do this safely.

Being in complete darkness can be frightening; stay calm and take stock of the situation. Check that you have no source of lighting on you. If you are moving in a group, make sure that everyone stays within touching distance of the next person. If you have a rope or lifeline, rope everyone together, placing the weakest in the centre.

Unless a life really depends on it, do not try crossing a river in darkness – it is extremely dangerous. Likewise, while it is a good idea to follow a stream or river on the flat, never follow water down a steep mountainside, as it will inevitably have a waterfall somewhere. Even if the waterfall is small, it will be enough to cause injuries if you fall over in the dark.

Working in complete darkness produces what is known as night sight, a condition where the eyes adjust to the low level of available light. This will be interrupted if a torch or naked flame is used; always close one eye against bright lights. All the human senses become heightened when enveloped in darkness, and these should be used to their best advantage. However, be aware that heightened senses mean that even familiar noises may sound much louder and closer, which to some people can be unnerving. Stay calm, and talk to yourself or each other if necessary.

Prior to darkness falling, check the ground you intend to cross and memorise your route. If your memory is good it will assist in maintaining your route during the darkness. Distances can be confusing, as you will be forced to move more slowly. Try, if possible, to locate features which can be easily identified. Your sense of touch will be particularly useful when it is totally dark or when you are moving over steep and rocky ground. Again, always move downhill, using your hands as if you were a climber, keeping three points in contact with the rock at all times.

Use your hands and arms to make sure that the immediate space before you is clear of any obstacles and is secure to step on. If the ground is uneven or if there is the possibility of a dangerous drop, crawl on your hands and knees. Stop when you hear water, as this almost certainly indicates a drop of some height. Try throwing a stone and listen for the sound of it hitting earth or water; this should indicate distance and depth. If walking in a forest at night, stretching the arms out in front of the body will ward off low branches, etc.

Light contrast between the trees and the sky helps when walking in the forest at night.

Keeping the mouth open during darkness increases sound reception. Furthermore, whenever danger is imminent the senses often produce a tingling sensation as a warning. Learn to recognize these signs and accept them without interpretation – remember that we are, after all, only animals.

Unless your life depends on it, don't attempt to cross water in the dark.

Movement in the dark.

Light contrast is a good aid to night navigation. Snow-covered ground reflects any starlight and moonlight, but be aware that it also hides pitfalls below the surface. On a clear moonlit night it is possible to see for up to 100m (330ft) over open terrain. In wooded terrain there is also a contrast between the dark forest and the lighter sky; this contrast will act as guide if you are following a track through woodland - simply look up, and observe the treetop silhouette. Certain weather conditions provide a fair amount of lightning which will constantly illuminate the surrounding area, although somewhat briefly.

Local Population

The hazards of surviving in desolate terrain may seem to be over if you make contact with the indigenous people - but this may be far from true. Many travellers have found themselves held hostage for ransom, or have been imprisoned for breaking some fundamental local law. That said, there are few places on Earth where meeting up with the local people will not bring your survival situation to an end, provided that you obey some very basic rules.

Only the most hostile of environments are totally uninhabited, since both man and animals have adapted to virtually every type of terrain and conditions. The nomadic Tuareg have survived in the central Sahara, while the Inuit have eked out an existence in the Far North. Today many tribes have become engulfed by the trappings of Western civilization, but many still cling to their former ways of life. In many cases these isolated peoples will have some form of communication with the outside world; if not, then at least they will have food, water and shelter, and offer a hopeful means of repatriation.

In the event that you make contact with such a community, there are a number of basic rules to observe.

- Unless you are at death's door, wait outside their village until welcomed.
- Lay down any weapon, but do not let them take it.
- Spread out your palms to show you are unarmed before shaking hands.
- Have an escape route planned beforehand in case you have to run.
- Take any drink or food that is offered, and remember to thank your host.
- Treat all people, customs and religions with respect.
- Explain your situation - use simple drawings in the dirt.
- Talk to the men; do not openly approach or talk to the women.

- Other than for medical reasons, do not remove your clothes in public.
- Explain that you must move on as soon as possible.
- Thank them for their kindness when you leave.

LIFESAVER

Acquired Immune Defficiency Syndrome

Despite their isolation, many tribes have become infected with the AIDS or HIV virus. This is a potential risk, to any survivor, especially in Africa, where AIDS is very prevalent. The risk will depend on the individual factors involved, but this is something to keep in mind when travelling to, through or over any country with a high occurrence of AIDS. The two main causes of AIDS transmission are via exchange of blood – e.g. the use of unsterilised hypodermic needles - or by sexual contact.

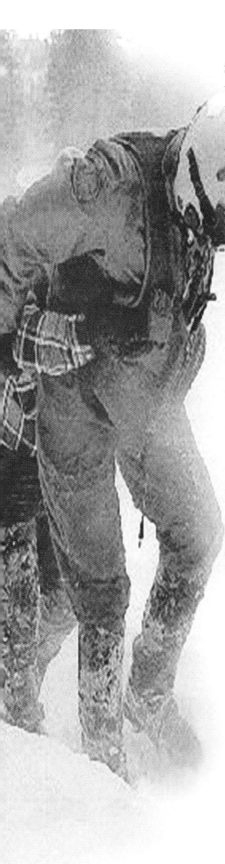

RESCUE

Search and rescue contingency plans will come into operation at the first sign of trouble. This is initially done when a radio distress call is received, or waypoint call-in procedures have been missed. All air traffic is monitored very closely, especially commercial aircraft flying on a set route. The introduction of radar during the Second World War was a huge step forwards; and the more recent adoption of the satellite Global Positioning System means that almost all transport vehicles, from aircraft to super-tankers, can be tracked constantly to within a few metres. Consequently, aircraft that have been forced to make emergency landings or ships that are foundering at sea can normally expect rescue assistance within a matter of hours at worst.

If for any reason the location is not known, then Search and Rescue (SAR) teams will be called in to make a search. The area covered will be based on the best available estimate of the last known location. How the search is carried out will be determined by the size of the area to be covered, the terrain, the weather and operational necessity. A search plan will be devised, and search patterns allocated to the aircraft.If radio communications can be established or a beacon signal is received, then a contact search will be initiated. This is designed to concentrate rescue efforts on a relatively small area, thus increasing the speed with which rescuers can get to you. Unless there is accurate knowledge of the location of the party to be rescued, it will be futile and even risky to send out search teams during the night.

The basic search patterns are as follows:

• **Area search** This involves dividing up the area into smaller areas using natural features as landmarks, giving boundaries in which individual team are to search.

• **Sweep search** The rescue party will spread out in a line and search the area in a disciplined and organised manner.

• **Contour search** In mountainous country a contour search, spiralling around tall features and flying several times along steep valleys, allows maximum thoroughness.

• **Contact search** A search focussed on a smaller area but based on the principles of the sweep search.

Rescue teams are highly skilled at extracting survivors from the most inhospitable places – but they have to locate you.

Signalling

Signalling is a means of communication which can take the form of shape, sound, silhouette and sight. Sound can encompass anything from shouting or blowing a whistle to using a radio, while sight can mean attracting attention by using anything from a signalling mirror to a smoking fire. The signalling methods you choose will depend on what equipment is available and the conditions in which you find yourself. A direct link radio or satellite phone will produce rapid rescue results; by contrast, the light from a signal fire will only be seen once the search aircraft is flying over your location.

Signal Fires

A signal fire needs to be kept ready to be lit at a moment's notice. All the tinder and wood must be dry. The fire is constructed so that the tinder is in the middle, ready for lighting. The aim is that once the tinder is alight all the other fuel should light easily and burn without too much effort on you part. This type of fire needs to be sheltered from the wet. If you are able, build three of these fires in a triangle, 30m (100ft) apart. Make sure that the ground around the fire is adequately cleared of vegetation so that the fire will not spread beyond its boundaries once lit. Using any oil or petrol that you may have can speed up ignition.

Your rescuers may appear at any time of the night or day, so when the moment arrives remember that you need to produce contrast; to work properly the signal fire must stand out from its background. At nighttime it should produce tall, bright flames which are easily seen. However, in the daytime (except in Arctic winter conditions) you will need to produce more smoke than flame. White smoke works best on a clear day, and can be made by adding green or damp vegetation to a very hot fire. On a cloudy day, black smoke will be seen more easily, and can be produced by burning oil or rubber (aircraft or vehicle tyres). In all cases the most important thing is to make sure that your signal fire is going to light quickly and burn fiercely, thus increasing your chances of being seen and rescued.

Helicopter search patterns depend on the type of terrain they are covering and the number of search aircraft taking part.

Tree Signal Fire In many cases it will be possible to construct a signal fire using a single growing tree.

Use one that is isolated or growing on the fringe of a forest. Make sure that when it is set alight the fire will not spread to the surrounding trees; clear smaller trees to isolate it if necessary. Thicken your signal tree by stripping branches from other nearby trees and interweaving them. Next build a small fire under the base of the tree; this will act as a booster, and will be partially shielded by the wide branches at the base. This booster fire will need to ignite immediately; either have a container of combustible fuel handy, or – if available – use a salvaged aerosol can (hair spray is excellent). Your signal fire tree should be protected from the snow and rain if at all possible by covering it with a parachute or similar canvas. If nothing is available, check it daily and shake it to detach fallen snow or water molecules.

Pyramid fire A pyramid fire needs a raised base and plenty of dry fuel. The aim of the base is to ensure quick ignition and a good air supply once alight. As with any sig-

You may only get one chance so make sure that your signal fire is prepared, and that it will fire quickly in any conditions and produce the required smoke or brightness.

nal fire, the fuel should be instantly combustible and stacked in a manner that allows air to permeate and feed the flames.

If you have a suitable salvaged aerosol can, half-bury this in the ground at an angle pointing upwards at the pyramid base. Have ready at hand a large flat stone heavy enough to depress the release button, and a torch made from a length of stick with rags wrapped around one end. At the first sign of rescue aircraft light the torch, put the stone on the button, and place the torch in the spray. Turn your back on the fire when you do this. Once the fire is burning well, distance yourself until the spray can is finished or has exploded.

Warning: Setting fire to aerosol spray is highly dangerous, and should only be attempted in a dire emergency.

Even in a survival situation extreme caution is advised, as the can will almost certainly explode.

Phones Although mainly restricted to land usage, the

global telephone network is extensive and accessible in many remote places. New portable satellite phones are little larger than a laptop computer, and will operate in every environment. Anyone

Personal Locators

There are many devices used for contacting and locating those who have become lost, and most have similar functions and operations. One example is the SARBE 6 (Search And Rescue BEacon), which is designed for use as a survival radio by civil or military aircrew. On activation the unit transmits a continuous, internationally recognized, swept-tone radio distress signal in the UHF 243Mhz 7.5kHz or VHF 121.5Mhz 3.75kHz distress frequencies. It also provides two-way voice communications between the survivor and approaching rescuers. Built-in self-test facilities allow a simple confidence check to be carried out for correct functioning of the unit and battery state.

The unit is activated by the removal of an operating pin, either manually or automatically by such functions as liferaft inflation or ejector seat operation. Simultaneous, omnidirectional transmission of both VHF and UHF signals then continues automatically for a minimum of 24 hours to facilitate detection by search aircraft or vessels or by any other land, sea or airborne installation monitoring these frequencies. Pressel switches located on the side of the unit allow the survivor to select the voice mode, permitting two-way communication with the rescuers. Voice communication is on both distress frequencies simultaneously. This mode is intended for use only when the survivor can see or hear the rescue craft. The SARBE 6 is waterproof to a depth of 10m (33 feet).

Be sure to have maximum contrast against your landscape when signalling.

Look through wreckage for any mobile phones or other communication instruments.

A heliograph can be purpose made or improvised from a vehicle mirror

High intensity strobe lights are good for signalling, but be sure to conserve the batteries.

planning to travel or spend any time in regions where survial situations might occur should investigate beforehand access to all forms of telecommunications, from land lines to mobile phones.

Searching the passengers and luggage from any wrecked aircraft will produce a variety of communication equipment, which even if not operable from the present position may connect later on.

Mirrors and Heliographs Any type of mirror – the larger the better – is excellent for signalling providing you have bright sunshine conditions. It is simply a matter of reflecting the sun's rays toward a search plane or party to attract their attention. All aircraft or vehicles carry a number of mirrors any one of which will serve as a signalling device. A more accurate method is to use a purpose-made heliograph. Modern variations of these are smaller than a computer disk, measuring just 5cm x 5cm (2in x 2in), yet they have the capacity to accurately reflect some 85% of sunlight up to a range of some 20 kilometres (12 miles). Mirrors work exceptionally well in the desert and areas where sunlight is guaranteed. Once any rescue aircraft gives definite signs of having spotted you, stop signalling - you will only dazzle the pilot.

Light Light is obviously the ideal means of attracting attention at night, even after you have made radio contact. Light can be emitted from any number of sources: a naked flame, torch, strobe, camera, or flare.

Although they are extremely effective the problem with most flares and torches is that they are either

Contour Search Pattern

All pyrotechnics are dangerous, make sure you read and conform to the instruction for use. Pistol and rocket flares should be pointed skyward.

Use a reflective blanket to enhance any light signals at night (bottom).

limited to a single use, or are useful only for the duration of the batteries. All survival flares come with operating and safety instructions; make sure you read these before commencing any operation. Consider whether hand-held flares might not be better used to ignite a larger signal fire.

Parachute and Missile Flares
There are many different types of missile flare on the market. Some simply fire a glowing light which lasts a few seconds; some have a parachute attached, which will retard the flare's descent thus making it visible for longer. Always read the instructions carefully and follow them to the letter. The important point is always to keep the flare pointing skywards. Parachute flares are

one-shot devices, so make sure their use is justified. The number of flares supplied with any normal pistol is around nine maximum.

Torches and Strobes Any torch is a bonus at night, but for signalling purposes a large, broad beam is required if any rescue aircraft is to see it.

Personal Locator Radios

• This is the survivor's best friend - but its battery life is limited. The 'beacon' setting uses least battery power.

• Reception and transmission are generally limited to line-of-sight – so don't waste the battery by leaving it switched on for long periods when you can't see or hear SAR aircraft.

• Try to use the radio from high ground.

• Transmit an SOS or Mayday at sunrise, noon and sunset. Try to transmit during a consistent time period, e.g. from the hour to 20 minutes past the hour.

• Transmit for two minutes each time; then switch off for one minute. Switch on for three minutes, then off for three minutes. Switch on for ten minutes, then off until the next transmission period. (USAF guidelines for use of standard PRC-90 radio.)

Radar reflective balloon.

Ground marker panels.

Marking a trail indicating direction.

Moving the torch from left to right in a slow arc will help attract attention, as will shining it onto a reflective surface - it is not the light which the search aircraft crew will see, but the movement of light. Strobes are designed to create this effect by emitting an extremely bright pulsating light. On a clear night a strobe can be seen some 16km (10 miles) away, and is effective in all terrain.

Vehicle Lights Providing certain elements are still intact a good signalling light can also be generated from vehicle and aircraft lights. These lights are best aimed at a large surface, such as a flat snow surface or mountain wall, with the light being fanned to animate movement. If done properly this will create an effect that can be seen for many miles. Remember that the system is reliant on bat-

tery power; recharge if possible before it becomes too weak to fire the engine.

Camera Flash A modern camera flash gun also makes a good signalling device, but as with other battery-powered systems it has a limited life and needs to be used sparingly. In cold climates batteries are best kept warm to maintain their performance.

Whistles and Sound Whistles have improved a great deal over the past few years, and many new models can be heard several kilometres away - provided that the air is still, or the wind is blowing in the right direction.

However, the main purpose of the whistle in many survival kits is to attract the attention of other survivors directly after the disaster. This is particularly so at sea, where all survivors should find a whistle attached to their life vest. On land any-

thing that will amplify sound, such as beating a metal drum with a stick, should also be considered. Obviously, if the survivor is luchy enought to have a firearm, firing a shot will also attract attention; but this should only be done if you have reason to believe a rescue party is nearby.

Warning: Never make a loud noise in snow-covered mountainous areas where avalanches may be caused.

Balloons Radar-reflective and colour-detectable balloons come in a variety of sizes. The coloured versions are primarily designed for use in the jungle. Normally constructed of bright orange polythene, they are inflated by mixing chemicals with water to produce helium gas. As the balloon fills it is raised on a line until it is above the dense forest canopy, and then tethered where it can be clearly seen by search aircraft. (The water bag and tin which are part of

the kit may be employed for survival purposes.)

Radar-reflective balloons are more compact, and are more automated in their operation. Inflation is initiated by removing a safety pin; this activates a helium cartridge which fills the balloon. The balloon is tethered to the life jacket, from where it rises to around 30m (100ft), where it will remain even in strong winds for up to five days. The 10m (33ft) radar reflective signature can be detected by search vehicles up to 30km (18 miles) away.

Rescue Panels and Streamers These come in various shapes and sizes, but all provide a fluorescent marker which can be seen from the air. Panels are normally 2m x 0.5m (6.5ft x 16ins) or 2m square depending on the design. Two or three of these can be formed into various shapes which indicate your requirements and situation - that you need a radio, or you have wounded with you, etc. Distress streamers are used in much the same way but are much narrower and longer, up to 10m (33 feet). These can be spread over the ground surface or floated on the sea behind a liferaft.

Contrast Signals Disrupting the normal pattern of the terrain creates contrast. Do this by introducing regular shapes which do not occur naturally - circles, squares, triangles, letters or straight lines. A large circle with a minimum diameter of 3m (10ft) can be made using stones. It can also be broken or trampled-out in snow, but a trampled signal is improved by the addition of some contrasting material – earth, campfire ashes, even marker dye if a dinghy is found among the wreckage. On sand use rocks, sticks, cacti or seaweed. Choose the things which make the best contrast against the particular background surface. If air marker panels are available use these first and construct improvised signals secondly. Make any ground-to-air signals as large as possible, and add extra shapes if space, time and energy permit.

Increased contrast is gained if you incorporate brightly coloured wreckage, clothing, blankets, etc. in your signals.

Flying Signals Signals can also be hung from trees. Anything shiny or brightly coloured which is moving will

be even more eye-catching. A flag pole will increase the distance over which signals can be seen from the ground. If any possible rescuers are seen or heard, use any available clothing or material as flags, and keep waving. If there is some suitable material that is not required for other uses during daylight hours, it is useful to have it ready, attached to the longest pole you can easily handle for the sake of maximum signalling movement. Two men holding a survival blanket, flag or other brightly coloured sheet can, by keeping it taut, manipulate it to show flashes of light or colour. These will catch a searcher's eye more readily than the display of a static sheet.

Ground Information Markers If you move from your location you may need to blaze a trail or leave ground markers to indicate direction of travel. It is easy to get lost or move off course, especially if no compass or map are available. To aid your progress and to make sure others can follow in your footsteps you will need to blaze a trail. This can be done either by chipping markers on tree trunks or leaving a prominent ground sign.

Trees should be cut at head height on both sides, making a single cut on the side ointing away from your last position, and two cuts on the side pointing towards your last position. This will allow others to follow and

Contrast signals can indicate your intentions or your requirements allowing others to find you quickly.

you to retrace your footsteps if the need arises. Always look back from time to time, making sure that your spacing between marked trees allows the next one to be seen from the position of the last.

A second method is to deliberately place natural items such as stones, sticks, grass, etc in such a way as to mark your direction. The distance apart is determined by the natural path you are taking. For example, if you are on a prominent path you need only mark direction changes at junctions. In a vast field of grass you will need to knot the tussocks on a regular basis, so that each one can be seen from the last.

Shapes for Specific Ground Signals

N	Negative
Y	Yes
I	Have seriously injured
X	Unable to move
→	Have gone this way
△	It is safe to land here
SOS	Save our souls

Helicopter Rescue Procedures

Most SAR teams are organised along military lines. They are highly skilled and have access to excellent resources, including fixed-wing long range aircraft and helicopters. Most carry personnel and facilities for front line medical care. However, it would be a dangerous mistake to assume that they will always be there to get you out of danger.

Severe weather conditions can keep search aircraft grounded for hours or days. Even once you have been located helicopter crews can take a considerable amount of time assessing the problems of trying to reach you. Over rough seas or jungle terrain it is not uncommon for the pilot to make several attempts to establish a hover close enough to the casualties to be able to get a winchman or mountain rescue team to their position. Having arrived at a workable hover, the next priority is to assess the safest method of rescuing the survivors.

To ensure that no important aspect of the situation is overlooked SAR crews use a standardised system of priorities:
- **Aircraft safety**
- **Winchman safety**
- **Survivor safety.**

Landing Areas Where possible the helicopter will land to evacuate survivors. To make this viable the survivor should do everything possible to provide a good landing pad (LP). Factors to be considered include the size of the clear area, the ground slope, the type of surface, and the direction of wind and approach. First check that the surface will support a helicopter, i.e. that it is not waterlogged ground or obstructed by large rocks, fallen trees, potholes, etc. Next, make sure that it is free of any looses debris that could be blown about by the rotor downdraft. Check the helicopter's approach path, which will be into the prevailing wind; make sure there are no tall obstructions to the rotor blades. Mark the centre of your LP with some form of marker such as an H-shape; and indicate the wind direction by improvising a wind sock or making smoke.

Rescue Strop The helicopter rescue strop is designed to facilitate the rescue of survivors. It can be used at sea or on land to lift uninjured survivors of any size with relative ease. The strop is manufactured from nylon webbing. A 'D'-ring is incorporated at each end of the strop; the centre portion is cushioned with a rubber sheet comfort pad tapered at each end and covered with polyester fabric. A

Stand where the pilot can clearly see you and indicate the best area for him to land on.

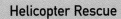

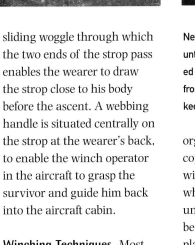

Helicopter Rescue

• Wait until the helicopter has landed, and either the pilot or a crew member has clearly indicated to you that you should come forward.

• Never approach a helicopter from the rear, or by descending down a slope - both will put you in extreme danger from the rotor blades.

• The best approach angle is on the cabin door side, from three-quarter front.

sliding woggle through which the two ends of the strop pass enables the wearer to draw the strop close to his body before the ascent. A webbing handle is situated centrally on the strop at the wearer's back, to enable the winch operator in the aircraft to grasp the survivor and guide him back into the aircraft cabin.

Winching Techniques Most helicopter rescues involve lowering a crew member to assist those being winched aboard. During this double lift the survivor will be secured by the winchman and they are raised together. In certain circumstances this may not be feasible, and a one-man lift will be

Never approach a rescue helicopter until the pilot or crewman has indicated that you can do so. Then approach from the front towards the open door keeping your head bent low.

organised. When the helicopter is positioned int the wind overhead the survivor - who must be conscious and uninjured - a rescue strop will be lowered. The survivor places the strop over his head with the winch cable to the front. It should be adjusted under the armpits, tightened the webbing ring woggle, before signalling to the winch operator that he is ready.

Stretcher cases will always be supervised by a lowered crew member.

SURVIVAL IN THE
ARCTIC

THE POLAR REGIONS
Clothing and Equipment
Surviving Forced Landings

MEDICAL HAZARDS
Frostbite
Hypothermia
Insects

SHELTER
Construction
Fires
Camp Life

FOOD
Plants
Hunting and Trapping
Fishing

TRAVEL
Considerations and Dangers
Means of Travel
Rivers, Lakes and Ice
Signalling and Rescue

THE POLAR REGIONS

As with any other environment, the Polar regions can be dangerous, but the same basic rules of survival apply: blend and integrate with the elements, and resist the urge to fight them.

It is difficult to imagine that anyone would deliberately go unprepared into a Polar region. The most serious situations arise when an aircraft crash-lands in the frozen tundra, or some other form of transport breaks down during a deep penetration into the wilderness. In all cases, providing you are uninjured, your chances of survival are good. In both winter and summer the northern Arctic offers an abundant supply of water and food; shelter can be found in the tree line, or created even on the barren ice floes. Provided that you successfully protect yourself against the risk of freezing to death your chances of survival and rescue are good.

Even in the worst cases, when you have been plunged into a survival situation by a plane crash, you should still be able to salvage enough equipment to survive for several months. Even in wartime, prisoners who have weighed up their chances realistically prior to any escape from, e.g., an Arctic prison camp and who have prepared themselves and their equipment intelligently have found that the Arctic, despite its vastness, offers survival conditions that most of us can deal with.

Latitudes higher than 66 degrees 33 minutes North define the area known as the Arctic Circle. It covers some 21 million square kilometres (approximately 8 million square miles), of which two-thirds are occupied by the Arctic Ocean. More than half of the ocean is permanently covered with layers of pack ice.

In summer the Arctic temperature can reach -38°C; in winter it falls as low as -65°C. Winters in the Arctic are long and severe, with the ground frozen much of the time. Summer lasts for around four months during which the ground thaws sufficiently to allow moisture to reach the roots of the trees and plants. The northern landmass changes as you move south, from pack ice to a rich grassy vegetation (the tundra), and on into a wide forest strip; in parts this is up to 1500km (900 miles) deep from North to South. Man and beast have occupied this inhospitable area throughout the history of mankind; depending upon the time of year, it is rich in plant life, fish and wild animals.

By comparison the Antarctic continent surrounding the South Pole is a forbidding land almost devoid of plant and animal life. Scientists have found a variety of lichens and insect life, but insufficient to sustain life for survival purposes. The landmass is greater than that of Europe, and is entirely covered by a dense sheet of ice which averages over 2000m (7,000ft) thick. The Antarctic is much colder than the northern Arctic, with temperatures falling as low as -89°C (-128°F) and never rising above 15°C (59°F). Animal life is mainly restricted to birds, seals and penguins, the latter spending most of their life in the water.

Modern materials mean that man can survive in the most severe conditions, but the layer principle of dressing will help maintain a comfortable temperature during periods of activity and rest.

Winds in the Antarctic can reach speeds of up to 160kmh (100mph), driving snow 30m (100ft) into the air. It is imperative that any survivor takes shelter from such a snow blizzard; apart from the lack of visibility, the wind forces down the air temperature, creating deadly hypothermic conditions. Short-term survival is possible, but would depend upon making early contact with one of the many scientific research stations which are dotted around the outer edge of the Antarctic.

Arctic Clothing & Equipment

To venture into the Arctic without the proper clothing and equipment is to invite disaster. Man is a tropical animal whose body functions best between 96F and 102F; above or below that relatively narrow range the health may start to decline. The maintenance of body temperature will help prevent cold injury. The main factors to protect against in the Arctic are low temperatures, wind, and ground conduction. Modern clothing materials such as Gore-Tex make ideal outer protective shells, but the inner layers are equally important. Safeguarding heat loss from your head, hands and feet will play a major part in any Arctic survival, and again the layering principle can be employed.

How the Layer System Works

Body heat is produced by activity; the more strenuous that activity the more heat is generated. By using the layer system we can control this heat. For example, blankets on our bed trap our body heat and provide warmth while we sleep; too few blankets and we get cold, too many and we overheat. The same principles apply every time we dress ourselves. However, in the Arctic we will need several layers of the right fabrics to control our body temperature. Removing a layer reduces trapped heat, adding a layer increases it. By doing this we also control sweating, and the damping of clothing next to the skin. The layer system applies to the whole body, overlapping where need be. The inner layers are used to provide insulation while the outer layers provide ventilation.

- Clothing next to the skin should be made of a thin, cotton material, loose-fitting and able to absorb perspiration. This layer must be kept clean.
- The second layer should ideally be made of tightly woven wool with adjustable fastenings at the wrist and neck.
- A third layer should consist of a fleece-lined shirt or jacket with a hood. This layer should be easily removable.
- The final outer layer needs to be both waterproof and windproof, with a large hood. For Arctic temperatures this garment should be filled with a padded insulating material similar to that used in sleeping bags.

Keep Clothing in Good Repair

- In a survival situation you can seldom replace your clothes – it is important to ensure they last and continue to function properly.

- Dirty or ripped clothing will not insulate or protect you – repair and wash clothing as soon as necessary.

- Layers next to your skin will need frequent washing to remove ingrained sweat and dirt.

- In sub-zero temperatures, wet clothing can be hung up to freeze. The moisture turns into ice particles that can then be beaten out. This works best with tightly woven garments.

- If you are in a static location, building a Yukon stove (see section on fires) inside your shelter will provide the means to safely dry clothes while keeping you warm.

Remove inner clothing before digging into the snow. This will prevent undue sweating. Replace your dry garments before entering the snow hole.

Protecting the Head

The head accounts for around 47% of heat loss, and its protection is vitally important.

An insulated hat with pull-down earflaps will stop much of your body's heat loss, but make sure it does not fit too tightly. The military use a 30cm (12in) long woollen tube which they call a 'head-over'. This is used under the hood of any outer garment; it slips over the head forming a seal at the neckline. In extreme cold conditions when it is necessary to remove the outer hood, the head-over can be pulled up to protect the ears and head.

Loosening the neck aperture and temporarily removing any head protection is the best way of venting excessive body heat. In extreme cold the face can be shielded by a special face mask.

Protecting the Hands

If your hands become too cold you cannot build a shelter or fire; and you cannot wal on numb feet. A thin pair of woollen finger type gloves should be worn under a set of insulated, waterproof mitts of Gore-Tex or some similar material. If you must handle metal as part of your daily routine in the Arctic you would be well advised to use special contact gloves.

The loss of a glove in the Arctic can be disastrous; make sure they are securely fastened to your body by a length of cord. Spare socks will make good mittens in an emergency; they can be protected from the wet by covering them with polythene bags and securing them at the wrist. Muskrats and other similar animals are eas to snare; their hides, if properly removed and turned inside out, make excellent gloves.

Protecting the Feet

Boots should be calf-length, watertight, and loose enough to allow the wearing of two pairs of socks – one thin pair under a thick, knee-length woollen pair. As with your upper body, loose, comfortable layers will not restrict the foot's blood supply. To make sure that the circulation in your feet is working properly, keep moving and wiggle your toes every few minutes. Check for any signs of numbness, as this is an indicator that your feet's blood supply is being trapped. Always carry at least one spare pair of socks and if your feet become wet, change them. If you are wearing normal leather boots, cover them with gaiters; the type which cover the whole boot are best in snow. If you intend staying out overnight, or standing around for any length of time, carry a pair of mukluks.

There is little to beat a good mukluk to keep your feet warm during the Arctic winter. The modern day mukluk is a thick felt sock with a wide, flat rubber sole and a waterproof outer. They make walking in snow easier than with normal boots; but their best advantage is their warmth in winter. They also protect against trench foot if travelling during the early spring or late summer.

Frozen hands kill – never risk losing a glove.

Surviving Arctic Aircraft Emergencies

Most aircraft will have sent out a distress call prior to any crash-landing. Most large commercial aircraft are automatically tracked, thus registering their precise position prior to making a forced landing. Aircraft which make emergency wheels-up landings in snow have an excellent chance of survival.

Some military aircraft may offer the crew an opportunity to bail out. If this is done the captain should appoint a centre man. The centre man should fire a flare or make a visible signal once on the ground so that the rest of the crew can converge on his position.

The time of year, weather conditions and location of impact will determine the ice conditions. An aircraft that has landed on summer ice may well sink – this can take anything from a few minutes to several days. If large sections of the aircraft hull are still intact and there is no indication of ice movement in the immediate vicinity, then it should be utilised and improved to make a more permanent shelter.

Certain safeguards should be carried out:
- Selected survivors of strong physical build should enter the aircraft first to remove any dead bodies. These should be neatly placed outside the aircraft and covered with a layer of snow. All personal effects should remain with the body for later identification.
- Check the aircraft or vehicle for all usable components. Make use of any hot water from storage tanks before it goes cold. Organise forage parties to search the hold baggage for clothing and any other useful items. Remove seats to make beds for the injured and extra sleeping space.
- All cigarettes and lighters should be removed from any survivor and kept for safety in a special container. This is to prevent any accidental fire on board the aircraft, as aviation fuel will have spilled from ruptured tanks. Monitor carbon monoxide if you have an internal heat source.
- Separate the injured, and divide any survivors into groups depending on age, fitness and ability. Organise on-going care for the injured, children and the elderly.
- Establish emergency procedures. Operate radio and rescue devices and prepare visual location signals. Organise a roster to keep watch for any sign of search and rescue.
- Always keep a detailed log of who has done what. As the days slip by people will become increasingly unwilling to stand outside in the cold – a log will help avoid arguments over the fair division of duties.

If you have to make a forced landing you are best to stay with the aircraft unless the situation seriously dictates otherwise.

Arctic Forced Landings

- Evacuate yourself and others at least 100m upwind from the aircraft.

- Care for the injured; administer first aid.

- Return to the aircraft only under instructions from the crew, or when considered safe.

- Remove life rafts to use for emergency shelter; secure them in high winds.

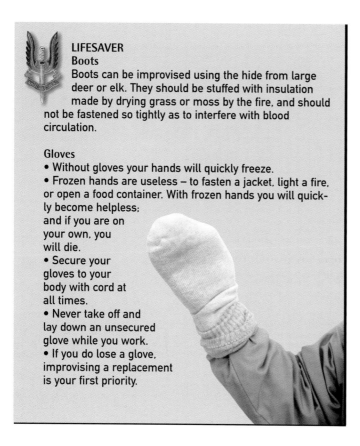

LIFESAVER

Boots

Boots can be improvised using the hide from large deer or elk. They should be stuffed with insulation made by drying grass or moss by the fire, and should not be fastened so tightly as to interfere with blood circulation.

Gloves

• Without gloves your hands will quickly freeze.
• Frozen hands are useless – to fasten a jacket, light a fire, or open a food container. With frozen hands you will quickly become helpless; and if you are on your own, you will die.
• Secure your gloves to your body with cord at all times.
• Never take off and lay down an unsecured glove while you work.
• If you do lose a glove, improvising a replacement is your first priority.

Equipment for a Cold Environment

Travelling in a cold environment should mean that you are already well clothed and equipped. Make sure that your survival kit contains the extra items to cope with cold priorities: warmth and shelter. This means including a good means of fire-starting, several heavy duty polythene bags, and some good fishing equipment (see Survival Essentials). If you find yourself in an Arctic environment due to some unforeseen accident then your equipment priorities will mean salvaging what you can from your aircraft or vehicle.

• Most aircraft carry a good survival pack containing a wide range of useful items.
• Every aircraft that flies over water should have a life raft. This in turn will contain most of the items needed for survival. The raft itself will provide an excellent emergency shelter, and the raft case can be turned into a sledge.
• Most commercial aircraft and vehicles carry a medical pack.
• Aviation fuel, diesel, petrol and oil all make excellent fuel for your fires. To a lesser degree, duty-free alcohol carried on commercial flights will also burn.

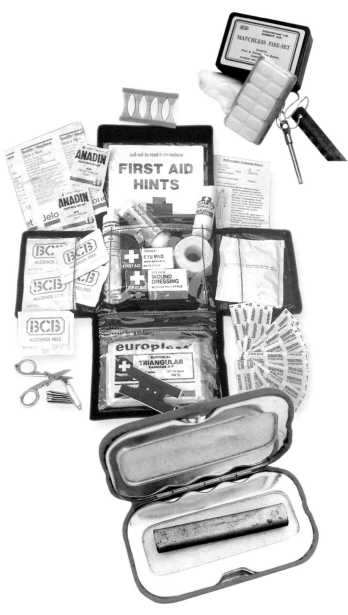

• Any spare clothing or sheeting should be utilised. On a downed commercial aircraft check the hold for suitcases, etc.
• Any item that stops the wind should be used for constructing shelter – canvas and polythene sheeting, parachutes, passenger blankets, etc.
• A commercial aircraft carries a great deal of food in foil trays, most of which can be preserved by freezing.
• Providing you have the means to make fire there is no need to worry about water in the Arctic.
• For signalling, tyres of all descriptions burn extremely well and produce a vast amount of black smoke.
• For Arctic navigation maps are of more use than a compass, but having both is better still.

ARCTIC MEDICAL HAZARDS

Medical problems almost always accompany an accident, especially an air crash. Victims will require immediate attention (see Survival Essentials). Arctic temperatures present their own additional dangers; frostbite, hypothermia and snow blindness are the main hazards, while efforts to keep warm and exclude draughts can lead to lack of oxygen and carbon monoxide poisoning. The first two are caused by excessive loss of heat from the body. Wind will accelerate the cooling of the body because its movement decreases air temperatures. Being wet also increases the risk, as water will conduct the heat away from the body; garments that are wet or damp, with either water or sweat, will lose their insulating properties and will begin to actually drain heat from the body.

Hands and Feet Hands and feet are at the extremes of the body's circulation system, and so need extra attention if they are to maintain heat. Make sure that any fastenings at the wrists, ankles, neck and waist are snug enough to prevent heat loss but not so tight that they cut off circulation to the extremities. As much as possible, keep the hands covered. If they become cold, warm them either between the thighs or under the armpits.

Moving the feet and wiggling the toes can warm frost-nipped toes, and warming them against a companion's body is also very effective. Pay attention to your footwear and try to keep your feet as dry as possible. If you have a pair of spare socks, keep them close to your body and try to change into a dry pair at least once a day. Overboots are also a great aid in protecting the feet against the cold and wet. If you do not have any, try to improvise by putting a spare sock over each boot. If you are not moving around, take off your boots and give your feet a good ten-minute rub every few hours.

Frostbite Symptoms When the body becomes cold it puts priority on retaining the core heat rather than warming the

Arctic Forced Landings

• Use life jackets, in-flight blankets and extra clothing for insulation.

• Locate any emergency radios or beacons and remove any batteries from their housings. The batteries should be kept warm.

• Remove all food from the galley.

• Prepare signalling devices.

• Drain oil; if no receptacle is available, drain directly onto the ice.

• Check surface ice conditions.

• Rest.

• If your position is threatened, or no rescue attempt is indicated after five days, consider your options.

The cold can be a real killer; adopt the buddy-buddy method and keep an eye out for one another.

extremities; it therefore shuts down the blood vessels in the skin. In extreme cold weather the parts of the body at the limits of the circulation may actually freeze and cause tissue damage. This is the condition known as frostbite. Frostbite can creep up on a person so gradually that they are not aware that they have it until the last minute. You will need to be on guard against this dangerous condition, as if it becomes serious it can lead to gangrene and loss of the affected part. The first symptoms to be noticed will be a feeling of 'pins and needles' in the affected part, which may also become stiff

and numb. Later the skin of the area will turn pale, then white, before becoming a mottled blue and eventually black as tissue death occurs.

As exposed skin is most prone to frostbite, check uncovered areas frequently – especially the nose, fingers and toes. Other areas which should be checked are the ankles and wrists. If you are with someone else, make sure that you check each other frequently for any warning signs that frostbite is occurring. Any frostbitten areas that are discovered should be slowly warmed by some natural means. Skin-to-skin contact provides the best method of

slow warming. If warm water is available, use that, but make sure that it is not too warm (do a 'baby-bath' test). Any frostbitten casualty should be removed to a shelter as soon as is practicable, and should be insulated against further heat loss with blankets and extra clothing. Hot drinks and food should be given to the casualty as soon as possible.

Hypothermia Hypothermia occurs when the body temperature falls below 35°C and body heat is being lost faster than it can be replaced. At this stage body functions start to slow down, and may stop

altogether if the condition is not treated. Exposure to cold, wet weather is a major factor in this condition, as are wet clothing, immersion in cold water, inadequate clothing, exhaustion and shortage of food and drink. It is important to be aware of the symptoms, especially if you are subject to any of the conditions described above.

The symptoms of hypothermia are:

- Uncontrollable shivering.
- Skin pale, dry and sub-normally cold to the touch.
- Muscular weakness, lethargy, need for sleep.
- Dimming of sight.

- Irrational behaviour.
- Personality changes –
  an extrovert may become
  introverted, a quiet person aggressive.
- Slow, weak pulse.
- Slow, shallow breathing.
- Eventual collapse and
  unconsciousness. Possi-
  ble cardiac arrest.

As soon as hypothermia is
suspected it must be treated
by restoring lost body heat.
This means getting the casualty out of the wet and cold
and into shelter as soon as
possible. Use dry cloth-
ing/covering to replace any
wet clothing. If the victim has
been totally submerged in
water, remove all clothes –
they will reduce body temperature faster than nakedness.
If you have a metallised survival blanket, use this to
reflect any radiated heat loss
back to the body. If the casualty is conscious, hot food and
drink are helpful. If another
healthy survivor is present he
will be able to share his body
heat with the casualty.

The casualty may become
unconscious with no signs of
breathing or pulse; proceed
immediately with assisted
ventilation and chest compressions. The casualty will
still need to be warmed. Even
if the casualty's body temperature has fallen to 26°C, do
not automatically presume
that he is dead. Carry on with
resuscitation techniques until
he has reached normal body
temperature; if he cannot
then be revived, death can be
assumed.

Wrapping in a reflective blanket
conserves vital body heat.

Remember that if one per-
son is suffering from
hypothermia, others may be –
check everyone in your party.

Immersion Foot If you are
travelling across the Arctic
tundra during spring/sum-
mer your feet can be
immersed in cold water or
bog for a long time. If the feet
are not adequately protected
they will develop a condition
termed immersion foot; this
can occur even when the
temperature is well above
freezing. The first symptoms
are that the foot becomes
white, numb, cold and
swollen. If the condition is
allowed to progress the skin
becomes red, hot, broken,
ulcerated and extremely
painful. Prevention is better
than cure. Keep the feet dry
and out of water – if possible
wear rubber boots. If you do
get water in your boots, take
them off, empty them out and
wring out your socks, replacing them as soon as possible.
Check the feet frequently and
rub them for five to ten minutes.

If symptoms appear:
- Gently dry the feet and
  wriggle the toes.
- If the skin has been broken, apply an antiseptic
  cream.
- Protect the feet by wrapping them loosely in
  bandages.
- Allow the feet to warm

If you discover frostbite:

- DO NOT rub or massage
  the affected area (except in
  the very early stages).

- DO NOT apply snow or ice –
  this will only serve to make
  the condition worse.

- DO NOT use direct or
  strong heat such as hot
  stones or a fire to warm the
  area.

- DO NOT give alcohol to
  drink, as this can lower body
  temperature further.

- DO NOT allow a casualty
  with a recently frostbitten foot
  to walk.

- DO NOT break open any
  blisters which may occur.

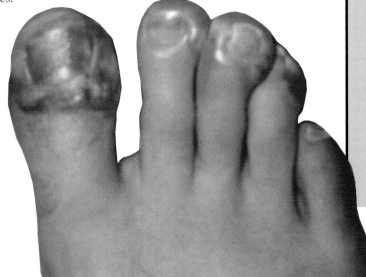

Prevent snow blindness by wearing goggles or improvising protection.

up slowly and naturally. Do not expose to direct heat.
- Elevate the legs to relieve the swelling and pain.
- Do not walk until your feet have recovered.

Snow Glare/Blindness When crossing snow in bright sunlight the eyes are exposed to reflected rays diffused by snow particles that strike the eyeball from every direction. Snow glare is a painful and watery inflammation of the eyeballs which causes a burning sensation. The first signs are a gritty sensation in the eye, which can proceed to intense pain and loss of vision. Snow blindness can be distressing but it is not a serious condition. Prevention is the best answer – protect the eyes with sunglasses or snow goggles. If neither are available a strip of cardboard, cloth or bark, with narrow slits cut for vision, will suffice. Use charcoal to blacken beneath the eyes to reduce glare.

Mosquitoes and Midges
Mosquitoes are found in most regions of the world including the Arctic and sub-Arctic.

They are not generally dangerous but constitute an irritating presence. While summer in the Arctic may seem preferable to winter for the survivor, it brings a number of its own problems. The ground gets very soggy as the snow melts, which also heralds the onslaught of biting insects such as clouds of midges. While small in size these swarm in their millions, making life unbearable; they have literally driven men and animals crazy. The survivor should do all within his power to fend off mosquitoes and midges; covering the whole body and protecting the head with a net is the only real answer, as insect repellent has little effect.

Arctic Hygiene It may seem impractical to remove all your clothes and wash yourself in the Arctic, but if you are to avoid infection and skin rashes it is vital. Providing you have a fire and shelter you should take a snow bath on a daily basis, preferably before you retire for the night. Take a handful of clean snow and wash yourself with the snowball. Concentrate on the areas of perspiration, under the arms and between the legs. Dry the body if a cloth is available, and get dressed again. Once your body is clean concentrate on your feet.

Remove one boot at a time; if no spare socks are available, beat the one you have just removed against a stiff object and allow it to air; dry it by the fire if damp. Give your feet a good scrub with fresh snow, cleaning between the toes and around the heel. Check for any blisters or sore spots, and treat them immediately. Dry and replace the sock. Repeat the process on your other foot, then get into bed.

ARCTIC SHELTER

In Arctic winter conditions shelter must be the first priority: get out of the wind – you will die if you remain in the open for any length of time. Arctic storms can last for several days, causing drifting snow to bury your shelter. Time should only be spent in building if conditions allow or you have no other choice, i.e. you are above the tree line on flat, snow-covered ice. If you have access to an immobilised vehicle or wrecked aircraft, use these rather than looking for any other means of shelter.

Natural building materials in the Arctic vary with latitude and season. On the northern ice floe you will be limited to snow and ice; the tundra has the added benefit of short bushes and moss; while the forest below the tree line offers an abundance of building material. Snow will vary in depth and level of compaction; this will be a deciding factor as to the type of shelter to be built. While some are simple to make, others require a degree of effort and time, especially if they are to be used long term. If building in a forested area, watch out for rotting or falling trees, and beware of heavy snow-laden branches breaking off. In mountainous areas look for caves or overhangs, but be aware of the danger of avalanches or rock falls.

As a guide to Arctic shelter, consider the traditional living habits of the Inuit inhabitants of such regions. During the winter most lived in shelters made from sod, constructed before the winter cold set in. In many cases the floor was dug down into the earth, which makes them warmer. The dome-shaped igloo we normally associate with these peoples was used more as a temporary shelter while hunting, although many Canadian Inuit did build them as permanent homes. Tents made of animal skins were used in the summer; these normally had a frame of whalebone or timber covered with caribou or seal skin. Both summer and winter shelters where fitted with several coverings of animal skin which formed the seating or sleeping areas. Heat and light was supplied from soapstone lamps burning rendered seal oil.

The type of shelter you build will depend on a number of criteria:
- Where you are and what weather conditions prevail.
- What you need shelter from – wind, snow, rain, cold or insects.
- What materials and tools are available.

Getting Under Cover

- Even the most desolate regions and climates can provide survivors with the means of shelter.

- In Arctic forest, use trees and branches.

- On the tundra, use bushes, moss and earth.

- If nothing else is available, the snow itself can protect you.

At best, travel in the Arctic is slow and dangerous, if the means are available build a good strong shelter that will last until rescue arrives or better conditions prevail.

A digging tool for snow can be improvised from cloth and a branch.

Digging out a drift cave.

Shelter Construction

Improvised Digging Tool If no purpose-made tool or more obvious materials are available, then improvise in the following way. Use any spare clothing such as a tee-shirt, and place it over a forked branch leaving a long enough stem to act as a handle. Wet the fabric – urine will do if nothing else is available – and allow the whole lot to freeze. The end product will be a very effective snow-digging tool.

Aircraft and Vehicles Aircraft and vehicles make excellent shelters in the summer; their major advantage over improvised shelters is that they can be sealed to protect against biting insects. Their use in winter will depend largely on how well you can insulate the interior. Most commercial aircraft are extremely well insulated and will provide excellent shelter; small outputs of heat from candles or a contained fire will raise the temperature enough for people to survive. Most commercial aircraft which fly over the Arctic carry as part of their survival equipment camping stoves which burn aviation fuel. If proper care is taken they can be used inside the aircraft for both heating and cooking (always check for carbon monoxide poisoning). If the aircraft or vehicle hull is not insulated, you are better off building a snow shelter outside.

Life Rafts Life rafts designed for survival at sea make excellent emergency shelters on land, and will accommodate a large number of people. They are easily inflated, thus providing instant protection against the wind and snow. Some form of insulation will be required if they are placed directly on a cold surface. Care should be taken not to puncture the outer rubber (a repair kit is included), especially if you intend to use the raft on water at a later date. All life rafts come complete with survival and medical packs, including food and water. Most models are packed in a plastic outer case which, if straps are attached, can be pulled along as easily as any sledge. One-man preparation time: 5 minutes. Location: anywhere.

Fir Tree Den

1 Dig the snow out from around the base of the tree.

2 Pile the snow up around the edges to form a wall.

3 Light a fire in a position that will not melt snow on overhanging branches.

LIFESAVER
Building a snow shelter even in temperatures of -30° C will cause you to perspire. Remove an inner garment (retain any waterproof outer) before you start building, replacing it the moment you are snugly inside your shelter. Whatever form of shelter you build you must have ventilation, especially if burning a fire inside your shelter.
These two elements are vital to your survival.

The Snow Grave

1 Dig out a trench as deep as time and conditions sllow.

2 Insulate with any available foliage.

2 Construct roof out of snow blocks, foliage or sheeting.

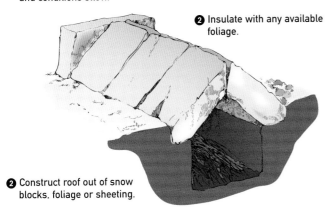

A simple snow trench.

Quick Snow Shelter In flat, snow-covered areas above the tree line it is possible to make a quick snow shelter by simply forming a mound and covering it with a sheet of some kind. Snow is heaped on top of the sheet and compressed firmly; this layer should be about 30cm (12ins) thick. Your mound can be based upon anything from your rucksack to foliage, wreckage, or – if you have nothing else – simply snow. It is vital that you have some form of covering over most of your mound, as this enables you to remove the contents after the compressed snow has frozen to form a sufficiently hard outer shell. Cut a hole on the leeward side of the snow dome large enough to recover your rucksack or other contents of your mound. If you are forced to use snow to form your inner mound then scoop this out; once you have removed about half the snow the rest can be pulled clear by removing covering. Don't worry if small parts cave-in -these can easily be repaired. Leave a small hole in the roof to breathe through. When you enter your shelter for the night close the entrance with your rucksack, or a giant snowball. One-man construction time: 30 minutes. Location: ice pack, tundra.

Simple Snow Trench The simplest form of protection is to dig a trench or tunnel-type shelter in the snow.

This tends to be a temporary or emergency measure used when hit by a snowstorm or unable to travel due to injury. It has only one purpose: to keep out the wind. A roof can be added; this can be made of snow blocks, if it is packed hard enough. Otherwise use branches, or some form of sheeting such as a poncho. These shelters can be built completely into the snow, partially sunken, or on the surface, depending on snow conditions and thickness. One-man construction time: 10 minutes. Location: ice pack, tundra.

Fir Tree Den In wooded areas a large fir tree forms an excellent basis for a winter shelter. Natural hollows in the snow can usually be found around the base of the trunk, especially on the lee side, and these will provide a good starting place for your shelter. Dig out the rest of the snow in the hollow and pile it up on the sides of your shelter area to give you greater protection from the elements. Roofing and bedding material can be made from the lower branches cut from the other side of the same tree. A fire can be lit, but make sure that it is a little further around the trunk away from your shelter – the heat from the fire will melt the snow from the overhead branches. One-man construction time: 30 minutes. Location: tree line.

Snow Frame The snow frame is ideal in Arctic tundra areas and where the vegetation is reduced to short scrub. If time and materials allow, this

Snow Shelters

- Building a snow shelter, even in temperatures of -30°C, will cause you to perspire. Remove a inner garment before you start building (keeping on any waterproof outer layer which you have). Replace it the moment you are snugly inside your shelter.

- Whatever form of refuge you build, you must have ventilation, especially if burning a fire inside your shelter.

- Always take you digging tools inside the shelter – you may have to dig yourself out again.

- Mark the exit to the shelter – since you may need to find it in a hurry.

- Once inside, remove loose snow from clothing before it melts.

- If you have a cooker, don't boil water for too long – it causes a lot of condensation.

The Snow Igloo

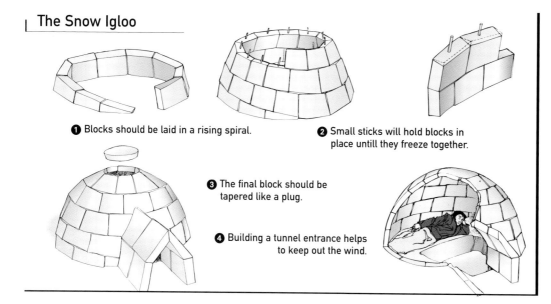

❶ Blocks should be laid in a rising spiral.

❷ Small sticks will hold blocks in place untill they freeze together.

❸ The final block should be tapered like a plug.

❹ Building a tunnel entrance helps to keep out the wind.

type of shelter can be made to provide a comfortable home for any number of survivors. Select an area where the short brush is thickest, and outline your shelter by stamping down the snow. Cut/break and remove any vegetation within the shelter perimeter. Carefully (they will break when frozen) bend over saplings on either side and interlace to form an arch (where no sapling is available, use those you have removed from the shelter floor). A side weave of saplings will help support the frame and give it strength. In winter the frame can be covered with a combination of piled branches if available, or tundra moss on top of which snow can be packed. Use a rucksack or giant snow ball to block the door, and vent the shelter by making a hole in the roof. One-man construction time: 2 hours. Location: tree-line, tundra.

Drift Cave To make a drift cave shelter the snow will need to be at least 2m (6.5ft) or more in depth – a snow-drift or cornice is ideal. To construct a comfortable shelter you need to tunnel into the snow, and add as many as possible of the features shown in the illustrated cross-section. The inside of the roof should always be dome-shaped – anything else will probably fall on your head by morning. Packed snow is often hard to cut through, and this type of shelter may require much effort and time on the part of the survivor. It will also require the use of some digging tools. One-man construction time: 1 hour. Location: pack ice, mountains.

Snow Igloo A snow igloo requires real effort and should only be built if time and tools are available. The igloo is a semi-permanent shelter, designed to withstand strong winds on a exposed treeless expanse. That said, a well-constructed igloo will provide a comfortable long-term shelter for two or more survivors. The tools needed for its construction are a saw or flat spade, and a long-bladed knife. Although a lone survivor could build an igloo, the work will be much easier and quicker with two or three. The other essential ingredient is cold, compacted snow.

First, the snow of the area where the igloo is to be built will need to be stamped down flat. Then the snow blocks should be cut: 80-90cm long, 50cm wide, and 10-15 cm thick (32-35ins x 20ins x 4-6 inches). The blocks are upwards from a circular base in a spiral form which is angled both upwards and inwards. Cut the blocks uniformly and place them care-

The Snow Hive

Where the snow is not suitable to construct an igloo, a snow hive can be built.

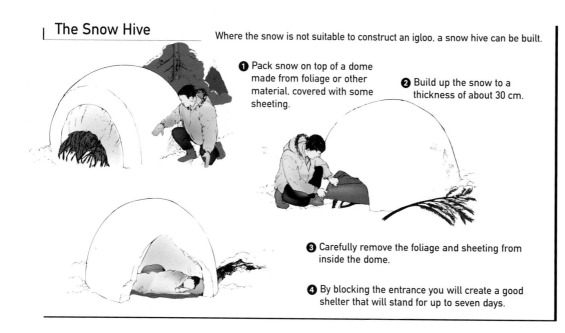

❶ Pack snow on top of a dome made from foliage or other material, covered with some sheeting.

❷ Build up the snow to a thickness of about 30 cm.

❸ Carefully remove the foliage and sheeting from inside the dome.

❹ By blocking the entrance you will create a good shelter that will stand for up to seven days.

Drift Cave

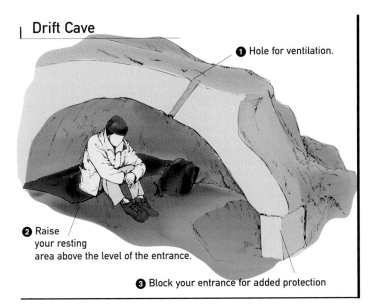

1 Hole for ventilation.

2 Raise your resting area above the level of the entrance.

3 Block your entrance for added protection

fully. Use a knife to chip away any uneven surface when laying one block on top of another. Dig or build an entrance tunnel on the lee-ward side of the igloo. Igloos retain any heat generated inside – even a single candle placed in the middle will pro-duce an amazing amount of warmth. One-man construc-tion time: 2-3 hours. Loca-tion: ice pack, barren areas. SAS Tip: I have found the biggest problem when build-ing an igloo is getting the walls to angle in correctly when trying to form a dome. This can be quickly achieved if small sticks are placed between the blocks as pegs, securing them until they have had time to bond by freezing.

One-Pole Snow Tepee The snow tepee is used mainly while travelling or where time does not allow the building of a proper shelter. Whenever travelling in the Arctic you should equip yourself with a sturdy 4m (13ft) pole. Apart from helping with navigation and when crossing ice, such a pole will also form the framework of your tepee. Stamp down the snow and drive your pole (tip towards the wind) into the ground at a 30⁻ angle. Next drape over your covering – you will need something at least the size of a military poncho – and secure it. Some form of ground insulation and a fire will improve the tepee. One-man construction time: 5-10 minutes. Location: any-where.

Double Lean-to If you are surviving in the winter tree-line and there are several people in your party, then you might consider building a double lean-two. This is basically the same as a nor-mal lean-to (see Survival Essentials) except that two open sides face one another with a fire in between. This

has the advantage of reduc-ing the amount of fuel need-ed. The windward side needs to be completely blocked; and the sloping sides need to be at least a metre apart at the apex in order to vent the fire properly.

Cold air sinks so make the entrance to your shelter lower than your resting space. Make the entrance large enough to crawl through and small enough to block with your ruck sack.

Fire

Warning: Believe it or not, the most common cause of accidental death in the Arctic is not freezing but fire.

However, fire remains the single most important element in survival under Arctic conditions. If you are leaving your shelter for any length of time always make sure there is a fire laid ready with a reasonable supply of fuel. Even if you are travelling and it is not your intention to return, unforeseeable circumstances may force you to do so, and finding a fire ready to light at once could make the difference between life and death.

Fire in the Arctic.

Oil, Aviation Fuel and Petrol

It is assumed that no one finds themselves surviving on the ice pack without arriving in some form of transport. As soon after an accident or crash as it is judged safe to return to the aircraft or other vehicle, drain off any available oil from the engine before it thickens with the cold. High octane fuel can be left in the tanks, as it will only freeze in extreme temperatures. An emergency fire can be lighted quickly by mixing the oil with one-fifth aviation fuel. This should be done in a metal container, no larger than 5 litres (say 1 gallon) in size, and well away from the aircraft. Give it a good stir; then, from a distance, use a rag soaked in the fuel on the end of a pole to light the fire. Once burning it is safe to approach. The aviation fuel will quickly burn off, but in doing so it will warm the oil enough for it to sustain itself. Draining a vehicle sump and mixing it in the same proportion with petrol will achieve the same effect.

Warning: Mixing any combustible fuel is dangerous, and should only be done in extreme conditions such as the Arctic.

An emergency fire can be built by pouring petrol or aviation fuel onto most consumable materials; even snow ca be set alight. Be careful where you place your fire, making sure it is far enough away from the main fuel supply. If you build your fire on a sheet of aircraft aluminium remember that this too may ignite.

Seal Fire It is impossible without inflammable fuel to start a fire on snow or ice. A base must first be established; this can either be aircraft wreckage, rotting timbers, or a thick layer of animal fat. The base should be large enough to support your fire; small fires serve little purpose as they provide very little heat, so you should only attempt to light a fire in the Arctic when a good supply of fuel and shielding is available.

On the ice pack the only natural fuel is that derived from seal fat and bone. It is not a good combination, being difficult to light and burning with little heat; the flame is also easily extinguished. However, in an emergency and with nothing else to hand it is worth trying.

Moss Arctic moss can be found in abundance and has several major uses to any survivor. In all cases the moss is best dried by placing it loosely around a fire, or by speading it out on a flat metal surface which can be placed over the fire. In either case care should be taken not to let the moss burn, converting it to charcoal dust.

- Dried moss makes an excellent tinder for lighting fires, especially when in a hurry.
- It can be used to pack around your glowing embers in a fire-carrying container.
- Boots and mukluks can be insulated with a layer of dried moss.

Hot sand Any survivor who finds a deposit of river-washed sand is advised to collect one or two kilos (2-4lbs), carefully removing any small stones. Sand can be heated either by using it as a base for your fire, or by placing it in a container. Its great advantage is that it retains the heat for a long time, and this can be extremely useful in Arctic conditions.

- Hot sand can be used to dry out wet boots.
- A small can full carried while travelling will provide an excellent hand-warmer.

Drift Wood Drift wood can be found along some Arctic coastlines. Pieces that have been out of the water for some time will burn best. Remember that wood, wreckage and flotsam can drift for thousands of miles.

Scrub and stunted willow

trees grow well above the tree line, extending well into the tundra. Many of the evergreens are so rich in resin that they will burn even when wet. The lower forests of the Arctic are rich in white birch trees; in earlier times their bark was used by the inhabitants to build canoes, make houses and provide torches.

Lighting a Fire at Night and in Bad Weather Lighting a fire in the Arctic is extremely difficult. For many months of the year these regions are shrouded in darkness and buffeted by strong winds and snowstorms. Under such conditions you will need some form of wind break and a permanent flame in order to achieve any success with fire lighting. While aviation fuel and petrol will burn, the wind and snow will douse it if it is not properly shielded. It is best to use a candle in a tin, in such a way that it is easy to light, easy to get a light from, and provides light so that you can see what you are doing. Place a small amount of combustible material over the can and let the candle heat it until it catches fire.

The governing factor here is heat, as the fire will not burn unless you can build its heat to a degree higher than the prevailing temperature. This factor is also true with many forms of cooker, which will require heating before they will burn properly. One way is to wash the burner (not the fuel tank) with petrol or some other volatile fuel,

and set fire to it. Always do this in an open space outside your shelter.

When travelling, hot coals can be carried (see Essentials of Survival); however, in the Arctic they need to be well insulated with a slow-burning material. The advantage of this method is to guarantee a fire at the end of your daily journey. Semi-burnt charcoal from the outer edges of the previous night's fire is best, but Arctic moss and birch twigs will prove equally successful.

Oil and Water Mixing oil and water will produce a flammable mixture that provides a very hot fire. Place the two fluids in their own separate containers, into which a long stick-like plug has been inserted near the bottom. This plug is to control the amounts of oil and water in the mixture: 2 drops of water to 1 drop of oil.

The mixture should run on to a platform (although it is possible to drip it onto dry earth) where it can be ignited. The oil will not ignite even if heated by the fire's radiation, but as a matter of caution it is best to leave a distance between the dripping containers and the burning platform.

Yukon Stove Constructing a Yukon Stove should be a serious consideration if you are planning to stay in one place for longer than 24 hours, and given that the materials are available. It is one of the best ways to use fire for cooking and other purposes. It is also

fairly safe, and can withstand a certain amount of bad weather.

Its advantages over an open fire are that it will burn unattended; its heat is retained; and fuel consumption can be controlled. Importantly, it can also be constructed inside a large shelter to provide safe heat and to dry clothing.

The stove is made from rocks, stones and mud, in the shape of a tortoise shell. A hole is left on the windwarside (best offset a little in the Arctic) for fuel and ventilation, and there is also a hole at the top acting as a chimney. If you have a metal box or can available, this can be built into the back wall to make an oven.

Before any food can be cooked in it, however, a layer of twigs must be put down first, otherwise the food will burn on the hot metal. These twigs will eventually turn into charcoal, which can be saved and used to deodorise purified water and for medicinal uses. A large flat rock should cover half the chimney outlet for use as a griddle. If you wish to use your Yukon Stove inside your shelter, make sure that you have adequate ventilation, as the stove will produce carbon monoxide gas.

Hot sand in your boots will dry them out.

Camp Life

If you are part of a group then leadership will normally fall to the captain, pilot or senior crew member, although this authority may be bestowed on a more qualified person. Always work in pairs so that you can watch each others' faces for signs of frostbite. Everyone should be allocated work in order to occupy their time; those who are not seriously injured but immobile can still tend fires, watch and listen for rescue, keep a written log, and make emergency tools.

Ensure a Good Night's Sleep

We normally spend one-third of our day sleeping. In a survival situation, particularly in the Arctic, this can increase to as much as 12 to 14 hours while waiting to be rescued. Provided that you are warm this can be beneficial, as it prevents fatigue and exhaustion. Sleeping in the cold can be made easier by lying on some form of insulation mat – this can be either animal skin, foam or even cardboard. If you have them, life jackets provide good insulation and extra comfort. Protection from the wind can be achieved by simply covering the body with a plastic survival bag. Sharing body heat with other survivors is comforting – forget the inhibitions and huddle together. Place older people and children in the middle.

If conditions allow and there are no limiting factors, daily exercise in the form of hunting and foraging for fuel will also help ensure a good night's sleep.

Arctic streams are a good source of food and water.

Fur Blanket or Poncho It you manage to catch several large animals you are best advised to use their skins to make a blanket or poncho. It needs to be around 1.5m wide and 4m long (5ft x 13 feet). Even in long term survival situations, forget about any stitching or sewing: simply tie the ends together with dried animal gut. This makes an excellent poncho by day or sleep-

In the absence of a man-made poncho as illustrated here, one can be made from animal hide.

There is always something to be done in camp to improve comfort such as making kindling.

Always take your digging too

LIFESAVER
Overnight Tips

❶ Wet clothes can be left to freeze, at which stage the ice can be removed by beating and shaking vigorously.

❷ Wet boots can be dried by placing a warm stone from around the fire inside (use a couple of stick to lift it). Check that the exhaust emitting from the boot is steam and not smoke. Several smaller stones are better than one large one. In some terrain hot sand from around your fire can be used in the same way.

❸ If you have a survival gun or other metal weapon it is best left outside your shelter, thus maintaining a constant temperature and avoiding condensation. Cover the weapon with cloth to protect against the snow and frost.

❹ By contrast, ammunition is best kept in your pocket.

Sleeping in the Artic

- Make sure your shelter is windproof.

- Sleep on a good bed of insulating material.

- Have a plentiful supply of fuel handy.

- Eat your main meal just before you go to bed.

- Exercise to warm your muscles, but do not perspire.

ing bag and insulator by night. A warm hat can be fashioned out of a smaller animal such as an Arctic hare.

Finding Water Even in Arctic winter you will need a minimum of 2 litres (3.5 pints) of water daily to replace normal fluid loss. Thirst is reduced under Arctic conditions, and the average intake of water becomes less – but as a result the body suffers from progressive dehydration. The first signs are excessive lethargy leading to the desire for continuous sleep. This is easily corrected by drinking more water and monitoring your daily intake.

Finding water is not a problem as the surfaces of both Polar regions are covered with either snow or ice. The problem is converting these to obtain a daily supply of water; this can only by done by heating. Avoid eating

loose snow or ice as it can cause damage to the delicate membranes inside your mouth as well as causing dehydration. If you really need to drink and snow is the only thing available, crush it into a snowball with your hands. Continued compression will cause the snow to melt, and you can let the water drip into your mouth. Ice is much easier to melt than snow due to the lack of air between the water particles. Breaking the ice into smaller pieces or crushing it will speed this process further, and you will not need as much fuel to melt it.

In summer Arctic water is plentiful. On the tundra and tree line you will find abundant lakes and streams. The water may look dark brown and taste brackish, although growing vegetation helps keep it fresh – always boil your water. Don't waste valuable fuel; melt only what you need, and drink while it is still warm.

- Strip and rub your body with a dry towel.

- Put on extra clothes and socks.

- Wear a hat to bed.

- Visit the latrine trench just before you go to sleep.

- Four hours' sleep before midnight is better than four after.

- If you cannot sleep, plan what you will do the next day.

nside the shelter as you may have to dig yourself out.

Glaciers and Icebergs A good source of drinking water can be found in the blue ice of glaciers or icebergs, as this ice will not contain any salt. On the ice pack in summer look for small hollows in the icebergs – these will be full of fresh water. Remember that although ice and snow may look clean, there is no guarantee that the water will not be contaminated. If you are in any doubt as to its purity, sterilize it first either by using purification tablets or boiling.

Snow Melting If you plan to stay at your camp site for some time, you can consider using the warmth of any sun to improvise a solar-powered snow and ice melter. This will take much less effort and fuel than lighting a fire. All you need is a black plastic sack or something similar. Open it out and lay it over pebbles, rocks or sticks to raise it off the ground. Make sure that it has a gentle slope to it, and that the centre line is depressed into a trough. Once the sheet has warmed in the sun's rays, take some loose snow and scatter it thinly over the plastic. The snow will soon melt and the water run down the trough into your collecting container.

If you do not have any black plastic, find a large flat rock. Place it where it can warm up in the sun's rays, and proceed as before. Wrapping snow in spare clothing or parachute material and hanging it near the fire over a container will also produce water. Make sure that only fresh snow is used; and that the bundle is placed where it will benefit from the radiant heat without any risk of getting scorched.

Glaciers and icebergs are an obvious source of blue ice for drinking water.

COLD CLIMATE FOOD

Searching for food in the Arctic may seem a forbidding task, and in severe weather conditions it can be. That said, the Arctic has an abundance of wildlife in the form of animals and fish. You will find that in the areas where man is an infrequent traveller other creatures have flourished. Even in the extreme North the ice and snow may look barren but the water is full of fish, lobsters, seals, walruses and penguins. The further away from either Pole one gets, the warmer the climate, and the greater the variety of food resources including animal, insect and plant food.

A recent programme screened by Russian television illustrated a significant contrast in attitudes to life in a challenging Arctic environment. The programme depicted people of the northern Siberian 'gold rush' towns, who due to the collapse of support from central government in the way of wages, fuel and food had been forced to abandon their homes.

By comparison, when the same interviewer talked to members of the nomadic tribes who have lived in the same area for thousands of years, they smiled and gave the reply: 'We have reindeer. We have water. Life is good!'

For the most part the Inuit following their traditional way of life lived on meat, with a small addition of berries, roots and plants when they appeared in summer. Seal, caribou and fish account for 90% of their food intake, the remaining 10% being provided by birds, Polar bears and musk-oxen. Because of the lack of fuel for burning, and given that the oil stoves they used did not provide sufficient heat for cooking, most of the food was eaten cold.

There are several poisonous plants in the Arctic, and all fungi are best avoided; but these are in the minority, and for the most part fresh Arctic plants make good eating. A selection of edible plants and lichens are listed as follows, but if you are not 100% sure refer to the edibility test. There are no known Arctic plants which produce contact poisoning.

Starvation

During the Second World War a number of parties of servicemen – mostly aircrew – became marooned in the Arctic wasteland; and most of them died. They perished because few ventured far from their crash sites; they made no attempt to catch fish, hunt game, or even to travel south. Of those who were later found, none had prepared a rescue signal; and of the dead, most had died not from cold but from starvation.

The natives of the cold regions have survived for many generations on reindeer, fish and water.

Despite the barren appearance, the Arctic region does sustain certain plant life.

Arctic Plants

Cloudberry (Rubus chamae-morus) Cloudberry inhabits the mountainous areas of cold temperate and Arctic regions. It is a herbaceous, bramble-like plant which grows 15-20cm (6-8ins) high. It has lobed leaves and a single white flower, followed by a large orange-red fruit composed of many segments. It is these fruits or berries which may be eaten raw; they have a pleasant taste. Medicinally, the bark of the root and the leaves are astringent and are therefore helpful in cases of diarrhoea.

Bilberry/Whortleberry/Huckleberry (Vaccinium myrtillus) Inhabiting heathland, moorland and woodland from temperate regions to the Arctic tundra, the bilberry prefers acid soils and is often found growing with heather.

It is a hardy, deciduous branched shrub with erect stems. The leaves are light green; small, globular green-pink flowers ripen into single black berries. When fresh these berries, high in vitamins B and C, are sweet to the taste and can be eaten raw. Medicinally, the fruits can be dried, and a decoction will help treat diarrhoea, enteritis and other inflammations. The dried leaves can also be used in the same way, but must not be taken for too long a period at any one time as this can lead to hydroquinine poisoning.

Rock Tripes (Umbillicaria) Rock tripes are a lichen which attaches itself to rocks by means of a large, central stalk. They are found in rocky locations all over the Arctic and northern regions. They can take many forms but are usually roundish in shape, rather like a blister, and grey or brown in colour. Some are smooth but others can present a warty appearance. Lichens of any kind must never be eaten raw as they contain an acid which can cause severe irritation. Before eating they must be soaked for several hours, and then boiled thoroughly. They are available all year round, and are highly nutritious.

Arctic Willows (Salix sp.) Arctic willows, a smaller cousin of our better-known willows, inhabit the tundra regions. They are small shrubs no more than 0.6m (2ft) in height, which form dense mats. The leaves are rounded in shape and shiny. The shrub produces yellow catkins. Many parts are edible – the leaves, young shoots, young roots (peeled), and the inner bark. Arctic willow is very rich in vitamin C.

Bilberry

Cloudberry

Hunting

Much of the Arctic is fairly exposed, making stalking difficult; therefore traps, snares and ambushes offer the best opportunity. Historically the Arctic peoples used a variety of weapons including bows, and harpoons tipped with stone, whalebone, deer antlers and ox horn. If you have a gun, bow or catapult you are advised to stay concealed downwind and lie in ambush. If stranded on ice floes the best hunting is around the edge, or by a seal breathing hole. Seals will haul themselves out onto the ice to sleep during the spring; by crawling quietly it is possible to get close enough to kill one by clubbing or harpooning.

Always use your height to observe game, but do not silhouette yourself against the skyline. Watch over open ground, preferably downwind. Be silent; be patient; let the animal come to you. Fire or throw your weapon from a concealed position. If travelling for any distance, make sure that you mark your progress – it is easy to get lost while tracking in a strange environment, so use strips of a brightly coloured material to mark the trail back to your shelter.

Animal Sign Animal sign can be anything, from a hoof-print to the biting of tree bark, which indicates that there is animal life present. Learning to interpret these signs can take a professional hunter years – time which the average survivor does not have. The markings on a tree may or may not mean the presence of an animal, whereas animal droppings will leave little doubt. The shape, size and colour of any animal droppings are of little concern other than to indicate the size of the beast. Tracks and prints are easy to follow during the winter, and in most cases will lead directly to the animal's habitat.

Arctic hunting requires practice, patience and experience. Knowing what to look for and where to look is a great help. Larger game such as caribou live on grass or 'caribou moss.' Wolverine and bear will live mainly in the forest, while the ice pack remains the home of Polar bear and seal. In the lower regions animals such as ground squirrels and porcupines can be caught by hand, although beating them with a stick is safer. (The spines must be burnt off the porcupine prior to skinning, and while the flesh is not very tasty it will sustain life.)

Although the exposure makes stalking difficult, the ease of locating animal tracks in the snow is a major advantage when hunting in the Arctic. They are easy to follow and give a great deal of information about the animal that you are tracking. Do not worry about recognizing an individual animal from the spoor; the size of print and distance of the pace will let you know how large it is. Make sure that it is alone; shooting a three-foot bear may not seem such a good idea when its six-foot mother comes along. If you think you have made a kill, always make sure that the animal is dead – even a small wolverine will put up an impressive fight. This is best done by touching the animal's eye with your gun muzzle or

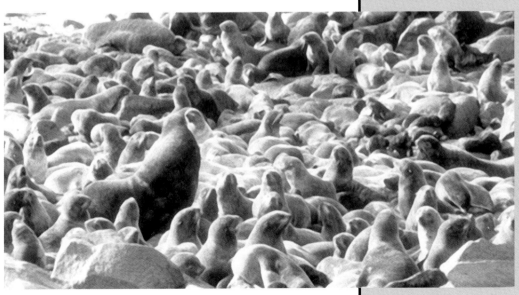

Seals are the primary source of wild food in the Arctic.

the tip of your spear; at the first sign of movement pull the trigger or stab it.

Seal For any Arctic survivor the seal is likely to be the best source of food, protection and means of lighting a fire. Seals are easily recognized by their torpedo-shaped body. They are superlative swimmers and spend most of their time in the water, but they must surface to breath from time to time. For this purpose they make small breathing holes in the ice. The best way to kill a small one is to wait by a breathing hole and club it, before dragging it onto the ice. Larger seals need to be clubbed or shot on land. (The elephant seal, which lives in waters near Antarctica, can grow to 6m long and may weigh up to 3000kg – 20ft, and 6,600 pounds.) Seals also give birth to their young on land between March and June – new-born seals cannot swim.

Seal meat has a very strong flavour but is perfectly edible. Remove the skin and cut away the layers of blubber, meat, bones and intestines. Freeze or cook the meat before eating.
Warning: Avoid the liver – like that of the Polar bear, it contains poisonously heavy concentrations of vitamin A.

The blubber can be used for cooking and for burning in oil lamps. The skin and intestines can be used to make waterproof clothes, boots, shelter and boat-covering. The blubber and bones will make a weak fire in an emergency.

Walrus Walruses live in shallow Arctic waters around both ice floes and land. They can be found across the entire Polar basin. They are recognized by the long tusks projecting down from the upper jaw of the male, by prominent whiskers, and by their size – some grow as large as 3.5m (11.5ft) and weigh up to 2 tons .
Warning: While walruses may look slow and cumbersome they are very dangerous; leave them alone unless you are armed with a good rifle.

Lemming The lemming is a tennis ball-sized animal related to the mouse. They dig into the soil to build their nests, living under the snow during winter. The females give birth to three to eight young as often as ten times a year. A young lemming can be fully grown and ready to breed in three months. Lemmings feed on Arctic grass, and most other animals feed on the lemmings; for snowy owls and Arctic fox they represent the only source of readily available protein. Lemmings are good to eat, but the flesh is best cooked. Living off lemmings for an extended period of time will cause fat deficiency, however.

Arctic Hare The Arctic supports two types of hare, the Arctic hare and the tundra hare; but for the purposes of this book they are as one. They are to be found in large numbers in Canada, Alaska and Greenland, most living on the rocky uplands of the Arctic tundra. They move very quickly, so snaring or netting offer the best chances of trapping them. Prepare and cook as for rabbits.

Ptarmigan This small chicken-like bird is commonly found on the Arctic tundra. Their plumage is brownish with dark stripes in summer, changing to completely white in winter. This camouflage is excellent for hiding in rocks or bushes or feeding on a carpet of snow. Ptarmigan can fly but they usually walk, feeding off berries and leaves from the tundra plants. Approach them with care, circling if need be, until you are close enough throw a stone or stick.

Arctic Fox This small fox lives mainly on the far northern tundras of Europe, Asia, and North America. Its fur, which is grey in summer and pure white in winter, provides the Arctic fox with perfect camouflage while hunting its prey. It can be found as far north as the ice floes, but has a tendency to migrate south with the seasons. Unfortunately, due to its valuable fur its numbers have been reduced through hunting. The Arctic fox is a scavenger, often living off other animals' leftovers, and is best caught using a baited deadfall trap.

Prepare it as you would a small deer.

Wolverine The largest of the weasel family; adults average some 1.1m long (3.6ft) and may weigh up to 25kg (55 pounds). The long, shaggy hair is mottled dark brown with black patches, giving them a bear-like appearance.

The wolverine is extremely aggressive, and will defend its kill even against Grizzly bears; it is also adept at taking food from other animals. In recent years it has been over-hunted for its fur. Its meat is said to be very tasty and rich in protein. Best caught with a baited deadfall trap.

Mountain Goat Mountain goats/sheep can be found mainly in the northern alpine ridges, although they do venture down to lower pastures. Their remarkable agility in the steepest mountain terrain is a form of protection from predators. Lambs are born around May/June and within a week are capable of walking around their hazardous environment. Mountain goats normally live within the same group for life. In summer they deliberately shed their wool by rubbing against rocks and branches. This wool was collected and used by Native Americans to make ceremonial blankets. Hunt mountain goat only if you have a weapon which is accurate and deadly at some range, i.e. a gun or a bow; trying to chase down any type of mountain goat is a waste of time and could prove dangerous.

Caribou The caribou is basical-

The further south one travels in the Arctic the more prominent the amount of wildlife. Beware, even small mamals such as wolverines can be excessively aggressive.

Birds and Eggs

• Arctic birds are to be found everywhere.

• Most are fairly tame and will not run away if approached quietly.

• Some will allow you to literally pick them out of trees; hold them with the wings folded against the body so that they do not flap and frighten the others.

• The Inuit would place small bits of meat around the air hole in the top of their igloos in order to attract birds; alerted by the flapping of wings, they would quickly grab the birds' legs.

• Nests can also be found in the lower latitudes and forest country; always check for eggs during spring and early summer. All eggs are edible and offer a good source of long term protein.

• If you are travelling in the Arctic and come across a source of eggs they can be cooked by wrapping them in moss and adding the bundle to the top of your fire-carry. These will cook while you travel and supply a warm meal on the move; they normally take around two hours to bake solid.

Arctic Trapping

• The Arctic wastes may look hopelessly empty, but have confidence – they do support game, and the predators which feed on that game.

• The bare snowscape can work to your advantage. Hungry animals have to forage far and wide, too – which increases the chances of them passing near your trap.

• Their senses will detect and lead them to your bait over far longer distances than you could hope to spot and stalk them if you were hunting. Their hunger will make them incautious when they find it.

ly an undomesticated reindeer. They live in large herds which are constantly on the move, feeding on the moss and lichen which grows throughout the Arctic tundra of Canada, Alaska, Greenland and Russia. If you come across a herd of caribou, search for one

that is injured and therefore slow on its feet. Caribou are not as shy as most deer, and are normally easy to approach if you move stealthily.

Musk Ox This striking-looking beast is easily recognizable by its long, thick, shaggy

brown coat, which covers its whole body and often hangs down to the ground. It can be found in small numbers throughout the Arctic (and has a close relation, the *takin*, which lives in the Himalayas). They average around 1.5m (5ft) tall and weigh 300-

The Polar Bear, Musk Ox and the Caribou, three of the largest land animals of the Arctic regions.

500kg (660-1,100 pounds). Although a herbivore and fairly placid, they should be approached with caution as they often use their hooked horns to chase off intruders. They are best hunted with a rifle; aim for the heart – the skull is extremely thick and capable of stopping a .22 survival bullet. Prepare and cook as for a deer.

Polar Bear The average Polar bear stands about 2.5m (8ft) tall, making it the largest of the bear family.

They live only in the northern Arctic and spend most of their time on ice floes hunting seals. Polar bears are excellent swimmers, but generally hunt seals out of the water, waiting by their breathing holes; a single blow is enough to kill even a large seal and the clawed paw will lift it out with ease. **Warning: Polar bears have a keen sense of smell, move fast, and are extremely dangerous; they regard humans as food. They should not be hunted with anything less than a high-powered rifle. Polar bear liver is over-rich in vitamin A, making it poison-ous to humans.**

Preparing Meat

Once you have caught your animal and are confident that it is dead, lay it on a fresh piece of snow or ice.

Bleed and gut the animal, removing any edible or valuable organs from the offal See Survival Essentials). If you are in a position to carry it, use the remaining offal to bait traps. Skinning is easier if performed while the carcass is still warm. Roll up hides fur side out before they freeze, and secure them with a carry strap by tying with a length of intestine. If the animal is too large, cut it into manageable portions so that it can be easily carried.

Remember that it is easy to cut meat when it is still warm and extremely difficult once it is frozen.

Some animals carry disease, therefore it is always best to cook or boil the meat before eating. Store any left-over food with care – there is always some other animal looking for a free meal.

Arctic Fishing

Arctic fishing extends from making a hole in the ice of frozen lakes during winter to more traditional methods in summer. If trapped on the ice floes, fish from the edge; if a life boat or raft is available, consider the risks of going out to sea, but be aware of wind drift and currents. Fishing through an ice hole can be done with a hook and line, although you will achieve better results with a net. In summer fish can be caught by damming streams and rivers and making traps (see Survival Essentials).

Ice Fishing The main consideration when fishing through ice is the thickness. In severe conditions the ice may be so thick that it is impossible to penetrate; by contrast, walking on thin ice is extremely dangerous.

Given that the ice is both penetrable and safe, there are two basic methods of fishing: line and net. In both cases you will need a tool with which to chop through the ice – a large knife will do, but an axe is better.

You will need to cut down until you have a 30cm (12in) wide hole; this can take time if the ice is thick.

The simplest method is to drop a single weighted and baited line into the hole until it hits the bottom. Raise the line about a foot and jerk it up and down. Securing the line to a pole which fits across the ice hole will allow you to leave and start work on a second hole. Fitting a cloth scrap as a flag to the line will indicate when you have a bite.

If you are able to cut several holes, then a net can be inserted under the ice by using a pole and line. The length of the pole governs the distance between the two holes. Tie one end of a line to one end of the net, and the other end to the pole; anchor the other end of the net securely at the first hole. Drop the pole into the first hole and manoeuvre it until the end shows in the second hole. Retrieve the pole and pull the line and the other end of the net out of the second hole. The net is now spread out under the ice between the two holes; make sure you have sufficient weights to fan your net out properly, and that both ends are anchored on the ice.

Always attach a stick which is long enough to brace across the ice hole, in case your anchors give way.

Salmon Salmon are found in many rivers and streams. They are born in a fresh water stream before making their way to the ocean, and return during late summer to their place of birth, where they spawn. During this arduous journey they become prey to a wide range of predators, including man. Pacific salmon do not eat during their spawning journey, but on occasions they will strike at artificial lures. The best method of catching them is by gaffing. Salmon can be caught easily once they have spawned; they are found floundering weakly in river shallows, and can be picked out by hand.

Trout Trout are found around the world but prefer the cooler waters of the Northern Hemisphere. True trout have dark spots on their bodies; tehre are many species, most of which live in fresh water streams and

Ice Fishing

1 Make two or three holes in the ice and push your pole through one end under the ice.

2 Manoeuvre the pole under the icewith the net attached retrieving it through the third hole.

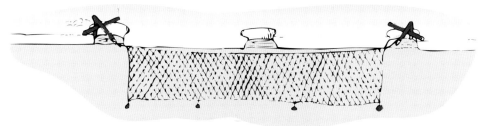

3 Secure the net. Use the centre hole to check for fish.

Cod There are few people who have not tasted this staple food fish, which is tasty and rich in nutritious value. It is normally grey in colour but there are also red and brown varieties. Both Pacific and Atlantic cod grow to between 0.6m and 0.9m (2-3ft) in length and weigh anything between 3kg and 15kg (6.5 to 33 pounds). For most of the year cod live on the ocean bottom, but in summer they venture closer inland, and can be caught in shallower waters of the coastal estuaries with a simple lure on a line.

Arctic Fish Preparation The Inuit clean their fish and lay boneless fillets on the ice to freeze. Once they are completely frozen they chop them into slices and eat them. They say that eating raw fish produces better internal body heat than that achieved by conventional cooking. I have tried this, and found the frozen fish extremely palatable; but one has to be careful to remove all bones prior to freezing, as they are not detectable until swallowed. If a fire can be made, prepare and cook as normal (see Survival Essentials).

Arctic Cookers Traditional Inuit used large oil lamps made from soapstone as a sort of cooker. They offered the best solution to a bad solution, but rarely produced sufficient heat to cook meat properly.

lakes. In slow-running water they may sometimes be caught by 'tickling' (see Essentials of Survival). Trout can be lured from their deep holes by flies, spoons and plugs, but you will need a strong rod and line to land many of the larger fish – these can weight up to 8kg (17.5lbs) and put up a hard fight. All the trout family gather to the feast while salmon are spawning.

Netting is one of the simplest ways of catching Arctic fish.

ARCTIC TRAVEL

The decision whether or not to travel must be made on a day-to-day basis, bearing in mind all your reasons for travelling in the first place. Once committed to travelling, you should continue your journey and endeavour to reach your goal. Unfortunately the weather conditions in both Polar regions are unpredictable, and getting caught in a snow storm in the middle of winter represents a serious threat to life.

One military solution is to adopt the 'time to shelter principle'. This simply means that if you are surprised by storm or have an accident, you must estimate the time it will take to construct a shelter given your surroundings. If this is longer than it would take to return to your last overnight camp, always turn back; if it is less, build a new camp.

ARCTIC TRAVEL PROBLEMS

Winter:
- Extremely low temperatures, high winds and snow storms.
- Permanent darkness for many months.

Summer:
- Melting snow turns tundra country into huge bogs.
- Clouds of biting insects cause maddening discomfort.
- Fallen, rotten trees covered in dense, spongy moss make walking uncertain and dangerous.

All year round:
- Strange and hostile surroundings, shared with some large carnivores for whom food is the No.1 priority.

Arctic Travel Considerations

The best option if marooned in the Arctic is to stay put, making the most of what you have available. If you arrived in your survival situation due to an air accident your surroundings will seem strange and threatening.

You will probably face more immediate problems, such as injury to yourself or other survivors. Build or adapt a camp site

SAS Experience

During one winter exercise my patrol parachuted onto the island of Senya in the frozen reaches of northern Norway. There, in the middle of winter, the only daylight we saw would sneak under the canopy of darkness for an hour at midday. As we dropped into a blinding snowstorm it soon became obvious that survival would take precedence over the exercise. Our sledge, containing all our fuel and rations, had been parachuted moments before us, but became lost in the darkness. For four days we walked knee deep (our skis were useless) in a blinding snowstorm in temperatures that fell below -30 degrees. Living on what we could carry in our rucksacks, the patrol faced a test of human endurance. We made shelter, built a fire, and waited to be rescued; in these conditions travelling would achieve nothing.

As the days went by we found ourselves making 'stone stew' a mixture of water and anything we could find in our rucksacks and pockets – boiled sweets, biscuits and a chocolate bar. On day five – the day of our rescue – we had made a hole in the ice of a nearby lake, from which we pulled three large fish. We were so pleased with our catch that we took them back in the helicopter to show everyone.

and make yourself as warm and comfortable as possible. The downing of a commercial aircraft will initiate a massive and prolonged search.

For an individual facing survival in the Arctic the choice is completely different. If he is 100% sure that rescue will come and that they will be able to locate him, then he must stay put. However, experience has shown that the prospect of a lost individual being located in the Arctic is very slim, and his best chance of survival lies in getting himself back to civilization. Despite its obvious difficulties this is in fact best achieved in the winter, when travel is a good deal easier; lakes and rivers are frozen, as is the marshy tundra. The tundra can be a nightmare to cross in warm weather – it can take an eight-hour day to walk less than a mile.

The going is slow in dense forest areas, mainly due to the number of fallen and rotting treetrunks. Avoid stepping on them if possible; they are extremely slimy and treacherous, and one slip causing serious injury could be fatal. In places these treetrunks can form such dense platforms, disguised in summer by thick vegetation, that it is very hard to pick a course which keeps you at ground level. It is always difficult to navigate through dense forest; it is best to follow an animal track, as this will eventually lead to a clearing and a water source.

Where the land meets the sea the Polar ice pack is in constant motion due to the currents and wind. Again, this makes travel extremely difficult and wildly inaccurate. Throughout the winter the ice is fairly solid, but as the summer gains strength the ice recedes. Sitting on an ice floe when this is happening is not a good idea, as you have no means of knowing where you will end up. Additionally summer ice is very wet and slushy. At times thick fog and misty rain fill the air. These conditions do not aid the survivor, and one should look for firm ground as soon as possible.

Direction Finding Basic navigation under Arctic conditions is the same as anywhere else (see Survival Essentials), although several special problems do arise. When too close to the magnetic Pole a compass will be subject to great inaccuracies. If you are unsure, double-check using the stars or another survival navigation method. Navigation can be improved by the use of GPS or an electronic compass, but as always these rely on batteries, and care should be taken to keep these warm to prolong their working life.

Overcast weather condi-

Planning a journey must take into account several factors including the time of year, the weather and your available supplies and equipment.

Staying together and working as a team will increase your chances of completing a successful journey.

tions and snowstorms often prevent navigation by the stars, so when a fix is possible a direction of travel must be clearly marked on the ground. The vast territories covered by the ice pack and northern tundra are mainly featureless when covered with snow, which makes it difficult to pinpoint a distant landmark for reference. It is a good idea to keep a log book of your daily movements; in the event that you discover you have made a mistake you should be able to correct it. Drawing a sketch map of each leg of your journey can also be extremely helpful.

Staying Together Staying together as a group while travelling through the Arctic winter darkness can be a problem. However, sound travels a greater distance in cold, clear weather, helping to maintain local communications. This same phenomenon will also give advance warning of approaching aircraft or any other type of activity in your area.

Opening your mouth and closing your eyes will help determine the sound direction.

If possible, avoid summer travel in Arctic forest and tundra.

Means of Travel

Arctic travel can be made easier if you improvise equipment to match the conditions. Make yourself snowshoes, bushwhackers, a sledge, or anything that will increase your speed across the terrain.

Travel Pole Many survivors will cut a staff and use this for a wide variety of purposes, from a walking stick to a shelter pole or even a cooking stick. In the Arctic the use of a longer, more substantial pole is advised – at least 4m (13ft) long, and strong enough to support your weight. The pole aids navigation, acts as a safety device while crossing ice, provides the basis for a shelter, and helps fit a net while ice fishing.

Snowshoes The snowshoe is little more than a 'tennis racket' attached to the sole of your boot. If commercial snowshoes are not available you are advised to make a pair, as it is difficult and laborious to walk in soft, deep snow. Find some hard, flat material that will suit the purpose – seat bottoms, cargo strapping and other metallic parts can be pressed into service. Many survival books advocate making snowshoes out of saplings such as willow. I have tried this with several different types of tree, taking time over their construction; but they did not last very long, and soon fell apart. Shoes made from strong plastic or aluminium and firmly attached to the boots by rope or webbing are best. Check your snowshoes daily and repair them if necessary. Remove your snowshoes if the snow surface is hard enough to support your weight, you will move much quicker.

- Use a flat platform about 30cm wide x 50cm long (12ins x 20ins), preferably perforated if possible.
- Use webbing to form a simple toe attachment for your boot.
- Devise a heel strap that will keep the toe in place but will allow the heel to rise from the shoe as you walk.

Ski Poles Ski poles are a great aid if you are walking with either snowshoes or home-made skis. They can be made from lengths of either wood or hollow metal; strong aluminium is the best (so check out the aircraft).

Hand straps of canvas or leather can be improvised, and the opposite end can be beaten flat. In conjunction with your pole they can form the framework of your travelling shelter.

Snowshoes

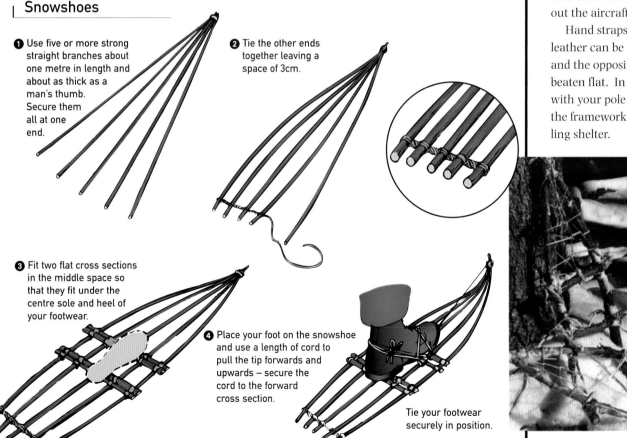

❶ Use five or more strong straight branches about one metre in length and about as thick as a man's thumb. Secure them all at one end.

❷ Tie the other ends together leaving a space of 3cm.

❸ Fit two flat cross sections in the middle space so that they fit under the centre sole and heel of your footwear.

❹ Place your foot on the snowshoe and use a length of cord to pull the tip forwards and upwards – secure the cord to the forward cross section.

Tie your footwear securely in position.

Improvised Sledge

Bushwhackers Bushwhackers are a cross between snow-shoes and skis. Providing material can be found they are well worth making. Once again, although they can be fashioned out of wood, they are best made from metal or sturdy plastic. Bushwhackers are good for walking in soft snow, especially in the tree line. Their major advantage comes from their ability to glide quickly over hard-packed or snow or a downhill slope. Use them with ski poles.

- Use a flat strip of aluminium or strong plastic about 15cm wide x 80cm long (6ins x 32ins).
- Bend up the first 15cm of each strip (beat if metal, heat if plastic) to form a ski tip.
- Use webbing to form a simple toe attachment for your boot; avoid the webbing going under the ski if possible – make holes and thread bolts, nails, or screws through them.
- Devise a heel strap that will keep the toe in place but will allow the heel to rise from the ski.

Sledge You should first consider what load you will be carrying, or if an injured person is to be transported; the answer should indicate if you need a sledge or not. A sledge will carry a lot of equipment, tent, rations, fuel, etc; if that equipment is available and you intend to travel then you will need a sledge.

However, be warned that even in the best of conditions pulling a sledge is difficult and requires a vast amount of energy. A crashed aircraft will supply enough sheeting and other items to construct a near-perfect sledge.

In certain conditions the snow will bind to the bottom of an improvised metal sledge. This can be overcome by attaching a sealskin or animal fur jacket to the underside.

Rafts See Survival Essentials.

Life Rafts If a life raft is available it is preferable to float down a river rather than attempt to travel across country. Due to the nature of its construction the raft's roof covering may need to be removed first, and the bottom of the raft modified e.g. by removing the sea anchor to avoid snagging on sub-surface rocks. The months of July and August are about the best time to cross or travel on Arctic rivers and lakes.

Wind Travel can be greatly speeded if the prevailing wind is at your back. Explore the possibility of making a sled from wreckage, and play around with sail power. A parachute will pull you along even in a mild wind; but do not use this method in high winds, as you will be unable to control it and may loose it to the elements.

During the Second World War Norwegian Resistance workers used parachutes to pull them along on skis, and were able to cover vast distances in a short time.

Arctic Travel Problems

Winter:
- Extremely low temperatures, high winds and snow storms.

- Permanent darkness for many months.

Summer:
- Melting snow turns tundra country into huge bogs.

- Clouds of biting insects cause maddening discomfort.

- Fallen, rotten trees covered in dense, spongy moss make walking uncertain and dangerous.

All year round:
- Strange and hostile surroundings, shared with some large carnivores for whom food is the No.1 priority.

Journey Planning

- The Inuit know that the only meaningful unit of measurement for an Arctic march is how many overnight stops the journey takes – and this will vary with the seasons.

- In good weather the going is twice as quick in winter, over snow, than in summer, over boggy tundra.

- Factor possible weather changes into your calculation – visibility can make a major difference to your speed across country.

- As journey time increases, carried rations are expended. If the rations run out while you are still travelling, you will have to allow extra time for hunting.

175

Rivers, Lakes and Ice

Arctic travel will mean trudging through water in some shape or form. The form will depend on the season, prevailing weather conditions and terrain. The closer to the Poles you are, the more severe the conditions; the further South you go the warmer it gets. Somewhere in between, any travel movement will be hindered by a wide variety of surface conditions – barren ice floes, firm snow, crevasses, slush, bog, large lakes and rivers.

While most Arctic travel is slow and exhausting, lakes and rivers can be life-threatening. In winter they may be hidden; in spring the ice surface will start to weaken; in early summer rivers can become roaring torrents.

Where water is not frozen the choice is simple: swim across, build a raft, or bypass it. Following a river downstream makes Arctic summer travelling easier (unless you have strong reason to do otherwise, always walk downstream). The survivor should find fishing, fuel and shelter. If the river conditions allow, consider making a raft from deadfalls, but make it wide and stable (see Essentials of Survival). Use any life jackets that are available when river crossing or rafting.

If you must swim due to the depth of the river, remove all clothes and place them in a watertight bundle which you can use as a floatation aid. Put your boots back on as they will give you better purchase when getting in and out of the water. Providing you are not in the water for more than ten minutes your body will withstand the coldest of temperatures; the secret is to relax and keep moving. Dress in your dry clothes as soon as you are across.

Never Trust Ice Frozen lakes and rivers provide the Arctic traveller with flat, easy terrain – but they are fraught with danger. No matter how cold the temperature, ice should never be assumed to be safe, especially in spring when the shoreline starts to thaw and sheet ice disintegrates into candle ice.

Locating a large frozen river can be of great benefit, providing you can establish which direction is downstream – this should guide you to safety. Check that the ice is solid and thick. The time of year and air temperature are good indicators of ice safety. If ice has not formed properly it means that the waters are very turbulent.

It is possible to make good progress on a frozen river. Stay close to the bank and firm ground; if walking in a group, make sure that the members are roped together at 5m (16ft) intervals with each carrying their own safety pole. Even if you are making good progress you are advised to stop while there is enough daylight to construct a shelter and build a fire on firm ground.

If travelling alone, as a basic safeguard always carry a long pole that is capable of supporting your weight.

Carry it by holding it with both hands in the centre like a tightrope walker – this will provide a bridge and extraction hold should you fall through the ice. The pole can also be used to test suspicious patches of ice.

Warning: Always make sure you have the means to light a fire, packed in a waterproof container, before venturing onto the ice. **If your foot goes through the ice, stop and lay your body flat on the ice surface; crawl back the way you came, standing only when you reach the shore or riverbank. Dry out your feet, socks and boots.**

Wading Partly frozen rivers and streams can be crossed providing you are aware of the greatest water depth and it is safe to wade across. If you do this, remove you socks (not your boots) and trousers before crossing, using your pole as a staff in

the water. Replace your dry socks and trousers once safely across. Your upper clothing should protect your body temperature, but be aware that entering ice-cold water can induce momentary paralysis.

Swimming Swimming in ice-cold water will greatly reduce your life-span. If you find yourself in this situation it is best to stay as still as possible, hanging in the water supported by a life vest or otherfloatation aid. Any movement produces body heat, which is lost to the surrounding water. Your body temperature is 37°C; when immersed in ice-cold water this will fall by 1°C every two minutes. When your body reaches 33°C you will drift into unconsciousness; and when it falls to 25°C you will be dead.

1982 – The Falklands

Never were the dangers of travelling in Arctic conditions better illustrated than when members of SAS teams were inserted into the Falkland Island of South Georgia in advance of the main task force. Men existed for several weeks in unbearable cold carrying out reconnaisance tasks. A party was dropped by helicopter on to the Fortuna glacier where conditions were so atrocious it was immediately obvious that to remain would mean certain death. The team was extracted at a cost of two helicopters which crashed in the apalling weather.

Falling through Ice

Surviving in the Arctic is hard enough, but falling through ice will almost certainly kill you, even if you do manage to crawl out. In such an event common sense and instinct must take precedence over any hard-and-fast procedures.

• If you fall through ice into water it will knock the breath out of you. Stay calm and act rationally – continuous hyperventilation can lead to unconsciousness, causing you to drown. You will ball up with muscle contractions, and there is the danger that younger and older people will die from heart attack.

• Try not to swallow cold water as this will both make you choke and speed the cooling of your body's core temperature.

• You must do everything in your power to resurface through the entry hole and pull yourself free. Extend and drop both arms out onto the ice; if the edge breaks free then keep trying until you have a solid purchase. If you remain clinging to the ice exposed parts will freeze in less than five minutes. Try orientating yourself towards the direction from which you came, and climb out over ice you have walked over. Grip on your pole to lever yourself out. Remain prone at all times, even when out of the water. Retrace you steps to the shore or riverbank.

• If you go under the ice you have little chance of survival, but there are several cases where people have come out alive. The best method is to kick at the ice above with your feet until you make a hole you can surface through; then follow the procedure above.

When You Reach the Bank:

• Rolling in fresh snow will act as a blotter, but this is only a temporary reprieve; you need to make a fire and shelter yourself from the wind – without either you will die. If you do not take immediate action you will start to lose consciousness in five to ten minutes, with death following 20 minutes later. Depending on the weather conditions this gives you around 30 minutes to build a fire before your hands, body and brain become useless.

• Take off wet clothing and remove as much water as possible by twisting and squeezing before they freeze. Put on extra clothing and exercise for a few minutes; this can take the form of collecting fuel for a fire if available. If there are several people in the party, share some of your outer clothes temporarily. You must replace your boots in order to walk around; place a layer of moss inside to act as an isolator while your socks are drying. It is better to be naked for a short while – you will survive longer than if you stay in wet clothes.

• Once you have fire and shelter, avoid panic. Take control of the situation. You must dry and warm your body first before your clothes.

• Water can be removed from frozen clothes by beating them with a stick. Do not place clothing too close to the fire – it may burn.

• Use the fire to the maximum: cook any available food or boil some snow for a hot drink.

• If you manage to survive, then you must rest. Once you have been thoroughly chilled it will take several hours for your body to return to normal; make sure you are fully recovered before continuing your journey.

Falling through Ice

Always use a long pole carried waist high in front of you when crossing ice. It can mean the difference between life and death. Get out of the water as quickly as possible climbing out in the direction you entered.

High Mountains

High mountain ranges are found not only in the Arctic regions but also in jungle and desert terrain, the common factor being their summits, which in many cases are permanently covered with snow and exposed to Arctic conditions. Additionally high mountains are a major contributing factor to air disasters, and account for over 30% of such fatalities. Winter mountains are always covered in thick snow and buffeted by strong winds, and are filled with danger for any survivor.

Staying with the aircraft is the best short-term option in most cases; you should have sufficient supplies to keep warm, eat and drink. The dangers of attempting to walk out are extremely perilous; but if rescue is not forthcoming travel may be your only option. Get out of the mountains as quickly as possible, travelling only in good weather conditions, in daylight,

using the safest route.

In such a situation you will almost certainly be forced to walk downhill on snow that is unpredictable. Ridge walking should be avoided, especially where snow cornices have formed. Be aware that steep-sided mountains may harbour areas of snow-covered scree, and while the upper surface may look intact the underlying snow structure may be prone to avalanches.

Avalanches It is almost impossible to predict when an avalanche will occur; even in Europe, where scientists have studied the problem for years it is still difficult to forecast a time or place. Snow forms as little droplets of rain pass through the cold upper atmosphere and turn to ice; these tiny specks of ice join together to form snowflakes. The temperature, wind, and amount of airborne water vapour will determine the shape, thickness and form of snowflakes that fall; a single crystal is star-shaped, but many of these bond together to form larger clusters. Once on the ground, depending on temperature fluctuation, the crystal will deteriorate back into a rounded blob of water which forms into hard-packed snow or even ice. Over a period of a week it is possible for several layers of snow to accumulate at one spot, lying on top of one another. Some may be hard with good cohesion, while others may be light with very little structural bonding.

On steep-sided mountains the snow is rarely cohesive enough to build up any great thickness. The depth of snow is very important, as avalanches rarely occur in snow falls of less than 30cm (12 inches). It is on slopes between 30 and 45 degrees of angle where the combined snow fall is more than 30cm that avalanches are most common. The ground itself may have been previously covered with a layer of old snow that has deteriorated due to temperature changes, building up a smooth, flat, hard surface. On top of this a much thicker layer of soft snow may have built up. The angle of the slope, the downward compression, the surface wind direction, and slip aided by gravity, are all fac-

Crossing Ice

- Always avoid dark-coloured or clear ice; white ice is safer.

- Cut into a section of the ice to check its thickness. The average adult needs a minimum of 5cm (2ins) to support their weight.

- If you are forced to cross thin ice, do so one at a time using a safety rope.

- Loosen any rucksack or snowshoe straps so that they can be discarded quickly if you fall through the ice.

- Put on extra clothing, and wear some form of floatation aid.

- Crawl on your belly if you are unsure of the ice thickness, and use a safety pole if alone.

tors which cause an avalanche. (There are many different types of avalanche, but the most common is the 'soft slab' slide described above.)

Walking through a mountainous area under survival conditions does not allow you to take full precautions against avalanches. You will not have the energy or equipment to climb, and you must take the easiest, flattest route.

This is extremely dangerous, especially in spring, and you are advised to keep a watchful eye on the mountain slopes.

Caught in an Avalanche If you are caught in an avalanche your best chance of survival lies with staying on top of the undulating snow. This is best achieved by using a backstroke swimming motion.

If you become covered, immediately make a breathing space for your nose and mouth by rocking your head back and forth – avalanche snow contains a lot of air, but grips you firmly as soon as it stops moving. If you are not sure which way up you are, spit out a small amount of saliva and feel which way it runs.

Try to dig yourself out before the avalanche snow has time to settle and freeze.

Glaciers Unless you are actually forced to cross, descend or climb, avoid all glaciers – they are very dangerous. You are best advised to circle round a glacier, and if this is not possible then try to find a stretch which appears to offer a safe crossing. Avoid any visible rifts and crevices. If snow covers the surface, probe with your pole to make sure the ground is firm. If you are not alone make sure that the party are roped together.

The quickest way down a snow slope is to slide under control using a makeshift ice-axe to act as a brake. Care should be taken when moving downhill while pulling a sledge. If the sledge is heavy it is possible that it will run away with you. To prevent, this always walk in front of the sledge using your body as a brake.

White-Out This term is given to a heavy snowstorm, or when the wind whips the ground snow above head height.

Attempting to travel in these conditions can only bring total disorientation, and the possibility of snow blindness – not from glare but from the stinging snow particles, which cause the eyes to water and freeze. In the event of a 'white-out', with visibility reduced to zero, your only option is to find shelter.

During a 'white out' do not attempt to travel – it will result in disorientation.

Rescue

See Survival Essentials section for general information applicable to the Arctic environment.

Signalling

If you elect to remain with an aircraft you should make sure that its metal surface remains free of any falling snow or heavy frost. This is to ensure that the aircraft shape remains recognizable from the air. If you have inflated any of the life rafts or emergency escape chutes, make sure that they are in a position where their high-visibility colour is of maximum value. The main considerations of Arctic signalling are the white snow surface during summer and the darkness of winter. Aside from the normal methods of signalling covered in the Essentials of Survival section, the Arctic survivor must concentrate on light and contrast signals.

Light Signals On a dark but clear day with good visibility it is possible for a search aircraft to identify the light from a candle or improvised lamp inside a snow hole from a distance of several miles – the brighter the light, the greater the distance from which you can be seen. A large, purpose-built signal fire can therefore be seen from 40km-50km away (25-30 miles). In practice, winter conditions will normally force survivors to stay inside their shelter; and while snow makes an excellent insulator against cold, it also insulates against sound. It is therefore vital to illuminate your shelter by using a translucent roofing material, leaving a large air hole, or using a thin layer of snow for your roof.

Contrast Signals Contrast is easily achieved in snow by making trenches. This can be done either by stamping down the snow with your feet, or digging with an improvised shovel. The deeper you dig, the greater will be the noticeable shadow. Make the trench in a North/South direction, about a metre wide, banking the removed snow uniformly along the southern edge to increase the shadow. Make shadow signals about 10m (32ft) long, each clearly indicating a letter or sign. Fir branches or any other dark material can be laid in the trench to increase the contrast. The same effect can be achieved in spring, when the melting snow starts to clear from the tundra, by clearing the snow away to reveal the dark earth beneath.

The larger your fire, the better your chances of rescue.

Assesing Avalanche risk

- Knowledge of any snow falls in the past week, the temperature and the wind strength all help in judging avalanche risks.

- Continue to adjust your assessment while travelling. Take into consideration any new snowfall, or if you feel a change in air temperature or the wind strength increasing.

- If you are climbing on a slope, take note of how the snow is reacting to your weight. Are the steps in the snow crisp and firm, or do they break and roll down hill? If you observe snow breaking away, even over a small area, you could be at risk: move to level ground.

- Avoid areas where snow has already slipped – several avalanches often fall in the same area.

SURVIVAL IN THE

DESERT

CLIMATE AND TERRAIN

According to the dictionary definition, a desert is an uncultivated, uninhabited and desolate area, devoid or almost devoid of vegetation due to low rainfall. Most deserts conform to this description, but they each have their own characteristics. Most of the Earth's deserts are strung along the Tropics of Cancer and Capricorn between 20 degrees and 35 degrees in both North and South latitudes. They represent about one-fifth of the Earth's total surface.

A feature of most deserts is the extreme fluctuation in temperature between day and night, sometimes in the order of 70° Fahrenheit. Some deserts are hotter than others; e.g. those of Mexico and Libya reach greater temperatures than the Gobi, sometimes recording 136°Fahrenheit. Such temperatures obviously threaten the survivor with heatstroke, sunburn and dehydration. On the other hand, nighttime temperatures are usually extremely low; in the northern Gobi and Siberian deserts they can fall as low as -50°Fahrenheit. This cold may also be accompanied by strong winds which will increase the chill factor. The sun's daytime heat is absorbed by the sand, gravel or rocks; but by night it radiates back into the sky, and without any clouds to contain it it escapes into the upper atmosphere, causing the desert to cool rapidly.

Deserts differ in the appearance and nature of their surface features, from mountainous plateaux to sand dunes. Rainfall, too, varies from one desert to another and also from season to season; one may receive 20cm (8ins) of rain in a year while another receives none at all. Mountainous deserts generally receive far more rainfall than sand dunes.

Contrary to common supposition, deserts do support life. Certain forms of animal and plant life have, through thousands of years of evolution, adapted themselves to live in this waterless environment. Various native peoples, too, have managed to make the desert their home.

Preparation

Anyone venturing into the desert, either by crossing it in an aircraft (other than a commercial flight) or by vehicle, should be prepared. In the desert the availability and ability to collect water is a priority, so pack items that will meet this need. Any desert survival will almost certainly involve some form of travel during which the bulk of any water supplies will need to be carried; and water is heavy. Clothing is needed that will protect the body from the sun's heat during the day and from the extreme cold of the desert night.

Navigation and signalling are important, so make sure you include a compass and a heliograph in any survival kit. While fire makes good signals, apart from engine oil and material from vehicle seating there will be little available fuel in some deserts. It is wise to fit vehicles with long range fuel tanks and sand channels if going off-road or crossing soft sand. An air jack will also be required to lift the vehicles for any maintenance or wheel changes.

Desert Dress Desert clothing should be loose and lightweight. Long-sleeved shirts and full length trousers should be worn to protect vulnerable skin from sunburn. Arab dress is

loose, lightweight and flowing, covering the body from head to foot – adopt the same principles. A hat is necessary to protect the head from the sun; use one which has a broad brim or a neck flap, or improvise. A sweat scarf or bandanna can serve a variety of uses. If worn loosely around the neck it will sponge up sweat; when wetted and worn in the same way it will help cool the body; and during a sandstorm it should be wetted and wrapped around the face, covering the nose and mouth to protect mucous membranes from the fine sand. If sunscreen is available this should also be used on any exposed skin, especially the face and neck.

Protecting the Eyes The eyes are most at risk, not only from the sun but from the sand. Tinted glasses are normally sufficient, but goggles will prove much better especially if travelling in open vehicles or in an area which is given to sandstorms. If no glasses are available them try using a lump of charcoal or soot from your cooker to blacken the skin underneath your eyes; this will at least cut down the reflected glare.

Boots Boots are subject to much abuse in a desert environment: the leather will dry out and crack in the heat unless cared for. Make sure that you remove sand, stones or insects from your boots; apart from being uncomfort-

able, they can cause blisters and wounds. However, having to constantly stop to remove them can be extremely irritating, so it is better to prevent them getting inside in the first place by improvising puttees. These can be made from strips of cloth 10cm wide by about 2-3m long, although one metre will do at a stretch (4ins x 6-10ft; 3 feet). Wrap these strips over the boot or shoe and then wind it upwards, over the trouser ends and the lower leg. Beware of tying them too tightly – you do not want to restrict the circulation to your feet.

Unserviceable Vehicles
Maintaining vehicles in a serviceable condition and protecting them from desert conditions will help prevent a survival situation occurring. If a vehicle becomes unserviceable then all efforts should be made to fix it. If the vehicle is totally immovable and no other assistance is available, i.e. another vehicle, then you should radio for help. If you cannot establish contact, then prepare to walk out. The easiest way to do this is by backtracking to the nearest habitable contact. The daytime heat in the desert can be very exhausting and will use up your water supplies faster, so use that time for resting and the nighttime for travelling. Travelling at night also offers the advantage that you will have the stars to navigate by.

Forced Landings: Immediate Action

Commercial aircraft forced to make a crash-landing in the desert should do so with a high degree of success. Providing there is time the pilot will have alerted the authorities to his situation and position prior to landing. Full instructions will be relayed to all passengers, both for the emergency landing and evacuation of the aircraft once on the ground. As with all forced landings there is the danger of fire, and all passengers and crew should get away to a safe distance and stay there until given the 'all clear' by the captain.

Depending on what information has been radioed to the authorities, and given that the bulk of the aircraft is intact, survivors are advised to stay with the aircraft. The chances of short-term survival and rescue are extremely high in the desert, with search aircraft usually less than 24 hours away. In the event that rescuers have not located your aircraft within four days, it is suggested that a small party should walk out.

Military and Light Aircraft

Military and light private aircraft should also try to land, although in the event of an onboard fire a parachute escape may be more expedient. Either way a radio message should be sent if at all possible prior to crash-landing or abandoning the aircraft. The pilot must use whatever altitude he still has to take a bearing to any prominent feature such as the coastline, city lights, roads, oil pipelines etc. If no compass is available a bearing in relation to the sun, moon or stars must be established. Those who have opted for a parachute exit can also use similar orientation methods while they have the benefit of height.

Medical Considerations

In all desert survival situations, whether the intention is to stay put or walk out, health and medical priorities must be established first. If there has been an accident there is a good chance of casualties; these must be dealt with before any other action is taken (see Survival Essentials). In addition to normal injuries the desert presents its own problems, of which heat and thirst are the most dangerous.

The intense heat of a desert is a threat to the body's ability to keep its temperature regulated within very narrow limits. Because the human body is made up of 75% water, it is essential for this amount of fluid to be maintained if the body is to work properly. A loss of one litre (2 pints) will seriously decrease efficiency – by around 25 per cent. Once the body's cooling system has been compromised, heat exhaustion or heatstroke will occur and may be fatal. Lack of salt intake will cause heat cramps.

Ensuring adequate water, salt and food intake will lessen the risk of becoming a victim of these debilitating and deadly conditions. Conserving body fluids by finding or constructing some type of basic shelter to provide shade from the sun's rays will also be important.

During the Gulf War of 1991 several members of the SAS operating behind the Iraqi lines were spotted by the enemy and forced to carry out escape and evasion tactics. This involved travelling vast distances at night, through the worst winter weather the region had seen for many years. All these soldiers suffered from hypothermia; and one died of it.

Environmental Effects – Medical Considerations

It takes about two weeks for the body to fully acclimatize itself to the heat of the desert. Even then the risks associated with such an environment will still be present. A survivor in the desert will still need an adequate supply of water and some shelter in order to stay alive. The desert can exhaust the reserves of both body and mind, so a strong, positive attitude will be needed. The human body functions best at certain temperatures, around 98.6° Fahrenheit (approximately 37° Centigrade). It maintains this temperature in a hot environment by conduction/convection, radiation, and sweating. Sweating – the most important – cools the body as the water on the skin evaporates. If you are in an area where the humidity is high the sweat will not evaporate easily. This is the worst of all scenarios: loss of bodily fluids and an increase in body heat.

A person in the desert will be affected by several environmental factors other than simply heat, and these need to be considered:

Radiant Light This is, of course, produced by the sun, but does not necessarily come from the sun's direction alone. Sunlight can also be reflected off the ground and any nearby rocks. The light from the sun contains radiation which is harmful to both skin and eyes, so both need to be protected as much as possible by light clothing and sunglasses or a hat. Sunburn happens very easily and quickly, especially to people with fair or freckled skin – but every skin type will be susceptible to some degree.

Sunburn Burnt skin is reddened and painful and will usually break out in blisters. Apart from leading to other forms of heat illness, extensive sunburn may have deleterious long term effects on the health of the individual. The effects can become even more pronounced when combined with either water (sea water or sweat in particular), or a persistent wind. The immediate priority in cases of sunburn is to get the casualty out of the sun and protect him from further exposure. Cool the burnt area, if possible with cold water or a tannic acid solution (see Survival Essential). Cover the burns with a dressing to prevent the possibility of infection, and do not move it unless essential to do so. The chances are that the casualty will also be severely dehydrated, so make sure that he drinks plenty of fluids and gets plenty of rest.

Desert Cold Lack of the right clothing or shelter during the intense cold of the desert night will, again, threaten the body's ability to control its temperature, and may well result in hypothermia or frostbite. Remember that any wind will increase the chill factor and make any temperature loss even greater. During the evening, as the air chills, more layers of clothing should be added as necessary. As the air heats up again in the morning they should be gradually removed. On no account should the survivor ignore the danger of hypothermia from cold nights in the desert.

Consider Your Options

If stranded in the desert, by whatever means of transport, make an immediate plan of action. The decision to stay put or walk out must be based on the following criteria:

- How confidently can you establish your location?

- What communications do you have?

- Who knows of your intentions and route – what are your chances of rescue?

- Is anyone injured too badly to walk?

- What water resources do you have, and how much can you realistically carry?

- The estimated distance to your intended destination?

- The estimated distance to your last known safe location – main road, village, etc?

Unless you have a good supply of water with your aircraft or vehicle, and good reason to believe that others will find you, then you must walk out. Previous incidents have shown that those who walk out fare better than those who stay at their crash site after any immediate expectation of rescue has been disappointed.

Hygiene

Just because deserts are barren does not mean that they are free of the organisms which cause disease. Plague, typhus, malaria, dengue fever, cholera and typhoid are all found in desert areas. If they cause vomiting and diarrhoea, the danger of death by dehydration will increase greatly, especially if the victim is already suffering from the effects of heat or cold. Most diseases will also cause a fever to occur, increasing the heat of the body and adding to the damage already inflicted by heatstroke or dehydration.

Assume that all desert water sources are contaminated, and use purification methods. Diarrhoeal illnesses are generally caused by consumption of contaminated water or food – contamination is usually from excreta. Most standing water will definitely be infectious. It is also important that clothes are not washed in polluted water, as the organisms can cause skin dis-

eases. The skin is also prone to the painful rash of prickly heat (brought on by excessive sweating) and fungal infections, especially if the humidity is high.

Maintaining a good routine of personal hygiene is important for a survivor. Infirmity through disease would be disastrous under these conditions, even where the disease is not usually fatal. Daily washing and care of clothes, where possible, will go a long way towards alleviating the conditions that encourage disease and uncomfortable ailments. If surplus pure water is available, clothes should be washed daily. Sweat will also accumulate within the boots; this may accelerate their rotting, as well as creating conditions for blisters and fungal diseases of the foot. At least once a day boots should be taken off and aired. Socks, too, will need to be dried or changed when they become wet. A short exposure (30 minutes) to the late afternoon sun should dry boots and socks and help prevent any fungal diseases developing.

Dangerous Wildlife

While the desert may seem lifeless, it is actually inhabited by many species of scorpions, centipedes, spiders, other insects and snakes. Most desert wildlife can be unpleasant to man, especially the insects, as they will view him as a source of moisture and food.

Insects likely to be troublesome in this way are flies, lice and mites, which are not just unpleasant but can also carry diseases such as dysentery and scrub typhus. Larger pests such as centipedes and some spiders may bite but are not necessarily fatal. On the other hand, certain species of desert-dwelling scorpions and snakes may inflict a lethal bite, especially if the survivor is already weakened by environmental factors. The most dangerous wildlife that may be encountered in a desert environment are as follows:

A Scorpion's bite will make you feel unwell but is not life-threatening.

Scorpions Scorpions are common and are easily recognized by their crab-like claws and high, forward-curving tail with a stinger on the end. Their size varies from about 2.5cm (1in) to 20cm (8ins), and their colour also varies over a wide range. They like damp, cool environments, and tend to come out at night to hunt. They have a great tendency to hide themselves in discarded clothing, bedding and shoes. The majority of scorpion stings are not likely to cause death; but they are extremely painful, and precautions should be taken to avoid them. If one of these creatures is crawling on you, knock it away in the direction it is moving – most scorpions, despite the speed of their sting once poised to attack, are unable to retaliate quickly.

Sandflies Flies are a troublesome pest in arid areas, especially around sources of mois-ture – which includes the human body. Common flies are major carriers of disease of all sorts. To protect against flies, use the same measures as you would against mosquitoes.

Make sure that any food supplies are covered over. Flies will also cause infection via any small wound or cut. Sandflies are small black flies usually found in the sub-tropics. They are carriers of sandfly fever, a disease that is more unpleasant than dangerous. The condition needs to be treated with rest and liquids. Ordinary netting will not give protection as sandflies are too small, but they may be deterred by insect repellent. However, it is worth noting that these flies stay fairly low to the ground, flying up no more than 3m (10 feet). They also dislike moving air.

lier civilizations in the deserts of the Middle East; these are often used as resting places by nomadic tribes, and consequently they are infested with lice and fleas.

Reptiles Many reptile species are denizens of the desert, especially lizards and snakes. Most lizards can be disregarded as – with a couple of exceptions in North America and Saudi Arabia – they are harmless to man. Snakes thrive in the arid conditions and range from the completely innocuous to the deadly poisonous. Snakes tend to

checked thoroughly before being put on. One aggressive species of snake, the Sand Viper, is particularly dangerous as it has a tendency to bury itself in the sand and strike out at any passing creature. Its presence can be detected by a distinctive coiling pattern on the sand. Another dangerous snake often found in deserts is the Egyptian Cobra. This species usually lives and hunts around rocky outcrops or old ruins. When confronted, it raises the upper portion of its body and spreads out its hood. Although edible, desert

In the Desert Remember:

- Most diseases are of the diarrhoeal or febrile types.

- Diarrhoeal illnesses are generally caused by contaminated water and food.

- Febrile illnesses are generally caused by bites from insects, such as flies and mosquitoes.

Snakes in the desert are extremely dangerous and catching one for a meal should be left to experts.

Fleas Fleas are carriers of plague and typhus. To avoid catching them, stay away from any camels, dogs, cats or rats. It is not uncommon to come across the ruins of ear-

seek shady hiding places under rocks, bushes and trees, so be wary when approaching such locations. Discarded clothing, bedding and boots should also be

snakes are extremely poisonous and should be avoided; the benefit of catching one to provide a quick meal is far outweighed by the risk of your dying from its bite.

WATER

The survivor must find a source of water or he will die, no matter how abundant the rest of his survival resources. Dehydration occurs slowly when the body is losing fluid faster than it is replacing it. On average a normal adult will start to deteriorate after four days, with death occurring within the first week if no water is consumed. Small amounts of water may slow down the process, but to function well a survivor needs at least five litres daily.

Deserts vary in the amount and frequency of their rainfall. Some may have a single day or less of rain annually; others may have showers throughout one season. Most desert rainfall comes with severe thunderstorms and tends to be torrential and highly localized, affecting only a few square kilometres at a time. These downpours produce flash floods, which rush through time-worn gullies and wadis. Some water does manage to soak into the ground during the rainstorms, but the limited ground water this produces is often far below ground. Any permanent or semi-permanent water source in a desert, such as an oasis or a well, is a rare and treasured source for any local population.

Distribution and Location

Water Rationing All commercial aircraft carry enough water and soft drinks to last for several days under rationing conditions. Life-rafts should also be inflated and their water rations used. At the same time it is important to conserve whatever water you have in your body and to use water supplies to your best advantage. If you are short of water do not eat any food – eating takes up valuable water in the body in both the digestion and excretion processes. It is wise not to eat or drink at all for the first 24 hours; after this time, plan a strict routine for rationing any water supplies you may have. You must plan ahead: how are you going to locate, collect, store and issue it?

Warning: The water from modern vehicle radiators should not be drunk directly as it contains harmful chemicals; the liquid can be converted by distillation.

Distillation Most vehicles and aircraft will have sufficient parts and fuel to enable the survivor to construct and operate a still. If this is done correctly all sources of impure water can be distilled into clean drinking water. This should be done prior to any walk-out attempt. The principle of a good working still is to heat liquid to the point where it produces steam – this will be free of impurities. Cooling the steam converts it back into water.

Rain It is a mistake to think that rain never falls in the desert. Rain normally falls on the coastal regions or in high mountainous areas. The latter can cause short-lived but violent flash floods at lower elevations (see Desert Travel, below). Rain water will quickly disappear, but pockets may remain where natural rock cisterns protect it from the sun.

Signs of Water Tracks in the desert, both animal and human, will almost certainly lead to any available water source, as most have already been discovered. Watch out for distinctive signs: concentrations of animal droppings, man-made rock constructions (desert peoples will protect any water supply), overhanging caves, and vegetation. The direction of flying birds will also give a clue, in particular such birds as parrots and pigeons, which never live far from water. Signs of the passage of humans or camels will always lead to water, although following single tyre tracks should be avoided. Desert roads can be very wide, and in soft sand there may be no tyre tracks, but the sand colour will be markedly different. The deserts of the USA are so populated or criss-crossed with roads that survival is a short-term problem and is more a matter of making contact as soon as possible with the nearest vehicle.

Ground Water Digging for ground water may be an option if there is no ready supply of drinkable surface water. A great effort will have

A desert cistern, Death Valley, USA.

easiest way to collect ground water is from a spring or a seepage in rocky ground. Certain types of rock will repay searching more than others. Limestone, for example, is easily dissolved by water to create caverns and springs. If the limestone is underlain by a less porous rock water may have collected over the years in a substantial water table beneath the ground. Lava rock, too, is porous, and water may be seen seeping from it. Study rock strata and forms. Springs may be found where the wall of a valley cuts across a lava flow, or within caverns. A layer of porous sandstone in a valley wall should be checked for signs of seepage.

Cisterns The run-off water may survive for longer in basins where it will sometimes form shallow lakes. These evaporate after a time, the high salt content of the water leaving behind large salt deposits on the surface. An example of this kind of desert terrain is the Great Salt Lake in Utah.

Dew The dramatic temperature variations in the desert cause condensation on any metal sheeting such as the hood of a car or the wing of an aircraft. Spare, clean clothing can be used to collect this dew by sponging the surface in the early morning; from a heavy dew you should be able to collect about a pint an hour. Avoid mopping areas covered with oil and grease.

Water in the Desert

• Most of the world's desert regions support significant animal life – which means there is water to be found.

Water seepage in rocky soil.

You can learn to:
• Locate it
• Dig for it
• Collect it from plants
• Distill it

to be expended, and it is recommended that you study the contours of the land and the type of soil before any digging attempt is made. Desert natives often know of lingering surface pools in low places; they cover these over, so look under brush heaps or in sheltered nooks, especially in semi-arid and brush coun-

try. Places that are visibly damp, where animals have scratched, or where flies hover indicate recent surface water. Dig in such places. If you have no special digging equipment, use a flat stone, a sharp stick or a strong bone from a dead animal.

Water from Rocky Soil The

Solar Still A solar still is designed to extract moisture from the air and convert it into drinkable water. Not only can it collect water from most environments, including the desert, but it can also purify impure water, seawater or urine. It is simple to make, requiring only a clear plastic sheet about 2m (6.5ft) square, a water collection container, and, preferably, a plastic drinking tube about 1.5m (5ft) in length.

❶ Make a hole in the ground about 1m in diameter and 75cm deep at the centre (3.3ft and 30 inches).
❷ Place the water container in the middle. If you have a drinking tube, put one end into the container.
❸ Place the plastic sheet loosely across the hole, weighting it down at the edges with rocks or sand to make it airtight. Make sure that the other end of the drinking tube is exposed.
❹ Carefully place a small rock or some other weight in the centre of the sheet, so that it sags in the middle just above the water container. Avoid contact between the sides of the hole and the plastic sheet, as this will drain away some of the moisture.

The solar still works on the principle of condensing the water in the atmosphere. The sun's rays pass through the sheet, warming up the ground below and evaporating any existing water. As the

The Solar Still

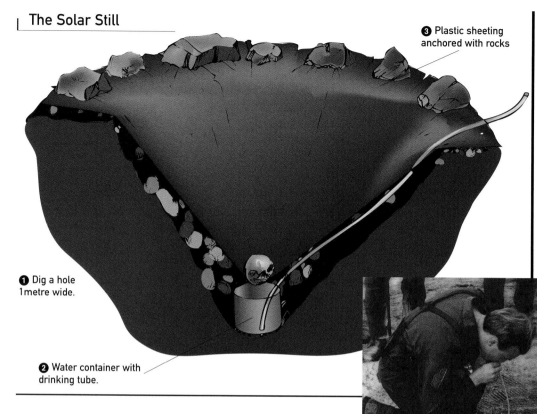

❸ Plastic sheeting anchored with rocks

❶ Dig a hole 1metre wide.

❷ Water container with drinking tube.

A solar still in practice.

water evaporates in the sealed space it saturates the air with water molecules. Eventually water will begin to condense on the underside of the plastic sheet, and run down the inverted cone into the water container. Depending on how dry the desert conditions may be, you can expect to collect between 0.4 and 1.5 litres (0.7-2.6 pints) in 24 hours. Lining the hole with any available fleshy plant material, sliced or broken up, can increase this figure to 2 litres (3.5 pints).

Urine Still Drinking urine will kill you quicker than not drinking at all, and it will probably be a painful death. However, urine can be used to wet the ground under a solar still; and it can be purified by the following method. You

will need two containers with small filler necks – large, clear plastic 3 litre soft drinks bottles are ideal. Urinate into one of the bottles until it is one-third full. Place the second bottle neck to neck and seal them together; if no tape is available use a couple of plasters from your medical kit. Gently lay them side by side on the ground, making certain that no urine enters the empty bottle. Cover the empty bottle with sand to form a cooling shade, while leaving the urine bottle fully exposed to the sun. If this process is done in the morning, it can be lifted at last light. Grab the bottles where the necks meet and lift together, separating as you do so. Depending on the heat available, you should find that at least half of the urine has

been distilled into pure drinking water.

Warning: Solar stills need to be moved every two days to produce the maximum amount of water. Even so, it is very unlikely that a single still will produce enough water to sustain one man for more than 15 days. Urinate only when you must, as this is depleting your body fluids.

Water-Providing Plants

Many plants with fleshy leaves or stems store drinkable water. Try them wherever you find them. Cacti have no root system worth mentioning, which means they store water in their bodies; in many cases this sap is safe to drink. Extracting the sap is not easy, as almost all cacti are covered with protective spines; these are difficult to remove from your skin, and cause sores if left in.

The barrel cactus of the south-western United States is a possible source of water, but use it only as a last resort and only if you have the energy to cut through the tough, spine-studded outer rind. Cut off the top of the cactus and smash the pulp within the plant. Catch the liquid in a container. Chunks may be carried as an emergency water source. A barrel cactus just over a metre (3.5ft) high will yield just over a litre (2 pints) of milky juice. **Warning: While the barrel cactus is an exception to the rule that plants with milky or coloured sap should not be eaten, the large, multi-fingered saquarro cactus, which grows mainly in Arizona, is extremely poisonous and should be avoided.**

Some desert plants, especially trees, store water in their roots, which are often to be found near the surface. These roots will need to be dug out of the ground and cut into lengths of about 0.6m-1m (2-3ft). The bark must be removed before the water can be obtained. The baobab, the desert oak and the bloodwood are examples of such water-containing trees.

Palms Palms are excellent sources of drinkable fluid and, in some cases, of food. The best palms for liquid collection are the sugar, coconut and nipa palms, as these contain a fluid which is sweet and sugary to the taste. To obtain this, bend a flower stalk downwards and cut off the top. This will start the juice flowing. A thin slice can be cut off every 12 hours to maintain the flow, which may produce more than a litre (2 pints) a day.

Coconut Fluid can be obtained from the fruit of the coconut palm as well as from the tree itself. Ripe coconuts can be used, but green ones produce more milk and can be opened easier with a knife. A good method of getting through the fibrous shell is to pierce two eyes with a sharp stick or a nail. If you have no other means you can smash the nut hard onto a sharp edge, e.g. of a rock, to break it in two. **Warning: The juice of the coconut has strong laxative effects, so do not drink more than three or four cups a day.**

Desert Vegetation Over many thousands of years of evolution certain plants have adapted to cope with extreme conditions of aridity. Their bodies have been adapted for storage of water and their surface area has been reduced to minimize moisture loss during transpiration. Most plants grow low to the ground and are rarely able to provide any real shelter from the sun. However, certain types of tree will give an indication of how deep below the surface ground water may be expected. For example, a palm tree will indicate water about a metre below the surface (3.25ft); psalters, within 2m (6.5ft); and cottonwood and willow trees, about 4m metres (13 feet).

Coconuts are a prime source of fluid and food.

Water in the Desert

• Shallow-rooted plants often store water in their fleshy leaves and stems.

• Desert trees often store water in their roots.

• Some cacti store large quantities of water in their bodies.

• Some palms secrete large quantities of refreshing fluid.

• Apart from safe species of cacti, avoid plants with milky sap.

A Rabbit ear cactus.

A Barrel cactus.

DESERT SHELTER

The one constant is that the desert is an extreme environment: daytime temperatures are so high that humans must seek shade, and the nights are so cold that protection is needed. The naturally occuring materials for constructing shelter are usually limited to rocks or sand. The circumstances that most commonly lead to a survival situation are connected with transport failure – either a plane crash or a vehicle breakdown. Initially, provided that you have a radio and are able to make contact, it will be better to stay in one place, usually with any wreckage, rather than to attempt to walk out.

Construction

Aircraft or Vehicle as Shelter
If you decide to stay put then your shelter depends on how best to use the unserviceable transport. Both the fuselage and the wings of an aircraft will provide a ready-made shelter or the means to improvise one. The shade from the wings is best used in the heat of the day, as the fuselage is likely to get too hot; draping a parachute over the wing will offer protection against sand,

flies and sun. The fuselage is best used at night as it will retain much of the heat it has absorbed during the day. If you are unable to seal the airframe due to excessive damage, then the life rafts will provide adequate protection against sandstorms – but they will need to be well secured. To a lesser degree vehicles also offer good shelter, especially if they are hooded. Any sheet materials should be used to provide shade during the day and to cover the body at night.

Sand Shelter Occasionally short, bushy plants can be found in temperate semi-desert areas, but you will usually be limited to sand or rocks. Scooping out a shallow hollow in the ground and covering it with a groundsheet or any other available sheet material can make a very simple emergency shelter. Draping a covering over any available rocks or vegetation is another alternative.

Stone Shelter The piled stone shelter or *sangar* is one of the earliest forms of man-made refuge and has been used since prehistoric times. In its simplest form it is little more than a circular windbreak constructed of rocks. However, with a little imagination the *sangar* can be transformed into a stone house. Either way it will provide shelter from the sun, wind, sandstorms, and cold.

The desert provides only stones, sand, and small, twiggy scrub for the building of shelters.

Benghazi Stove

Improvisation by the British 'Desert Rats' in North Africa during the Second World War produced this simple cooker, available to any survivor who has a source of liquid fuel from a vehicle (see Survival Essentials). One litre (1.75 pints) of petrol poured into a can half full of sand, and left to soak for a few minutes before being set alight by tinder on top, will normally burn for about five minutes, hot enough to boil water. Warning: A Benghazi stove is not dangerous, but care should be taken when setting light to any volatile fuel. Never add extra fuel while the burner is alight; and be careful to avoid burns from the can, which becomes extremely hot.

Warning: Rocky desert conditions are the preferred habitat of scorpions. Be careful when you pick up rocks – kick them over with your boot first.

Caves and Overhangs All mountain rages will offer some form of natural shelter. Try to find an overhang which is almost permanently in the shade, as this will be much cooler. Any natural feature can be quickly improved by the addition of a small rock wall in front of the cave or around the overhang.

Warning: If you move away from your unserviceable vehicle and into such a place of shelter, always remember that most rescue operations will take place in the daylight hours. This means that you may be hidden or resting up when the search party is looking for you. Make sure you always leave some form of visible marker to indicate your position.

**LIFESAVER
SHELTER IN THE DESERT**

- Get out of the daytime sun, if only by digging down into the sand.
- Find or build shelter from the nighttime cold, where you can start a fire.
- Rocks are plentiful in most deserts – piled walls and a groundsheet for overhead cover make a serviceable shelter.
- Remember that snakes and scorpions seek warmth, too – at night you may be the warmest thing around.

Fire

The survivor needs a fire as urgently in the desert as in any other environment, for cooking, warmth at night, and signalling. In some desert regions any fire will need to be kept small due to the lack of combustible material; by contrast, other deserts are covered with dry scrub. The kerosene plant of the Nevada desert is a good example, burning exceptionally well and producing a hot fire. Due to the dryness and thin structure of most desert scrub, this fuel does not last very long. Signalling fires will normally only be possible if the survivor stays with the vehicle or aircraft and uses any combustible material which it provides.

If the decision has been made to walk out, then a small amount of fuel and oil should be drained and carried; this should be kept for emergencies. The remaining fuel is best used to provide heat for distillation of radiator water and urine before travelling.

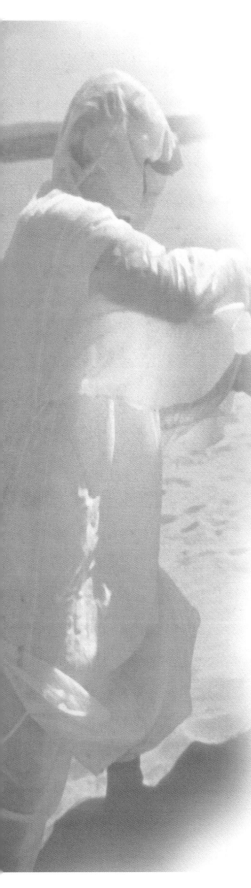

DESERT FOOD

Food is not a priority in desert survival; indeed if water is limited then it is best not to eat at all. This particularly applies to high protein foods such as dried emergency rations and the flesh of wild animals, which require water for digestion. Your life expectancy is governed by the amount of water contained within your body and whatever extra water supplies you can obtain. Eating is only a long-term survival factor, and even then you are advised to eat moisture-retaining plants wherever possible.

Desert Animals

Certain mammals have adapted completely to the desert environment. Camels are the largest mammal to be found in the desert, and are often used by native populations as a means of transport. Camels can consume up to 120 litres (27 gallons) of water at a time, storing it in their body tissue. Water loss through perspiration and urination is minimized, making the urine extremely concentrated. The camel's superb adaptation to its environment means that it is able to lose about 30% of its body weight and go without water for about a week before succumbing to the effects of dehydration.

Rodents are commonplace in the desert and tend to live underground in small burrows. They emerge to forage at night, and may become a pest to the survivor – any food supplies must be safeguarded. Rodents carry many diseases, including plague.

In places close to any human population the survivor will encounter packs of dogs. These should be avoided, as they may carry rabies or fleas. They will also be very protective of their territory and may attack.

Plants for food

Date Palm (Phoenix dactylifera) The date palm is a tall tree whose native habitat stretches from North Africa to India. They are always found near to water. They have long, slender trunks topped with leaves that can grow up to 4.75m (16ft) long. Both the fruits and the young growing tips of the tree can be eaten raw, but the young leaves need to be boiled to make them edible. In most cases the survivor will need to climb the tree in order to pick the fruit; unless the tree has been cultivated (most have) this can be extremely hazardous. The fruits sometimes fall to the ground, where they provide sustenance for a wide variety of animals and insects – check fallen fruit before eating it. Boiling the sap from the trunk will produce a sugary substance. The palm also provides excellent material for making shelters.

Mescal (Agave) Common in both desert and tropical areas, the mescal is distinguished by a basal rosette of spiky, tough, erect leaves. From the centre of these grows a tall, straight flower stalk which will eventually produce a yellow flower spike. The flower stalk can be eaten before the flowers appear, and tastes best when roasted. The juice from the leaves can also be dried and mixed with wood ash to produce a soap that will lather in salt as well as fresh water.

Desert Gourds (Cucurbitaceae) The cucurbitaceae family is an important food source, and includes plants such as melons, squashes, cucumbers, pumpkins, marrows and gourds. Representatives are found in most arid regions, from the deserts of the southern United States and Mexico, through the Kalahari and the Sahara to India. Wild gourds generally have a vine-like appearance, forming mats on the desert floor. The flowers produce orange-sized fruits. Nearly all the plant is edible: the young leaves can be cooked, as can the fruit, which makes it more palatable. The seeds inside the fruit can also be boiled but taste best roasted. The flowers can be eaten raw. The stems and shoots can be chewed to extract the water they contain.

Acacia (Acacia spp.) This common tree occurs in many variants from Africa to Australia. They are small to medium-sized thorny trees with small, feathery leaves. The flowers are small, globular, and depending on species are either yellow, pink or white in colour. Young acacia leaves and shoots may be eaten boiled, as can the seeds, although these are better roasted. The roasted seeds can also be ground down into a flour to make either 'damper' or porridge, and have been shown to contain more protein, energy and fat than rice and wheat. The roots contain water. Some types of acacia also ooze a resinous gum from the bark; this is highly nutritious and can be eaten raw. Gum acacia also has demulcent qualities, soothing inflammations of the respiratory, digestive and urinary tracts.

Stay Put or Walk Out

• Does the unserviceable transport offer enough resources to help you survive?

• How long will your resources last?

• Do you have good reason to expect rescue?

• Are you in good enough physical condition for a desert march?

Fire in the Desert

• Keep fires small – natural fuel will probably be scarce.

• Signal fires will depend on vehicle fuel and tyres.

• If travelling. try to carry an emergency supply of vehicle fuel.

• Gather any natural kindling and fuel you encounter as you march.

197

DESERT TRAVEL

Despite what many survival books recommend, walking in the desert at night is no more hazardous than walking in daytime. The exertion will also help you keep warm, and conversely the cold will reduce the rate of body fluid loss. Visibility is normally good, with the moon and stars providing enough light to see clearly up to a hundred metres at ground level. If no compass is available, then knowing your star constellations will guide your path as easily as the sun by day.

The types of terrain encountered differ depending on local factors such as rainfall, rate of erosion, geology and wind. These factors may produce sand dunes, wadis (valleys), escarpments and depressions. Desert terrain falls into three broad categories: mountain, rocky plateau, and sandy or dune terrain.

Mountain deserts consist of areas of desolate hills or mountains with flat, arid basins in between. The rainfall, which tends to be infrequent, usually falls on the high ground and pours into the basins, eventually carving deep gullies and ravines into the sides of the mountains. Rocky plateaux – such as the *hammada* of southern Algeria and Morocco, are characterized by flat expanses almost entirely covered with gravel and small rocks.

Sand dunes are what most people associate with the word 'desert'. These deserts are usually large in area, flat or undulating and covered with sand or gravel. Depending on the quantity of sand present large dunes, some as tall as 300m (1,000ft) and as long as 16-24km (10-15 miles) may be the dominant feature. Plant life is usually very sparse, but there may be some scrub in isolated places. Examples of this type can be found in the Empty Quarter of the Arabian desert, and the great *ergs* or sand seas of the Sahara.

Navigation

Establishing North, and therefore all other points of the compass, is easy in the desert due to the exceptional clarity of the stars in the night sky (see Essentials of Survival). Additionally the nature of most deserts makes it possible to see for great distances, and thus to pinpoint a distant feature on the horizon. The Prevailing winds dictate the direction in which sand dunes move, giving the careful observer a ready guide. These factors should keep most people on course, providing they know the direction to their final destination.

Maps Unless destroyed by fire all aircraft and vehicles will have a supply of maps from which the survivor should be able to pinpoint his position and estimate the distance to the nearest safe haven. All maps have a defin-

able scale; and in addition to showing major features such as roads, towns and coastlines, many desert maps show the position of water. In the event that no maps are available, a course to the last known visual or major feature should be established, i.e. a coastline or mountain range.

Obstacles & Hazards

Wadis are a natural feature of some deserts. These vary between steep-sided gullies and small depressions in the sand. They are usually easy to travel along and, in the case of some of the deeper *wadis*, may provide some shelter from the sun. However, be aware that they can be prone to flash floods (see below). Remember – it doesn't have to be raining in your immediate vicinity for a flash flood to occur.

Salt Marshes, when wet, will be difficult to negotiate on foot and totally impassable for

a vehicle. In the dry season trails across a salt marsh will be easily visible. In the wet season the only indication of their presence will be a line of standing water where the salt crust has been consolidated through the pressure of feet into a barrier impenetrable to water.

On higher ground in mountainous desert terrain you may come across another travelling hazard: during winter many mountain passes are often blocked by snow.

Mirages Mirages are optical illusions caused by light refraction through the hot air rising off the desert floor. Despite the storybooks they occur only along or near to coastlines. The image is normally one of small islands floating in a sea of water, which is generated by a combination of heat distortion and image reflection. Gaining a higher vantage point of several meters should allow the

Desert sandstorms can last for days and drive you mad – avoid if at all possible

survivor to see over the mirage. Fixed visual points taken at dawn and dusk will aid the desert traveler overcome this problem, as will the relevant position of the sun, moon and stars.

Sandstorms Deserts are prone to prevailing winds, although these may vary in direction at different times of year. For example, the Sahara has the khamsin wind which occurs in the spring and summer and can last for days at a time; Death Valley in America's Nevada desert suffers the same effect. These are very strong winds, with velocities sometimes reaching hurricane force, which stir up the dust and sand. The fine particles then become suspended in the winds, moving with such speed that they have a literally sand-blasting effect. Visibility can fall to zero, and combined with the abrasive blast of windborne sand this makes travel intolerable and almost impossible. These storms have a tendency to start and stop suddenly, and like all strong winds will cause changes in temperature. You can sometimes avoid the path of an approaching sandstorm by moving to firmer or higher ground.

If you become trapped it is vital to secure any essential equipment to prevent it blowing away. Be prepared to cover

yourself thoroughly, especially your eyes, ears, nose and mouth, as the fine sand will penetrate even the smallest aperture. Prolonged exposure to a sandstorm can result in death. If you intend to wait the storm out make sure you mark your directional heading with a permanent marker; be aware that when the storm moves away you may find your gear and your path buried under large quantities of sand.

Night or Day?

• Day marching exposes you to the worst of the sun, with consequent risks of sunstroke and exhaustion.
• This increases your fluid loss and water requirements.
• Marching by night keeps you warmer than lying still in the cold, while causing less fluid loss.
• Visiblity is usually good at night, and navigation easy – but:
• If you lie up in shelter by day, you may not spot search aircraft, nor they you.

The featureless desert can be difficult to navigate.

Flash floods can produce extraordinary amounts of water for short periods.

Communication lines will always guide you to civilisation.

Flash Floods Flash floods are caused by heavy rainfall in the upper mountains, normally along the coastline where evaporated seawater is blown inland in the form of clouds. As these are forced to rise by the mountains the vapour cools and turns to rain. The water falls quickly through the gullies until it forms one large body of water trapped in the lower wadis. The rushing water, arriving without warning, is rarely more than a metre deep but moves with great force, carrying with it rocks, sand and gravel swept up from the wadi floor. The force of the water and the debris it contains will kill anyone trapped in its path. The water usually dissipates as it reaches flat, open terrain, and quickly evaporates. Flash floods take place repeatedly in the same areas, leaving behind tell-tale signs of debris. Always be wary of travelling along the floor of steep-sided gullies which are difficult to leave in a hurry.

Communication Lines It is rare to find a road in the desert, and those that do exist tend to be simple affairs designed for commercial purposes, or for travellers to get from one large centre of population to another. Away from road systems vehicular travel is difficult over most types of desert terrain, although not always impossible. Travel on foot is easier but – due to the hazards of climate and the long distances – not recommended. If you are forced into this type of journey by circumstance, then you will need all your survival skills to stand a chance of living. Most deserts will have sources of water such as oases and wells, and will be criss-crossed by native trails; however, the ability to make use of either will probably depend upon some kind of contact with the local population. Other man-made features likely to be found in the desert are oil pipelines and wells, refineries, quarries, crushing plants, military installations and telecommunications equipment. Around areas of population there may be canals and other means of irrigation for crops.

Rescue

The chances of rescue in the desert will depend on your location and whether any responsible person is aware of your accident or the fact that you are overdue. If a serviceable radio is available and it is possible to give a precise location of your whereabouts then rescue is normally swift. In the worst event, where no one is aware of your situation or your position and you have no means of communication, your best hope lies in walking out. Either way, signalling your position must remain a priority second only to preserving and locating water.

Signalling

When travelling in the desert, location signals are doubly important. Since travel will generally only be possible at night, the location signals left at previous camps will be the searchers' main guide. In the same way the need to seek shelter from the sun during the day will mean that you will be hidden from search aircraft. Place large ground signs, or if in a party have one person on standing watch at all times. To pass the time have them continually sweep the skies with a heliograph.

Heliograph Next to a radio transmitter or beacon the heliograph is the ideal signalling device for any desert area. It does not rely on batteries, the sun is virtually guaranteed, and ground-to-air visibility is infinite. The newer heliographs are designed to reflect the sun's rays with pinpoint accuracy, thus allowing for the reflection to be directed at any rescue aircraft over a distance of up to 20km (12.5 miles). All liferafts contain a heliograph,

LIFESAVER

Due to the heat haze some low-flying search aircraft such as helicopters may be heard but not seen. If this is the case, operate your heliograph in the rough direction of the sound using a small circular motion. The flash from any heliograph is extremely noticeable to the eye.

Desert People

Populated areas will often be found around a source of water such as an oasis. In addition, deserts are the home range of nomadic peoples who travel from place to place with their flocks and herds, carrying their tents and belongings with them. While the majority of nomadic tribes still cling to the time-honoured Islamic tradition of hospitality to the stranger, times are changing.

Life in the desert is harsh and the people often extremely poor. Nomads, especially, may have little contact with any central government authority, and many tribes operate their own fundamental laws. On the plus side, local inhabitants will know of every local water supply. For notes on how to conduct yourself during contacts, see Essentials of Survival. To behave in an openly suspicious or aggressive way when making contact would be extremely foolish. Some of the most desperately poor communities can be astonishingly generous, particularly the sedentary groups; but be aware that the occasional group, usually nomadic, may be descended from many generations of bandits. The presence of flocks and families is more reassuring than groups of men travelling alone.

but if none are found then an ordinary mirror will suffice (see Survival Essentials).

Signal Fire Unless it is possible to produce black smoke and lots of it, daytime signal fires are of little use in the desert. Survivors who have remained with their transportation should prepare a signal fire burning tyres, seating and oil. However, providing there is enough scrub bush available nighttime signal fires should be prepared. Always keep a small amount of fuel in reserve and close at hand, ready to prime the fire instantly when signs of rescue are present.

For signals employing stones and panels, see Survival Essentials.

Air Supply Drops

The desert is a vast and apparently empty place, yet while it is possible for aircraft to cover great distances, it is highly unlikely that fixed-wing aircraft will be able to land. In such an event supplies will be dropped which should enable you to survive until a ground or helicopter rescue can be mounted. In such cases a normal supply drop will include a radio, water, food, medical equipment and shelter. The radio should be operated immediately and contact with the rescue aircraft established. In any event you should not move from your present position unless instructed to do so, as a fix on your position will have been reported. Your return to civilization may take several days, so make yourself comfortable and relax.

SURVIVAL IN THE
JUNGLE

JUNGLE ENVIRONMENT

Equipment
Clothing
Medical Hazards
Wildlife

SHELTER

Materials
Construction
Fires

WATER

Plant Sources
Hazards

FOOD

Plants
Animals

TRAVEL

Navigation
Obstacles and Hazards
Signalling and Rescue

THE JUNGLE ENVIRONMENT

Jungles are divided into two types: primary and secondary. When we think of jungles we imagine a densely forested area with almost impenetrable foliage; this is what is known as a primary jungle. But jungles can also include swamps, grasslands and cultivated areas. A primary jungle can be either a tropical rain forest or a deciduous forest, depending on the types of trees and plants found growing there.

Tropical Rain Forest This typically has very tall trees whose upper branches interlock to form canopies. Underneath the top canopy there may be two or three more canopies at different levels, depending on how much light can penetrate through. The lowest canopy may be only 10m (33ft) from the ground. The effect of these canopies is to stop any sunlight from reaching the jungle floor. Undergrowth is therefore extremely limited; there are, however, extensive buttress root systems and many species of hanging vine at these levels.

As its name suggests, the rain forest has a very high rainfall, and the tropical heat produces humidity levels which at times can be seriously exhausting.

The water-logged ground all but rules out any off-road vehicular travel, so realistically the only way to travel through this type of jungle is on foot. Due to the lack of undergrowth this is fairly easy in a tropical rain forest, especially compared to other types of forest. However, it does present its own problems: due to the dense canopy, no search-and-rescue crew will be able to see you from the air. Ground visibility is also limited to about 50m (165ft), and it is extremely easy to get disorientated and lost.

The jungle became a second home to the SAS during the 1950s and 60s.

Deciduous Forest This is found in semi-tropical regions. Here the weather tends to have a marked annual season of rainfall (usually called a monsoon) and a dry season, even a drought. During the heavy rains the trees produce leaves, and when it is dryer the foliage tends to die back. Unlike the tropical rain forest the trees are not so densely packed together and sunlight is able to reach the forest floor. This encourages a thick layer of undergrowth. Travelling through a deciduous forest in the dry season is reasonably easy, and visibility is relatively unhampered. However, during the wet season, when the trees are in full leaf and the undergrowth is at its thickest, movement is extremely slow and difficult, and visibility is hampered both from above and on the ground.

Secondary Jungle This occurs on the edge of primary jungles, and appears where forest has been cleared (frequently by man, using slash-and-burn methods) and then abandoned back to nature. Where the ground has had much exposure to sunlight certain types of plants take hold. These are usually weeds, grasses, thorny shrubs, ferns and bamboo. This sort of thick, difficult vegetation, often growing to a height of 2m (6.5ft), makes any movement on foot slow and difficult. Visibility is often no more than 2-3m (6-10ft), giving a feeling of claustrophobia. Often the only way to move through the impenetrable foliage is to slash your way through with a machete.

Equipment

There are few places in the wild where you won't have to deal with bugs to some degree, but this is especially true in tropical, swampy or forested areas. Every survival kit should include extra insect repellent. Those based on a solid wax stick are the best for the jungle, and give effective, long-lasting coverage.

Also adjust your medical kit so that it caters for skin rashes, snakebite, etc. In a tropical environment, or anywhere else where biting insects present a serious problem, taking plenty of mosquito netting will greatly reduce the number of bites needing treatment. If the area is extremely bad you should consider using a headnet for protection; use the type that have two hoops, top and bottom, to keep the netting away from your face.

The new jungle machete, developed by former SAS soldiers, is a major improvement on the former issue.

Jungle Survival Tool Any planned trip into the jungle will warrant taking a large knife or machete. This will be required to clear vegetation from your path and to construct a camp site. The Rockwell 55/57 has been developed after years of research in conjunction with former SAS soldiers, and is undoubtedly the most suitable tool for the job. It has a heavy chopping blade with which it is possible to fell large trees, but with a finer edge for skinning and food preparation. The broad, flat point makes an excellent digging tool, or can be used for boring holes. Engineered from 440a stainless steel, with a tough plastic handle, this tool will perform a multitude of tasks and withstand the most extreme treatment.

Sleep in dry clothes

SAS soldiers have regularly operated in the world's jungles over nearly 50 years, since the Malayan Emergency campaign of the early 1950s. They have pioneered many techniques of jungle survival and warfare – methods of insertion and extraction, and long operational patrols – sometimes staying in the forest for months at a time. They have developed one completely undramatic practice which makes a big difference to comfort, and thus to efficiency.

Although dedicated to travelling as light as possible, they carry two sets of clothing with them, one for daytime use and one for night. Just before they go to sleep they change out of their wet clothing, which is normally hung under the shelter or hammock to dry out. In the morning they change from their dry clothing back into on the damp set. It is an uncomfortable change, but one that guarantees a good night's sleep in dry clothes.

Jungle Clothing

While heat and humidity are undisputed facts in the tropics, the reports of discomfort being 'unbearable' are often exaggerated. The heat would be a lot easier to bear if the moisture level was not so high; this causes constant sweating and damp clothing. This is an inconvenience, but one can learn to adapt; the jungle survivor must accept that his clothing will always be wet, either from sweat or from rain. However, problems can arise during late evening when jungle temperatures drop and damp clothing becomes chilly. It will be cold enough to warrant a fire or wrapping a blanket or some other form of covering around the body for protection.

Lightweight, loose-fitting clothes that completely cover the body are best for the jungle environment. If you arrived in your situation unexpectedly, scavenge for suitable clothing, search personal effects or improvise with any available material.

- Shirts should have long sleeves, and should button at the wrist and neck.
- Trouser bottoms should be gathered and tucked into thesocks or boots.
- Secure all valuable survival items in pockets or around your neck on loops of string.
- Find or make a spare set of clothing and keep it for sleeping in.
- Wear a hat with a wide brim – it will help stop bits of the forest and its smaller inhabitants from dropping down your neck.

SAS soldiers operate in the jungle for weeks at a time with little more than what they carry on their back. Most jungle regions of the world supply all your survival needs

Clean Clothing Given that you will sweat constantly, your clothes will smell. Bits of jungle also get everywhere, and snagging vines are constantly ripping clothing. If you are forced to remain in the jungle for any length of time without a change of clothes then they will start to rot. The speed at which they do so will depend on how clean you keep them. If water is available then clothes should be washed every couple of days. Use any soap sparingly; a simple rinse in clean water is often enough to remove sweat and debris from the fabric. Do not beat your clothes against rocks, as this will damage buttons and zips, etc. Dry them by laying in direct sunlight; if none is available, then wring them out and wear them damp.

Footwear The best footwear is a pair of high, lace-up boots with water drainage, but these may not always be available. In this event the important factors are firmly fitting, comfortable footwear with a good sole, and a long pair of socks – with your trouser bottoms tucked inside, the latter are to protect your ankles and legs from being bitten. If you are wearing anything other than proper jungle boots you might consider making several small holes in your footwear above the sole about midway along the foot, to release any water trapped inside.

Selecting Equipment You would be astounded at the amount of rubbish untrained soldiers carry into the jungle. Prior to any operation every SAS soldier will strip his equipment down to the bare bones and carry only what is

In the 1950s the SAS developed special techniques and equipment to make parachuting into the jungle less hazardous – note the lowering ropes carried in a bag on each of their right sides.

To Jump or Not to Jump?

Normally there is no facility for a parachute exit from commercial aircraft and passengers are forced to take their chances when the pilot crash-lands in the jungle. However, the crews of smaller aircraft may have the choice, and it is up to the pilot to make a swift decision whether or not to bail out. This decision will be out of his hands if the aircraft is out of control, or if no suitable landing site presents itself – in this case he and the crew are better off jumping. If the aircraft can be controlled, and a suitable landing site can be seen (clearings, wide rivers, paddy fields and beaches all offer possibilities), then there are several advantages to attempting a landing. The crew or passengers will be together; the aircraft and its component parts will be available for survival use; and they will have avoided what is in any case a very dangerous procedure – the jungle canopy is far from the ideal landing zone for a parachutist.

If you are ever forced to parachute onto the canopy of the jungle, always aim to land on the centre of the bushiest tree available. This will prevent you falling through and getting hung up, helpless and far above the jungle floor.

Foot Care Overnight

• At night remove footwear and socks, to give your feet a chance to breathe – but remember to protect them from biting insects if you do not have a mosquito net.

• Place your footwear upside down on two metre-long sticks pushed into the ground underneath your shelter or hammock. This will help them dry, foil some of the intrusive wildlife, and keep them where they can easily be grabbed during the night.

• Dry socks by hanging them from your hammock strings.

absolutely necessary. There is little point in inviting exhaustion by carrying large loads in jungle terrain, and any equipment you need to carry should be carefully selected. Remember that the jungle will provide you with most of your basic needs such as food and shelter.

What you really need are your machete, compass, survival and medical kit, plus a supply of drinking water. Apart from these you should deliberate on items such as a mosquito net, spare clothing, and signalling apparatus, especially radar-reflecting balloons.

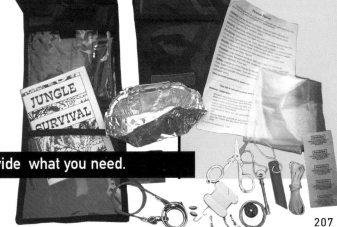

Do not overburden yourself with kit, the jungle will provide what you need.

Getting Down from the Jungle Canopy If your survival situation arises from an aircraft crash-landing or a parachute exit over the jungle, there is a good chance that you will become trapped high up in the forest canopy. Parachutes will obviously get entangled in the branches; but it is also more common than most people realize for aircraft to come to rest in the canopy, given that it will simply cushion most light fixed-wing types and helicopters. If this happens, and you are still alive, your problems have only just begun. The distance from the canopy to the jungle floor can be anything up to 30m (100ft) – a fall means certain severe injury or death. While you could try climbing down, you will undoubtedly come to a point where there are no more branches yet you are still dangerously high above the ground. The only safe way is to lower yourself on a rope (see box). Most pilots and parachutists who are active over the jungle carry some form of lowering device.

Immediate Action The ways of entering the jungle are fairly limited: either you walked or used a boat to get in, in which case you should be prepared – or your aircraft has made a forced landing. Military personnel who have been deliberately inserted into the jungle should have the means by which they can be extracted in an emergency. Whatever has caused your survival predicament, the same guidelines should be observed.

The immediate actions to be taken in the jungle are much like the imperatives in any other terrain (see Survival Essentials): first aid, position, rendezvous and contact. In the jungle first aid is particularly important, as the smallest cut or abrasion can quickly become infected. Fixing your position and rendezvousing with other survivors is also difficult due to the dense vegetation. Shouting and whistles will help at this stage. Only move when you are certain, and then move in the direction of the aircraft crash site or to a prominent feature specified by the pilot prior to jumping. Establishing communications before any emergency, or activating a personal locator beacon after the event, will greatly improve your chances of rescue. Finally, make sure that the rescue party, which will normally arrive in a helicopter, will have either a cleared landing zone or a suitable winching area.

Carry Equipment Before leaving to walk out, decide what equipment is vital to your journey and what you can easily carry. Do take spare parachutes, ropes, fire axes, medical and survival kits, and some container which will hold fresh water. Cut up seats and cargo webbing to make improvised packs, or use a pole to carry loads between two men.

Lowering Methods

If escaping from an aircraft trapped in the canopy, remember to remove all serviceable items, survival packs, rations, tools etc, and drop them to the ground before you lower yourself.

❶ Attach the lowering rope to a strong branch and drop it to the ground below.

❷ Make sure the rope is correctly fitted so that it runs through the lowering device smoothly.

❸ Hitch your body to the rope by means of the karabina and figure-of-eight.

❹ Wearing gloves if available, lower yourself slowly.

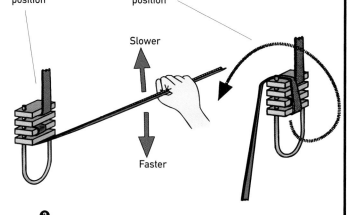

To anchor point

Descent cord

To braking hand

Descent position

'Locked off' position

Slower

Faster

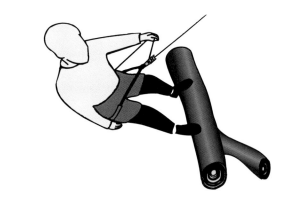

Jungle Medical Hazards

Fear The greatest danger for those who have never been in the jungle before is fear. Strange and startling animal noises, large biting insects, the dangers of sickness, and the sheer claustrophobia of the dim surroundings can make the jungle environment seem like a hostile place. While the jungle is noisy, smelly and teeming with animal life, it is not as dangerous as most people perceive; indeed, in many ways these forests are places of great beauty. The secret is to go with the jungle – if you try to fight it, it will fight back, making your life even more miserable and lessening your survival chances.

The forest will provide food, water, and materials to construct a shelter or make weapons with which to protect yourself. Most of the hazards are avoidable. Work with the jungle, as many native peoples do, and you may find opportunities to make your survival more comfortable. If you are uninjured, fairly fit, and able to use a little common sense, then you have little reason to fear the jungle.

Heat Heatstroke or heat exhaustion is common in the jungle. If the victim shows signs of becoming weak or giddy, and the skin is clammy and cold to the touch, you must suspect heatstroke. Find a shaded spot and let the victim rest, loosening his clothing to circulate the air over the skin. Pour cold water over the head and neck, and give water with a little salt in to drink. Rest until recovered; take things slowly to prevent recurrence.

Fungal Problems The heat and humidity provide the perfect conditions for the development of fungal and bacterial growth on the skin. This is why personal hygiene is so important. Any skin that is constantly damp and not exposed to the air will invite an attack by some type of fungus. Athlete's foot and ringworm are types of fungal conditions. Dhobi itch is another, which attacks the groin leaving itchy brown or reddish areas. Fungal infections rarely clear up on their own, especially in such conditions, and may need application of a fungicidal cream over a period of time.

Prickly heat occurs when sweat glands become blocked, causing a rash. It occurs when skin is moist and hot all the time, and is common in people not acclimatized to the tropics. Loose clothing will help to prevent this condition, and cold water poured over the skin will soothe it.

Wet Water Immersion Wet water immersion foot is rather like trench foot but occurs in warmer climates. Feet that are constantly immersed in water, such as when repeatedly crossing streams and swamps, will be susceptible to this condition. The soles of the feet become white, wrinkled and sore, and walking becomes very

Wild animals

Attack by wild animals is less of a risk than is commonly thought. Most animals – even predators – are shy of man and are not often seen. Unless cornered, startled at close quarters, or injured, they will seek to escape. Females with young are also likely to be protective and will attack anything perceived as a threat to their young. Large cats such as lion, tiger, leopard and jaguar will sometimes attack a human who appears vulnerable or weak, or if that animal has had a taste of human flesh before.

Far more dangerous are animals such as the hippopotamus, which accounts for more human deaths in Africa than any other animal; or even the placid-looking water buffalo of South-East Asia. These are not meat-eaters, but can be extremely aggressive when roused or when feeling threatened. Elephants, too, should not be provoked, and should be given way to at all times. Unless there is reason not to, make as much noise as possible when passing through the jungle; this will warn many animals, who will simply avoid you. The risk from animals and insects will depend largely on which continent you are on.

Crossing swamp for any length of time can cause problems for your feet.

painful. Chafing of the skin can occur when it is constantly exposed to soaking wet clothing; the crotch area, in particular, becomes sore and red through the rubbing of the wet material. Eventually it will become too painful even to touch. Both chafing and water immersion foot are helped by allowing the skin to dry out and heal.

Dysentery See Survival Essentials.

Pain Relief Smoking the below-ground root of the Strangling Fig has the effect of relieving pain. The roots, about the size of cigars, should be pulled out of the ground, washed and left to dry. The roots contain very large water veins which become hollow during the drying process; it is this that allows it to be smoked. Cut the root into lengths of about 10cm (4ins), and smoke the

whole root to gain any benefit.

Author's note: Although I have never smoked and always condemn those who take illicit drugs, in the interests of survival I have tried this remedy. The experiment was a little inappropriate, as I had no pain to relieve; but there were no visible side effects. The

Survival health cures come in the strangest form.

Iban trackers of South-East Asia, who regularly smoke the root, seem remarkably healthy.

Making Splints Broken limbs in the jungle can be supported by a natural plant splint. Many of the young palm tree stems provide an excellent splint, but the best stem to

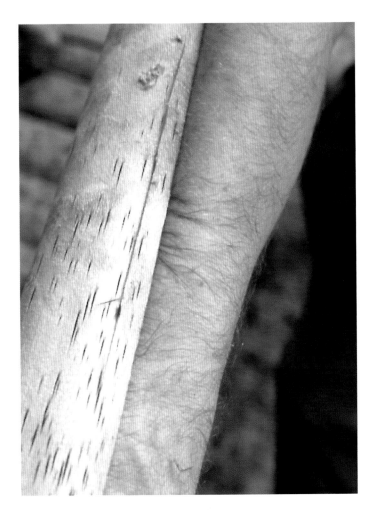

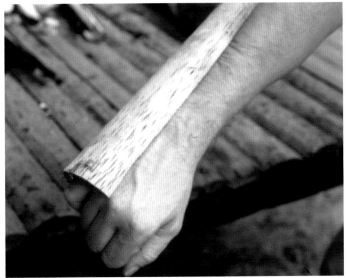

The peeled layers of the palm tree make excellent splints.; not only do they grip the limb firmly, but they have a beneficial cooling effect.

layer as your splint. The splint should be long enough to cover the damaged limb and can be bound into place with several lengths of attap string. The inner coating of the banana palm is smooth and cool to the touch; and the splint will automatically lock itself over the limb. Experimenting with this material can produce a splint the equal of those manufactured for the purpose. (Do not forget that in a survival situation the inner core of the palm can also be eaten, raw or cooked.)

Wildlife

Mosquitoes Any insect bite has the potential to introduce infection, but tropical mosquitoes are the carriers of several dangerous diseases and parasites which can prove fatal. Malaria, filariasis, yellow fever and dengue fever as well as various forms of encephalitis are all carried by the mosquito. Do everything within your power to protect yourself from their bites.

- Mosquitoes breed in stagnant or sluggish water and on swampy ground. Avoid making your camp near any of these; seek higher ground where possible.
- Make sure that any antimalarial drugs are taken as prescribed for as long as your supply lasts.

The People of the Forest

Jungle survivors have a good chance of contact with people living deep in the rain forest, who in most cases have no communication with the outside world. If the local tribespeople are friendly towards you then you may well be offered hospitality. Traditionally jungle tribes are shy, but if approached in a quiet manner will accept a stranger into their midst. Unfortunately, in recent decades some innocent tribes have been exploited during political uprisings, and their jungle villages have been used as training camps for guerrilla warfare. Others have been provoked into warlike attitudes by the expansion of commercial logging and farming interests into their forests. A knowledge of the current political system governing the region should indicate to any survivor what attitude can be expected when contact is made with the forest people.

use is that of a young banana tree. Locate a young palm with a stem around 10cm (4ins) thick, cut it off at the base, and trim at the leaf end. Split and remove the outer layer 1-2cm (0.4in-0.8in) thick, and use the next inner

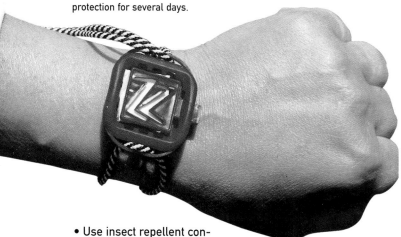

Insect repellants come in many forms, this bracelet provides protection for several days.

- Use insect repellent continually. Nighttime is when mosquitoes bite the most.
- Cover exposed skin wherever possible, with mosquito netting, parachute material, handkerchiefs, or anything else that you can improvise. Tuck trouser legs into socks and sleeves into gloves.
- Mud smeared over exposed areas of skin may help deter mosquitoes.
- Slow-burning, smoky fires will drive insects away.

Snakes The fear of snakes is common among survivors, yet in reality they do not present too great a risk. Of all the thousands of species less than 10% are dangerous, and generally they will not attack unless disturbed, hungry or provoked. Most snakes are very shy and will do their best to avoid you, attacking only in self-defence – though when they do strike, it is with lightning speed. That said, most snakes move over the ground quite slowly, and any healthy human should be able to outrun them. The one notable exception is the Black Mamba of Africa, which is not only extremely aggressive and deadly, but can also reach speeds of up to 48kmh (30 miles per hour). If you do find yourself in a snake-infested area, take a few precautions:

- Use a stick to turn over stones or logs and to probe thick undergrowth.
- Watch where you walk – some snakes are dopey when basking in the sun, shedding their skin, or digesting a meal, and may not hear you coming.
- Most snakes hunt at night and prefer dark areas to rest in. When walking at night, make enough noise/vibration to warn them of your presence.
- If you come across a snake, stay calm and still, and then back away slowly. Avoid sudden, threatening movements. In most cases the snake will slither away.
- Never tease, pick up, or corner a snake unless you intend it to be your next meal.

Treating snakebite Bites, whether from a venomous or non-venomous snake, can be very frightening. If you cannot firmly identify the snake as a non-venomous variety, treat the bite as if it were poisonous. The important thing, whether the victim is yourself or another survivor, is to stay calm and not to panic. More people die as a result of panic than from the actual bite, as the increased heart rate only adds to the adverse effects of the venom.

If a person is bitten the treatment must have two aims: to reduce the amount of venom available to enter the body, and to prevent the venom which has entered the wound from spreading throughout the system too fast. This will give the body a chance to deal with it at a reduced rate. Act calmly and resassure the casualty; make them rest. Find the site of the puncture wounds, and if possible position the patient so that the bite is lower than their heart. Wash the surrounding skin with water to prevent more venom entering the wound and getting into the circulatory system.

Despite what you have seen in the movies, never cut a snakebite, as this may introduce more venom into the bloodstream. Never try to suck the poison out; it may be absorbed through the lining of your mouth, and you may end up suffering like the casualty. Instead, use a bandage as a light tourniquet; put it on above the bite, and wrap it downwards towards the puncture marks. Make it tight enough to stop the return of venous blood, but not so tight that it restricts the flow of arterial blood to the area. You can make sure it is of the right tightness by checking to feel a slight pulse below the bandage.

The wound will probably bleed, but this is potentially beneficial as the blood will carry away some of the venom. Put a splint on the limb to lessen any unneces-

It is my personal opinion that most jungle snakes will avoid humans. If you come across one, stand still and let it slither off.

LIFESAVER
Snakebite: Immediate Action
• Remember that only a small minority of snakes are venemous.
    • Try to stay calm and reassuring at all times.
• Position the casualty so that the bite is lower than the heart.
• Wash the area of the bite.
• Do not try to stop the bite bleeding.
• Apply a tourniquet above the bite – i.e. between the bite and the heart.
• Immobilize the limb.
• If possible, immerse the limb in cold water.

Leaches are annoying but they cause little harm.

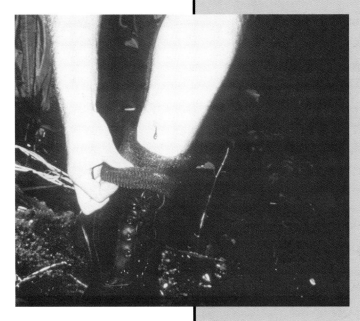

sary muscle movement, which will act as a pump for the blood in the veins. If you have the means, immerse the wound area in cold water; this will further slow the blood flow back to the heart. Continual reassurance of the casualty is vital; do not let him believe he is going to die, or this may lead to shock. After 15 minutes, if the bite area is not painful or swollen and the casualty has no headache or dryness of the mouth, it is safe to assume that the bite was not poisonous.

Ants Tropical ants, both large and small, can inflict severe bites, and if disturbed will attack in numbers. The bite of the fire ant, in particular, is noted for causing excrutiating pain. Unless you need them as a source of food you are best advised to leave ants alone. Both termites and ants move in continuous columns varying from a few centimetres to over a metre wide. If undisturbed they will pass by, and any isolated insects which crawl onto you can usually be brushed off without biting. Ants can be a problem for injured people who are unable to move, so

always lay them in a place free of ants.

Leeches Leeches are found in tropical and sub-tropical lowland forest, especially after rain. They look like fat black worms, and live by sucking the blood of any warm-blooded creature that passes. Their bites, although not especially dangerous, cause discomfort and loss of blood and open the way for infection. They wait for their prey in swamps and slow-moving water, or attach themselves to vegetation in moist areas. When moving through such terrain protect yourself by ensuring that your trousers are tucked into tightly-laced boots, or that your legs are covered with some sort of improvised wading gear. Check every few minutes to see that leeches have not attached themselves to you or your companions – their saliva has anaesthetic properties so you may not feel their bite. (If alone, you can use a heliograph mirror to check your back.)
    As long as the leech has

Despite their vast numbers, ants cause little harm.

not yet latched on you may flick it off; however, if it has already bitten do not try to pull it off – if you do, its jaws may remain in the wound and cause infection. The best way to remove a leech is to put salt or ash on it, or approach it with a glowing ember (such as the tip of a cigarette). You can also make

A Choice of Two Evils

• Your clothes will always be wet in the jungle.

• Pressure of wet clothing causes chafing and encourages fungal infections – but:

• The danger from disease-carrying mosquitoes and other pests demands that you keep your skin covered as much as possible.

• Try to keep clothing loose, though well fastened.

• Take any opportunity to dry off.

• Take care over personal hygiene.

• Carry supplies of fungicidal ointment.

Above all, remain calm when dealing with snake bites.

up a nicotine solution from left-over unburned tobacco wrapped in a piece of cloth; when this is moistened and squeezed onto the leech it will loosen its hold. Leeches will fall off naturally when they have had their fill.

Leech bites can be cleaned by gently squeezing the area, allowing the blood to carry away anything nasty. Despite the anti-coagulant properties in the leech's saliva the bleeding will stop after a while and a clot will form. Leave this in place for as long as possible to

Alligators, crocodiles and caymans are all flesh eaters and should be avoided.

protect the wound from infection.

Use your hands to scoop up water to drink – never put your face into leech-infested water. If a small leech gets into your mouth, throat or nostrils it could be very unpleasant and even dangerous. If it does happen, however, gargle or sniff up a concentrated salt/water solution to dislodge them.

Flukes and Hookworms

These tropical parasites can easily enter the body by piercing the skin. They remain in the bloodstream, and are the cause of serious, debilitating diseases such as bilharzia (schistosomiasis). They are found only in fresh water that is slow-moving or polluted, so be aware of this if you have to wade such water. Always check before bathing, and do not drink water from such sources without thorough boiling.

Bees, Wasps and Hornets

These stinging insects can all be very aggressive in defence of their nests. Nests can generally be identified as brown-coloured oval or oblong masses attached to treetrunks or branches at heights between 3m and 10m (10-30ft) above ground. If you are only a few metres away when a swarm becomes disturbed, stay very still, preferably sitting down, for at least five minutes. Once the worst threat has passed, crawl away slowly and carefully. Should a swarm attack you there are two ways to defend yourself. One is to run through the thickest and bushiest foliage you can find – the foliage will spring back after your passage and will beat back and confuse the insects. The other method is to immerse yourself in water completely, and stay under for as long as you can.

Spiders

Of the many species of spider in the world only a tiny minority are deadly poisonous, such as the Funnel-web of Australia. The Black Widow and its tropical relatives also present a threat to life, but only in extreme cases is their bite fatal; it is, however, very painful, dangerous and disabling. Apart from the Funnelweb, which is grey or dark brown, most of the other spiders to avoid are dark in colour and patterned with red, white or yellow spots. If in doubt, assume that it is poisonous. Any casualty bitten by a poisonous spider during a survival situation should be treated as if for snakebite.

Rice Borer Moth

This insect is found in the lowland jungles of South-East Asia. It is small, plain-coloured, and has a pair of tiny black spots on the wings. At night it is attracted to lights in large numbers. If one lands on you it should never be roughly brushed off: it has small barbed hairs on its body, which may enter the skin and cause a painful sore which takes weeks to heal.

Water Hazards

Crocodiles and caymans are flesh-eaters but will rarely attack humans; nevertheless, they are best avoided. Tropical waters provide far more dangerous but less obvious creatures than crocodiles. Piranhas inhabit the rivers of the South American rain forest, and may attack a human if he is in the wrong place at the wrong time; they are most dangerous in shallow waters during the dry season. Electric eels can reach 2m (6.5ft) long; the larger specimens can generate 500 volts of electricity and are extremely dangerous. Catfish and poisonous water snakes can all be found in tropical rivers and may present a danger to the unwary. One to beware of is the Amazonian Candiru, a minute type of catfish. It is reported that this will actually swim up the urethra of a person urinating in the water; once inside its back-folded dorsal fin acts as a barb, causing extreme pain and a very serious medical problem. You should remember this image when wading.

JUNGLE SHELTER

If you decide to stay where you are rather than walking out, then it is worth planning and constructing a more substantial shelter. Given the amount of materials readily available, with a little initiative you should be able to quickly build a shelter which will considerably increase your level of comfort. Shelters are necessary to give protection from the heavy downpours, and for getting a good night's sleep. As well as following the general principles of shelter-building (see Survival Essentials), in the jungle your camp should be sited on high ground away from swamps and dry riverbeds alike.

The term *basha*, meaning a jungle dwelling, has been adopted by the SAS for any form of sleeping place. Follow the SAS example, and always check the site of your basha first for snakes, ants, ticks, standing dead trees, and anything else that might crawl into or fall onto it. It is wise to check the surroundings for any large, well-worn game trails, taking note of the size of any pawprints.

If you can, raise the whole shelter off the ground; if this is not possible, then at least make sure that your sleeping area is raised – do not sleep directly on the jungle floor, which is alive with biting insects and home to other kinds of wildlife with which you will not enjoy sharing your bed. Consider all possible shelter options, from aircraft wreckage or parachute material to building a tree house (which is easier than it sounds).

Large aircraft crash-landing in jungle are usually completely destroyed on impact (the consolation is that they leave a clearly visible trail). Occasionally large sections remain intact enough for use as shelter by survivors, however. Make sure the airframe is firmly settled and will not move further. Remove seats to make space for sleeping, or for any injured; and make the fuselage as insect-proof as possible.

Sleeping in the Jungle

• Do not camp close to swamps, dry water-courses, or large animal trails.

• Camp on high ground where possible.

• Check the ground and vegetation for snakes and insects.

• Check above the site for rotten branches, and wildlife.

• Raise your sleeping place well above the jungle floor.

With a good hammock and poncho, jungle survival is easy.

Hammock If you arrived in the jungle on foot you should be carrying a purpose-made hammock or pole bed. In the unlikely event that you parachuted in, then you have the means to make one. Improvise using some form of fabric and cordage from a crash or abandoned vehicle; hammocks made from vines tend to break, however, so it is best not to attempt this method.

Jungle Materials

The forest abounds with building materials. Young saplings between 8cm and 10cm in diameter (3ins-4ins) make excellent framework poles. All species of bamboo are found in tropical or semitropical regions where there is sufficient rainfall. They are tall, fast-growing members of the grass family. The mature woody stems – which in some species can grow to a height of 25m (80ft) – are jointed and hollow. Bamboo is extremely useful as a building

material or for making utensils. Beware when harvesting bamboo, however – the tight-packed clumps of stems are often under great tension and may suddenly shatter or whiplash as you cut them. This can cause serious injury, as bamboo splinters are very sharp; and note also that the bases of bamboo shoots are covered with fine, stinging

A basic pole bed is designed to get you off the jungle floor (right).

The Jungle is full of large, broad leafed plants which are ideal for shelter construction.

hairs which may cause skin irritation. Vines make good tying material and can be pulled down from trees whenever required (but be careful to look upwards, and make sure that it is only a vine that you are pulling down).

Shelter Construction

Pole Bed My advice is to build your pole bed first and then construct a shelter around it – insertion may be tricky if you work the other way round. The bed itself can be made of bamboo or other small branches lashed together to form a frame – either a free-standing A-frame or one integrated into the hut itself. A simple A-frame is made by lashing two poles 2m (6.5ft) long together at the top and splaying the legs apart. With two frames, each resting against one of a pair of closely spaced trees, the bed frame

can be dropped over the top; the height of the bed is adjusted by opening or closing the A-frame legs. When it is satisfactory, tie the whole thing together with cords or string vine, and fit a poncho as overhead cover.

Attap Basha Many broad-leaved plants grow in the jungle, but attap is the most commonly used in shelter construction. The branch has V-shaped leaves growing down a central stem; although sharp, with careful handling these can be used to thatch shelter roofs and walls. Neatly interwoven on frames of bamboo or saplings, attap is a versatile building material used by villagers throughout South-East Asia. It is often possible to find four closely-growing trees to form the basis of your shelter without felling; these will give the firmest possible support.

Simple lean-to with bamboo floor.

A Jungle tepee.

A tree hut offers protection from beasts and insects, and is cooler at night.

Ground Hut This is the attap variation on the North American tepee, using a framework of poles angled together and tied at the apex. This can be covered with parachute material or attap branches. Crosspoles should be incorporated to form a raised platform inside, for seating by day and a bed by night.

Tree Hut Tree huts are common in South America and Asia, and are built to protect the inhabitants from flooding and dangerous wildlife, or simply to give them a different perspective from that of the forest floor. One tribe in Borneo build their homes on the roof of the jungle canopy, interconnected by swaying ladders and platforms of vine. For survival purposes there is no need to build more than 5m (16ft) above the ground. Cut your frame poles on the ground, leaving them long enough for an individual to reach down and pull them up to the construction platform. Once a level base platform has been completed, build an attap hut on it as normal. A long, thick log inclined against the tree and with steps cut into it will form a simple ladder.

Swamp Bed If you are forced to camp in a swamp or on habitually wet ground and have no hammock, you must construct a sleeping place above ground. Take into account the location – e.g., if near a coastline you must allow for tidal changes. Try to use the surrounding vegetation. For instance, in many swamps the trees can be very large, with fin-like buttresses at the base; by cutting into these fins it is simple to form a platform big enough to sleep on. Another method is to link two nearby trees by securing a pole at the same height on either side, and criss-crossing these with shorter lengths to form a platform. If sheeting is available, place another pole 1m (3.25ft) above the sleeping platform to support overhead cover. Bamboo is ideal for this sort of work, but any strong pole about 10cm (4ins) in diameter will suffice.

Fire

Fire in the jungle is mainly important for cooking and water purification. Although much of it is permanently damp, jungles are full of rotting vegetation, and there is no shortage of fuel. Starting a fire will depend on your available means and tinder. During the evening and night a smoky fire will help fend off insect pests.

Fire In Swamp Areas

In wet areas build your fire on a platform well above the water surface; use poles and other vegetation, finished with a thick pad of mud or silt on top of which you can set your fire.

Fire As Insect Repellent

The smoke from a burning termite's nest will keep biting insects away. Crawling insects do not like walking over ash, and it is a good idea to spread some around your sleeping area at night.

JUNGLE WATER

Tropical rainfall is usually far higher than in temperate regions. In some areas rain falls on most days, often at a predictable time; it comes suddenly, and is followed by clear sunlit skies. In other zones rain is seasonal, and in the wet season falls continuously without any breaks in the clouds. This predictability at least makes it easier to plan and organize your activities.

The tropical climate provides the perfect breeding ground for bacteria, viruses and parasites; it is very likely that any unprotected person entering these regions will contract some sort of disease. Although these are more prevalent in populated areas, where they are caused by lack of sanitation and clean drinking water, you should assume that all jungle water other than direct rainfall is contaminated, and should be purified – bad water can kill more quickly and painfully than no water at all.

Water from Plants

Some plants have a high water content and offer a water source in emergencies. Others have a drinkable sap. Some examples are given below; but it is wise to make a study of plants in a particular area before you go. Bear in mind that some are poisonous; you should never drink from any plants with milky or coloured juices (the two exceptions to this rule – coconuts, and the American barrel cactus – are described above).

Many jungle plants will act as water containers, catching any rain or moisture in the atmosphere. Try shaking hollow old bamboo stems to see if you can hear any water inside; if you can, pierce the stem carefully just above each joint and let it pour out. Bromeliads, which are part of the pineapple family found in tropical America, collect water in between their leaves. Other examples of water-holding or collecting trees are the baobab of Africa and Northern Australia, and the umbrella tree of tropical West Africa.

Plant Sources

Banana and Plantain Both these trees provide an ample supply of good drinking water. Cut the tree down, preferably sawing through the trunk 30cm (12ins) above the ground. Place your knife in the middle of the stump with the blade at an angle of 45 degrees, and hollow it out to form a bowl. You will find the water filling it even as you cut. When you have finished, scoop out any debris and wait for it to refill. Although sometimes bitter, the water is good. Cover the stump to protect it from insects, or use it as a means to catch them.

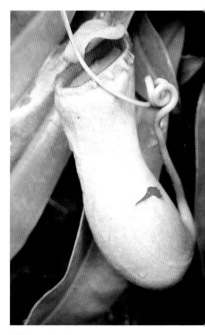

Pitcher plant.

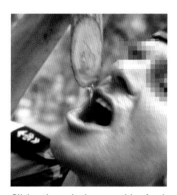

Slicing through vines provides fresh water.

Bromeliad.

Vines Some vines may also supply fresh water. Cut deeply into the vine as high up as you can reach, then sever it completely near to the ground. Allow the water to drip from the end of the vine into your mouth or a container. Try a little first; water from vines is normally crystal clear and sweet. If the liquid is murky and causes irritation to the mouth, stop immediately – this could be an indication of poison. Once the water has stopped dripping, cut another section of the vine and start again. Study the vine so that you will recognize it in future.

Pitcher Plants Found all over South-East Asia, this is a climbing plant which is mainly confined to the more mountainous areas. Many people mistake the pitcher for a flower, but it is really a leaf formation which can be found in a variety of different shapes.

Due to the poor soil the pitcher has evolved to supplement the nutrients it needs to sustain life by digesting the small insect and animal life that becomes trapped in the pitcher's water reservoir. Ground-level pitcher plants hold a good supply of water, but due to the plant's prey it is best boiled before drinking.

Avoiding Waterborne Diseases and Parasites

- Collect rainwater as it falls.

- Purify all drinking water, whatever the source, by filtration, chemical agents or boiling (see Survival Essentials).

- Avoid bathing in untreated water.

- If forced to cross water, do so fully clothed.

Water is plentiful in the jungle, but beware of its potential dangers.

Ten minutes of jungle rain will deliver several litres of drinkable water if you stretch out a poncho.

There are many plants that you can drink water from – beware of any previous occupants of the plant though.

Bamboo

- You can use lengths of bamboo to make any kind of shelter, platform, bed, raft, etc.

- You can use short sections cut close to the joints to make cups, water carriers, food containers and cookers.

- You can use split bamboo to make eating utensils, skewers, etc.

- When harvesting bamboo in thickets, check first that your cut will not suddenly release a stem under tension.

- Avoid cuts and punctures from sharp bamboo splinters.

TROPICAL FOOD

The jungle environment is rich in plant and animal life. Edible animals include monkeys, wild pigs, birds and rodents. Toads and salamanders can also be eaten, but have glands on their skin which need to be removed first. Fish are plentiful in the tropics, as are shellfish in swamps and coastal regions. Edible plants include wild bananas, mangoes, yams, oranges and lemons, breadfruit and taro.

Plants

Bamboo The young shoots can be eaten, although they have an extremely bitter taste and need to be well boiled, with a couple of changes of water. Bamboo flower seeds are also edible and should be cooked like rice.

Wild Yams Many species of wild yam occur in the tropics; they are perennial, and prefer light forest and clearings. Wild yams have twining, vine-like stems and a long, contorted rootstock or tuber, which is the edible part. Some vines also produce edible aerial tubers. It is best to peel and cook them before eating as a

Bamboo shoots.

few varieties are poisonous in their raw state. Yams have a high nutritional value, being a good source of carbohydrate and vitamin C. They also store well as long as they are kept in a dry place.

Baobab (Adansonia) This bulbous-trunked tree is found in open tropical bush from Africa to Australia. It has a very strange appearance, the diameter of its trunk being equal to about half its height. It produces large white flowers which mature into pulpy fruits about 20cm (8ins) long. The leaves may be eaten, cooked in soups, and the fruits and seeds are edible raw. The swollen roots will, more often than not, contain a good water supply.

Wild Fig Most wild figs are edible, although some will be more palatable than others. Wild figs grow commonly in both tropical and sub-tropical areas. They all tend to be trees with a rambling habit and tough, evergreen leaves. The fruits, usually pear-shaped, may appear either in clusters or in pairs at the base of each leaf. Wild figs can be eaten raw and are highly nutritious, containing high

levels of dextrose, calcium, potassium and iron, so should be considered as a very desirable survival food. Figs also have medicinal properties, being mildly laxative; they contain an enzyme which aids the digestive process. If they are roasted and split in two the inside of the fig can be applied with benefit to boils and abscesses, even those of the mouth.

Taro (Colocasia esculenta)

The taro plant is a member of the arum family. It is found all over the tropics where there is moist ground, and is an important food plant for many native peoples. The plant can grow up to 1.5m (5ft) tall and has large, leathery, heart-shaped leaves on stems rising from the base. It has an orange flower and a large turnip-like tuber; this tuber is the edible part but, as it contains harmful substances, it must never be eaten raw. The tuber should be cooked thoroughly; the result should be a root which has a taste rather like a potato. Taro roots are rich in starch.

Ti Plant The ti-plant prefers to grow in the shade. It is a shrub which can grow to a height of 4.5m (15ft); the leathery leaves have thick stems and are usually green, although they may also be tinged with red. Although it bears red berries it is not these which form the edible part, but the fleshy roots. These are full of starch and highly nutritious; they are best cooked.

Animals

Being able to observe animal sign is a valuable skill in the jungle. Despite the dense foliage signs are easily found in mud, streambeds, on trails and near watering holes. When animals move it is usually for a reason, and on a daily basis that reason is either to eat, sleep or drink. Tracks will give you information about their direction of travel, and an indication of their size.

Monkeys Huge numbers of a wide variety of monkeys live in all types of rain forest. Jungle tribes regard monkeys in very much the same way as Western people see rabbits: as a food resource. Larger species should not be hunted, as the males can be extremely aggressive. Monkeys can be caught in traps or shot with a bow or blowpipe. Traps vary; the baited perch type is one of the best ways of catching a monkey, with bananas being the favourite food. The bait ensures that the monkey is in the correct spot when the spear-laden arm is activated. The trap should be designed to keep any catch from being pilfered by other predators, as a monkey's scream can be heard for a great distance.

Mousedeer The world's smallest hoofed animal, the mousedeer is no larger than a domestic cat. Although found throughout the Far East its main habitat is the Malaysian jungle. It is an extremely shy animal and rarely seen during daylight. The best way to catch them is to search with a torch while they feed after dark; caught in the torch beam, a mousedeer will normally freeze long enough to be felled with a club.

Giant Capybara The largest of the rodent family, measuring about 60cm (2ft) at the shoulder and weighing up to 45kg (100lbs), this herbivore lives in large groups along the banks of South American rivers. It is semi-aquatic, usually diving into water at the first alarm. The coat is generally short, coarse, and pale in colour, but those living in colder regions tend to have longer, shaggier fur. Although it still has rat-like features, the face is deeper and the ears and tail are small; the feet are slightly webbed. They are often heard before they are seen, since they communicate with grunts, squeals and clicking noises. The meat is white and very much like pork.

Tapir Tapirs are found in Thailand, Malaysia, Sumatra, and Central and South America. They are harmless herbivorous animals with pig-like bodies which can grow to over 2m (6.5ft) long, weighing up to 250kg (550 pounds). The thick skin is covered with short, coarse hair. They can usually be found in and around swamp areas, sleeping by day and feeding by night. They are able swimmers and, if pursued, will seek safety in deep water.

Long-Legged Mara The mara lives on the grasslands of Argentina, where it can be seen grazing in small groups, or lying on its stomach basking in the sunshine. In appearance it rather resembles a hare with a large head, a blunt nose and big eyes, long legs and clawed toes. It often grows to 75cm (30ins) long and weighs up to 15kg (33 pounds). It usually moves with a hopping action, but is capable of speeds up to 45kmh (28mph) when disturbed. Maras are easily alarmed; when they run for cover flashes of white fur on the backs of the thighs act as a warning signal. They are burrowing animals, and return to their burrows at night. The entrances are easily identified by piles of droppings.

Tapir.

Wild Pig Wild pig are common in almost all rain forests, especially in areas adjoining cultivation. Pigs are omnivores; the wild species eat a wide variety of leaves, roots, fruit, reptiles, rodents and carrion. They are usually found living as a family group, although the male will spend much of his time alone. Mature boars have dangerous tusks, and in some areas of South America they are very aggressive, attacking without provocation. Pigs are creatures of habit; if their feeding areas or watering holes can be located they can easily be caught. Although a good food source, most wild pigs are infested with worm.

Ants and Termites Placing a tin can containing a small bait of rotting fruit directly in the path of the ants for several minutes will produce enough protein to last a human for a whole day. Give the can a hard bang on a firm surface, and place it on the fire for about 30 seconds; this will shake the ants to the bottom where the heat will kill them. Then put the can near enough to the heat that the contents will dry but not burn. See Essentials of Survival for preparation: crush to powder, add water, boil and skim. (Worms, beetles, wasps, grubs and very small fish can all be cooked in the same way.) The resulting protein-rich drink is normally tasteless.

Snakes Ground snakes do not move very quickly and can easily be killed with a stone or stick. Obviously, take care to avoid snakebite at all times – though normally shy, they will strike in self-defence. Once you have caught your snake, remove the head to make sure it is dead. Slit the stomach skin downward from the neck and peel it back until fully removed. Most of the organs are held in the inner stomach and are easily separated from the body. Snakes make good eating; the flesh is best boiled or fried.

> **LIFESAVER**
> **Snakes**
>
> • In Western culture snakes are regarded with a fear which is more supersitious than reasonable.
> • Many jungle peoples regard them as a good meal.
> • With common sense and reasonable caution, most snakes are easy to catch and kill.
> • Cut off the head; slit and peel off the skin; open and clean the body cavity.
> • Boil or fry. Some veterans claim that the taste resembles chicken.

JUNGLE TRAVEL

Your decision to stay at the crash site or walk out will – as always – need careful consideration. Choosing to stay put depends on somebody both knowing of your plight and having the resources to find and rescue you. Low-lying mist can frequently hamper aerial searches of jungle terrain. If your site is clearly visible from above, and you have workable signalling devices, you may choose to stay. If your chances of location seem poor, and you have a good idea which way to travel, walking out may be your best option – although it might take months, and demand the development of long-term survival skills. But do you have casualties? How many, and how badly injured? It takes a minimum of four healthy survivors to carry one injured person through the jungle, and even with this ratio the journey will be long and hard.

Dense Vegetation The jungle presents the survivor with an obstacle course; vegetation tends to be very dense, and cutting a path will be slow and exhausting. When travelling through this type of terrain normal progress will be about 1km (0.6 mile) per hour, or about 5km (3 miles) per day. It is therefore vital to choose your route following the largest opening in the vegetation that is roughly in line with your intended direction. Don't just look – penetrate the forest with your eyes. Move slowly, stopping regularly to orientate yourself. Native paths, game trails, dry water courses, rivers and streams or ridge crests all offer a slightly easier passage. Bear in mind, however, that animals will also use these trails, especially at night – after sunset it is safest to stay in camp. Take precautions to limit the discomfort and damage caused by insects and leeches; and always check for wildlife in your bedding, packs, clothes and especially boots before use.

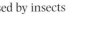

Don't Fight the Jungle

- Don't try to cut a path to follow a compass bearing rigidly.

- Seek areas of thinner vegetation, game trails, streams, etc, which lead roughly in the right direction.

- Follow ridge tops if possible.

- Move slowly, stopping for frequent compass checks.

- Don't travel after sunset.

Almost all jungle is laced with barbed bush and vine. Ridgelines, animal tracks and rivers offer a more speedy route through.

Navigation

Navigation in the jungle is difficult even for those with some experience. The heavy vegetation and irregular terrain often make travelling in a straight line impossible. Although the compass must always be used as a check on overall direction, it may be easier to follow a feature such as a ridge rather than hacking through endless stands of bamboo and clinging vegetation. River courses meander, sometimes increasing the linear distance three-fold; however, travelling down a river by raft is a good idea if it is feasible.

Tracks Many tracks can be found in the jungle, the smaller ones made by animals. Those that are well-worn normally lead to water – if you find one, follow it downhill to water. Man-made tracks may either link villages or be habitual hunting routes. Logging tracks may also be found, driven great distances into the jungle in search of particular types of tree.

Rafts Traversing jungle terrain by river is still one of the most popular methods of travel, due to its speed; but for the survivor it presents the twin threats of dangerous animals and dangerous water. Rafts are best built from bamboo lashed together with vines – these materials are plentiful and easy to work with.

Obstacles & Hazards

Swamps Low-lying jungle areas near to water or where the ground is poorly drained will have swamps. There are two types: mangrove or salt-water swamps, and palm or freshwater swamps. Man-grove swamps occur on coastlines subject to tidal flooding. Mangroves thrive in these conditions; they are small trees, usually from 1m-5m (3ft-16ft) high, although some can grow as high as 12m (40 feet). They have extensive, tangled root systems both above and below the water which can create hazards for the traveller, both on foot and on a raft. Due to the dense growth visibility is poor both on the ground and from above. These swamps may also harbour large crocodiles, leeches and biting insects. Despite the abundance of food they should be avoided, or crossed as quickly as possible.

'Freshwater' or palm swamps actually occur in saltwater as well as in freshwater areas. Undergrowth usually consists of small palms, thorny bushes, reeds and grasses, which can make movement and visibility extremely difficult; however, they often have channels navigable by a small boat or raft. This sort of swamp has much wildlife of survival value and fewer animal dangers than the mangrove swamp.

Fallen trees are one way of crossing small rivers.

Savannah On these wide, open stretches of grassland characteristic of much of Africa small shrubs may be found but tall trees are rare. The thick, broad-bladed, sharp-edged grass can grow from 1m to 5m (3ft-16ft) tall. Depending on its height, movement may be slow and tedious, and there is little shade from the sun. Visibility may be poor at ground level, but is reasonably good from search aircraft.

Signalling & Rescue

Radios rescue beacons, strobes and radar-reflective

Logging tracks provide a wide footpath through the jungle, just make sure you are going in the right direction.

balloons should be activated as available and required (see Essentials of Survival); where none are available, improvise. If you stay at a crash site you must use every possible means to signal any rescue aircraft or boat. The jungle density prevents sound from travelling and the noise of an aircraft will not be heard until it is close. You must therefore display some form of permanent signal; the best is the aircraft or parachute itself, especially if it is still up in the forest canopy. The canopy will hide and disperse the smoke from the largest fire (and if the surrounding vegetation catches fire you are liable to have more immediate concerns than your rescue). Ground signals can obviously be seen best where there is a break in the canopy, and any rescue aircraft will be check-

ing every clearing. Rivers and their banks are normally visible from the sky. Jungle rivers are often pitted with small islands large enough to build

a fire on; failing this, make a fire platform and tether it midstream. If a fire is not feasible use marker panels instead.

Quicksand

Should you fall into quicksand the danger you face is determined by its consistency and depth. Despite the movie version, most quicksand holes are very small; it should be possible to reach firm ground, or grab a purchase which enables you to pull yourself free. If you cannot do this, don't panic:

• Immediately throw yourself prone, and 'swim' using the breast stroke.

• In very wet quicksand you may go under, as you would in water; but the retention properties of wet quicksand are weak, and you should be able to surface and swim.

• Stagnant quicksand is more dangerous, as it will grip your body and slowly suck you down until you reach the bottom of the hole. In this case any abrupt motion may dig you deeper.

Jungle Extraction

Jungle survivors unable to walk or float back to civilization will usually depend on helicopters for any rescue. (Ground searches may occasionally be organized, but in tropical forest the chances of locating even something the size of an aircraft are not high.) Helicopter rescue also has its pitfalls, due mainly to the denseness of the forest canopy. This makes locating survivors extremely difficult; and the task of extracting them from the jungle floor presents special problems.

SEA AND COASTLINE SURVIVAL

SURVIVAL IN THE OCEAN

Man is a land animal, but seas and oceans cover nearly 75% of the Earth's surface. Human survival when abandoned at sea is perhaps the most difficult challenge of all. Survival duration will depend on a number of factors, the most immediate being whether you are in the water or in a craft of some kind. If you find yourself in the water, with or without a lifejacket, your survival will be governed by the water temperature more than any other factor. A person can survive for several days in warm water, although the risk from dangerous creatures is higher in tropical seas. However, this risk is as nothing compared to the difficulty of survival in cold water.

Wearing a lifejacket greatly increases the chances of survival.

For those lucky enough to gain a place in a liferaft or lifeboat there is hope of rescue, especially if the craft carries electronic communications equipment. Survivors may still suffer from environmental hazards – heat, cold and storms – but modern liferafts and their level of equipment have improved tremendously over recent years, significantly improving the survivor's chances.

Jumping into Water You should first try to climb down into the water, jumping only if there is no alternative. Check the area you will land in for other people or debris. Jump clear of any protruding obstacles. Keep your body vertical and your back straight; cross your ankles and fold your arms; put one hand over your mouth and nose, shut your eyes, and jump. The moment you are in the water, flatten out into the breast stroke swimming position, and surface. Move away from the ship or aircraft, as others may be jumping after you. Move upwind if possible, to avoid fuel-covered water – which can ignite at any time. Check your lifejacket and top up the air using the mouthpiece if required. Look for the nearest liferaft.

Floating and Swimming Good swimmers know that if they relax they will remain afloat. This is best done by lying on your back with arms and legs spread and head back, with just your face above the water. Swimming is only advised in warm waters, and then only with a specific objective, such as reaching a liferaft or other floatation aid, rescuing others, or making for land; float at all other times. If you have a lifejacket you should be able to remain afloat indefinitely, with the added bonus of keeping your head out of the water – this greatly increases your survival duration in cold water. If you have no lifejacket and there is no liferaft nearby, then you may wish to make a flotation aid.

Lifejackets The lifejacket or preserver consists of a lightweight waistcoat with integral blast-resistant pouch, a stole container, and an inflatable profiled stole. In military versions the waistcoat has pockets for a beacon and miniflare pack; ground/air emergency code card; heliograph, and whistle. Most lifejackets are coloured fluorescent orange and equipped with a battery and light assembly and whistle. Infla-

LIFESAVER
If you are forced to jump into water which is covered with burning oil, do not inflate your lifejacket. Swim underwater for as far as possible. If you must surface for air, do so hands first, splashing the water surface; take a breath, and submerge again immediately. Repeat this process until you are in safe water; then inflate your lifejacket.

Trouser Floatation Aid

1 Tightly tie the trouser legs at the bottom.

2 As you enter the water, grasping the waistband, swing the trousers over your head.

3 Splash the open waistband on to the water's surface.

4 Twist the waist to trap the air in the trouser legs.

5 Put one inflated leg under each arm for the best floating position

tion is by a single pull on a handle which releases carbon dioxide gas; there is also a mouthpiece for emergency inflation or topping up.

Trouser Floatation Aid If no other floatation aid is available you can use a pair of trousers. The reliability of such an aid is governed by the ability of the material to hold air once it is wet; jeans and other tightly woven fabrics are particularly reliable. Before you enter the water, take your trousers off and tie a tight knot in the end of each leg. If possible wet them thoroughly (although this can be done once you are in the water). Hold on to the waistband and swing them over your head as you jump. This will trap air in the legs, which can be secured by twisting the waistband. On average the air will last around five minutes before the need to reinflate. To do this, simply open the waistband, flip the trousers over your head with

Modern liferafts carry all you need to survive at sea and aid rescue.

the waistband open, and pull them sharply down again to trap the air once more – repeat as necessary.

Liferafts Liferafts of different sizes are designed to accommodate between five and 33 survivors, including aircrew wearing full equipment; and to provide the occupants with the highest possible degree of protection while awaiting rescue. The liferaft comprises twin super-

imposed buoyancy chambers, each chamber being an independent air-holding tube capable of supporting the designated number of persons should one chamber deflate. The assembly also features a through-the-floor baling device which avoids the need to open the canopy entrance in foul weather. A canopy is also inflated, covering the main body to protect against the worst weather conditions while also providing a rain-

Survival in Cold Water

Experiments have shown that the average adult immersed in seawater at a temperature of 10°C (50°F) while dressed in light clothing will not survive more than three hours. The basic factors governing survival are temperature, the amount of clothing, and whether or not the survivor has a lifejacket. The colder the water the quicker the body will cool to the point where unconsciousness leads to drowning. Several layers of clothing will insulate the body and prolong life. A lifejacket will not only keep the head above water, but will allow floating in the foetal position, thus preserving body heat. Swimming greatly increases loss of body heat, and should only be attempted when trying to reach a definite point of safety, i.e. a liferaft. If no liferaft is visible, pull your body into the foetal position; this can prolong survival time.

• Keep on as many layers of clothing as possible.

• Always wear a lifejacket – it not only keeps your head out of the water, but also allows passive floating, which conserves core body heat.

• Look out for a liferaft, floating debris, and/or other survivors; continue to blow your whistle.

• Do not swim, except to reach a definite point of safety within realistic distance – swimming greatly increases heat loss.

• Floating in your lifejacket in the foetal position can prolong survival time by up to 50%. Pull your knees up to your chest; loop your arms over your tucked-in knees and clench your fingers together; cross your ankles.

Righting a Liferaft

When they are launched or thrown into the sea some liftrafts inflate upside down. This possibility is allowed for in the raft's design, and a rope is attached so that the raft can be righted. While this procedure is easy in calm waters, it is extremely difficult in rough seas. Emphasis must be placed on balance; breaking the initial water suction; and following through as the raft starts to tilt. The task should be undertaken by the strongest person nearest the up-turned raft:

❶ Get on the side of the raft where the pull rope is stored.
❷ Pull yourself up into a kneeling position on the edge of the raft.
❸ Brace yourself by pulling backwards on the rope, and stand up.
❹ Keep your feet on the edge of the raft and fall back into the water; the far side of the raft will rise.
❺ Continue pulling on the rope as you fall into the water.

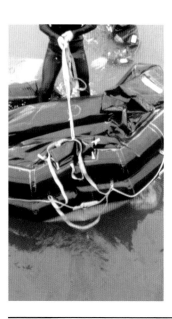

Once you are safely in the raft start rescuing others from the water and establish a routine.

Rescuing Others Once the liferaft is stable, check the inflation pressure and top up manually if necessary. Once the raft is seaworthy, check the surrounding water for survivors and help them aboard. Most liferafts are fitted with a rescue quoit on a line, which can be thrown to swimmers to pull them to the raft. If survivors are unable to catch the quoit then a strong swimmer should go into the water and recover them using the safety line. Once the raft is full those most able should see to the wellbeing of those less fortunate or injured – in cold waters this will mean preventing the onset of hypothermia. Remove any wet clothes, and if no dry clothing is available then wring out excess water and replace. Use the body warmth of other survivors while this is done. Wrapping the patient in a foil survival blanket can prevent further heat loss. Improvise a windbreak if the raft is open. Feed any available high calorie rations (e.g. chocolate) to those suffering from exposure.

Routines While Awaiting Rescue If you are at sea in a dinghy or lifeboat a full range of survival items should be available, including a radio beacon, radar reflector, flares, whistles, lights, heliograph, food and water. Most importantly, it will contain a set of survival instructions. These will cover the immediate steps to be taken, such as gathering together other survivors and setting up a radio or beacon. If a number of liferafts are in the same vicinity they should

water catchment area. Ramps for easy boarding and recovery of survivors from the water are fitted to the lower buoyancy chamber. Various accessories are attached as part of the liferaft assembly, including two independent lamps – one on the outside for location purposes and one on the inside for illumination – which are powered by water-activated batteries located in a retrievable retainer; a sea-anchor and line; and a locator beacon.

If no liferaft is available stay together; this will make your visual signature more prominent.

One-Man Raft

The one-man raft is designed for use by jet pilots who eject over water. Although small this dinghy is well designed to protect the pilot in the worst possible weather. It contains all the equipment associated with multi-person versions, and is connected to the survivor by a lanyard. If the gas inflation device does not work the raft can be inflated by mouth, although this is difficult in rough seas. Care should be taken not to puncture the raft when entering; check your body for any sharp objects. The raft is fitted with handles for pulling yourself aboard; but if injured or exhausted the best method is turning your back and getting the raft under your buttocks before falling backwards.

be lashed together for security, and to form a larger object for SAR aircraft to spot. An hourly check should be made of the condition of the raft, and the air topped up using the manual pump as required. If the raft loses air quickly or consistently then you must inspect for any leaks and carry out repairs. Decontaminate the raft of any oil or fuel as petrol can weaken the rubber glue at the joints.

Use your sea-anchor as per the instructions to stop drift (your position may change by 80km-130km – 50-80 miles per day); this will keep you closer to your last reported position and make rescue easier. If numbers allow, watches should be organized on the basis of two hours on, four hours off. Each watch should

be familiar with all the methods of signalling. Save any consumable signalling devices until there is a good chance of being seen or heard or until definite contact with a search aircraft is established. However, it is good therapy to have the watch make regular sweeps of the horizon with the heliograph whether or not any target is in sight.

If no signalling equipment is available when a possible rescuer is near, wave clothing or agitate the water as violently as possible with paddles. If survivors are fit enough, expand your visible size by making human signals in the water. The vast, bland uniformity of the ocean makes visual searching extremely difficult. Only the head and shoulders of an

individual floating body are visible; but a number of survivors banding together will have a much better chance of being spotted – a human circle or 'conga line' will form an excellent marker.

Deploy the sea-anchor and fit the spray shield before starting your survival routine.

Medical Emergencies

Medical problems at sea are either caused during ditching/abandoning ship, or as a result of long periods in the liferaft. The former can be anything from burns to broken bones, and should be treated as normal (see Survival Essentials) using whatever resources are available. Injuries caused by time spent in a liferaft will depend on the prevailing weather conditions and the duration of the ordeal (see relevant entries in e.g. Arctic and Desert Survival sections).

Protection from the Sun During long-term survival in a raft sunburn is common, and if no shelter can be improvised in extreme conditions then severe blistering and the sting of seawater can lead to an agonising death. Sun cream is part of the survival kit and should be applied at the first opportunity during hot conditions. However, the only long-term solution is to rig some form of shade over the raft. On still days the glare from the sun and reflection from the water can damage the eyes; wear sunglasses, or improvise them with a strip of some sort of material with narrow eyeslits cut into it.

Protection from Cold Second only to serious injury, cold presents the greatest danger to any survivor at sea; the majority of deaths are caused by hypothermia. A combination of cold air and cold water rapidly reduces the body's ability to function, and death can occur within less than an hour if no protection is provided. Hypothermia and frostbite need immediate attention.

Seasickness The motion of the raft will cause nausea and vomiting. This seasickness results in fluid loss and dehydration, and the survivor may even lose the will to live if the condition is prolonged. Once one survivor starts reacting others normally follow, making the whole of the raft unclean. Wash away any vomit with seawater to remove the smell and sight which induce others to retch. If seasickness tablets are available they should be taken immediately, before the onset of rough seas. Lying down with the eyes closed will help prevent seasickness, as can swimming alongside the raft – but be aware that sharks can detect vomit from a great distance.

Seawater Sores Wetting clothes to reduce the amount of fluid loss is a double-edged weapon and should be monitored carefully. Continuous exposure to seawater will produce a body rash or boils which soon turn septic. It will also attack any small break in the skin, causing puss-filled sores. Seawater sores should be drained and cleaned with fresh water if available, and treated with antiseptic from the survival kit. Washing both the body and clothes during rainfall is the best way of preventing saltwater sores.

Equipment Carried in a Liferaft

- Buoyant rescue quoit, attached to at least 30m of buoyant line ● Buoyant bailer ● 2 sponges ● 2 sea-anchors ● 2 buoyant paddles ● Knife (non-folding type) ● 3 tin-openers.
- First-aid outfit in a waterproof re-closable case
- 6 doses anti-seasickness medicine.
- Whistle or equivalent sound signal ● 4 rocket parachute flares ● Hand flares ● 2 buoyant smoke signals.
- Waterproof electric torch suitable for Morse signalling ● Efficient radar reflector, or radar transponder ● Daylight signalling mirror.
- Set of fishing tackle.
- Immediate action instructions ● Survival instructions.
- Food ration totalling not less than 10,000kJ for each person the liferaft is permitted to accommodate, kept in airtight packaging and stowed in a watertight container. Rations should be palatable, edible throughout the recommended shelf life, and packed in a manner which can be easily opened and readily divided.
- Rustproof graduated drinking vessel.
- Watertight receptacles containing a total of 1.5 litres (2.6 pints) of fresh water for each person the liferaft is permitted to accommodate, of which 0.5 litres per person may be replaced by a de-salting apparatus capable of producing an equal amount of fresh water in 2 days.

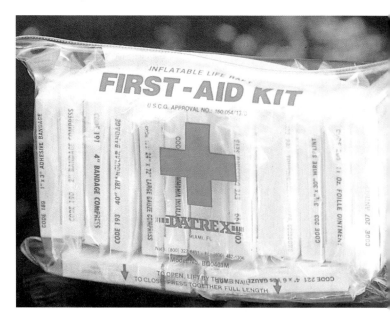

Dangerous Sea Creatures

Many creatures that live in the sea can either bite or sting, the latter usually with poisonous spines. In general, avoid touching (or eating) fish which are spiny, box-like or oddly shaped. Some spiny fish have outer fins and bone as sharp as razors. Some corals and sea anemones also possess stinging properties and are best avoided. If you come across something you are not sure about in tropical waters, it is advisable to treat it with the utmost caution until you are sure it is harmless.

The stonefish, as its name suggests, looks like a stone, but when stepped on or touched will deliver a painful sting. This fish is found in shallow water and among coral reefs, as are two others – the toad fish and the scorpion fish. In European waters you may come across the weever, a small fish with venomous spines around the gills and dorsal fin. Sea snakes will also deliver a venomous bite, but are unlikely to attack unless provoked. Other creatures that may prove dangerous if disturbed are the moray eel and the sea bass. If you do get stung by an aquatic animal, treat it as you would for snakebite.

Barracuda These large fish are found in both tropical and sub-tropical waters and around reefs. Barracuda are both inquisitive and aggressive, often attacking without provocation, especially if there is blood in the water. Precautions against barracuda attack are the same as those for sharks.

Jellyfish Most jellyfish carry a nasty sting; but the one to avoid at all costs is the Portuguese Man-of-war, which floats in shoals. This largest of the jellyfish can be identified by its buoyant bluish bladder with a flute-like sail. Trailing from this bladder are long, stinging tentacles. If you are caught in these you will suffer severe pain, shock and cramp from the toxins. The cramp may be enough to cause drowning, even to a strong swimmer. Clothing may offer some protection. If you are stung and you still have your emergency medical kit on you, take painkillers and antihistamines.

Sting Rays Found in warm coastal shallows, these flat fish tend to lie just under the surface of sand. If trodden upon or touched the stingray will lash out with the poisonous spine on its tail. The wound will be be painful, and if the fish is mature it may be fatal. It is wise when wading through tropical shallows to sweep the area in front of you with a stick – rays are not the only poisonous fish which like lying under the sand.

Crocodiles It is mistaken to imagine that crocodiles do not venture out to sea; many have been spotted miles from the nearest shore. However, for the most part they inhabit the mangrove swamps, estuaries and tropical saltwater bays of the East Indies and South-East Asia. Crocodiles are powerful even when young, so treat any crocodile over a metre long with the greatest respect. Crocodiles can be caught by using a large spiked deadfall trap (see Survival Essentials), and the flesh is good to eat.

Sharks

Despite their fearsome reputation very few types of shark are actually aggressive enough to attack. They are inquisitive, however, and will show an interest in anything strange. Many attacks have taken place when a shark has mistaken a diver or surfer for one of their more usual food sources, such as a shoal of fish or a seal. For the same reason any blood loss will draw sharks quickly to an area, and attack is then almost certain. Hollywood notwithstanding, sharks do not eat boats or jump out of the water and swallow people whole, so remaining calm while they investigate is your best bet. Shooting a shark will encourage others to devour it, and anything else in the immediate vicinity; unless you have the means to distance yourself this will do more harm than good.

In Shark Water:

• Remove any watches, jewellery, or anything else shiny, which to a shark may resemble a small fish.

• Do not make a noise, and swim smoothly without splashing – the breast stroke is best.

• Use shark repellents if available, and stay within the confines of the stained water – sharks find the chemical extremely distasteful.

• Avoid putting any bodily waste into the water: blood, urine, faeces or vomit will attract sharks.

Food at Sea

Food is not a high priority during survival at sea. Little exercise is possible, thus fewer calories are burnt off. Liferaft rations are not very appetising and are intended purely to sustain life (their digestion also requires a fair amount of water). Fish are obviously the main source of fresh food. Remember that some fish are poisonous, and do not eat any food that makes you feel nauseous – this only increases fluid loss.

Fishing Fish are a good source of nutrition, but there are some poisonous species which must be avoided. These are found mainly in tropical waters around reefs and atolls and in lagoons. When cleaning any tropical fish, throw away any gills, eggs, intestines or livers. They contain a virulent poison which cannot be destroyed by cooking, however thorough. Any fish showing the following characteristics should be avoided:

- Sunken eyes
- Odd, ugly shape with horny protrusions
- Thin shape with sharp spines and lack of scales
- Slimy appearance and feel, giving off unpleasant smell

Do not fish if sharks are present. Handle all fishing equipment with care; the lines can cut into both your hands and the rubber of the raft, and be very careful when preparing your hook. Take care of your fishing tackle – make it last. Be careful when landing large fish, as they can cause a lot of damage to the raft – cut loose any fish that presents a danger to the raft. Gut and bleed any fish you catch immediately, using the entrails for bait. Take care when using knives. Providing the flesh is cut into thin slices, portions which are not eaten directly can be hung up to dry – this is best done on warm, windy days. Air-dried fish will last for up to a week.

Birds All birds are edible (see Survival Essentials) and every attempt should be made to catch any bird that comes close to the raft. If a weapon is available you might consider shooting it, although this will seriously damage much of the flesh. A baited hook or safety-pin is the best method. Seabirds do not taste good but the flesh is perfectly edible, even uncooked.

Drinking Water

In the past the duration of survival at sea was controlled by the amount of stored water carried and the amount of rain water which could be caught. In recent years new portable equipment for converting seawater into drinkable water have become available. Even with such devices, water remains the most vital need, especially if adrift in hot tropical seas. The priorities must be to conserve body water and ration any reserves. Conservation means providing some form of sun shade, or wetting your clothing with seawater to cool the body if exposed directly to the tropical sun. Rest and sleep during the day, and avoid over-exhaustion.

Food is not a priority at sea, but starting a fishing routine helps overcome apathy.

Seawater Pump Seawater can be made potable by using a desalination pump. Using advanced reverse osmosis technology, these small, light, hand-operated devices will not only desalinate but also remove all bacteria and viruses. They remove 98% of salt (making their product less saline than normal tap water) at a rate of over a litre (1.75 pints) an hour, with a maximum capacity of 2220 litres (486 gals) per filter cartridge. Avoid using the pump if there is any evidence of fuel floating on the water; petroleum-based hydrocarbons will damage the delicate filter membrane.

Solar Still Available for a number of years, these are gradually being replaced by seawater pumps. The still is a clear plastic egg-shaped dome with several compartments. It is inflated, and seawater is poured into one compartment; through the action of the sun's rays this is distilled into fresh water, which is caught in a separate compartment. Stills differ slightly in design but all come with simple instructions. The still should be put to use at the first opportunity. Use it as a water reserve when rainfall occurs.

Rainwater Always be on the lookout for gathering clouds and prepare to catch any rain, e.g. by two survivors holding out a foil blanket or similar sheeting. Clean spare clothing can also be used to

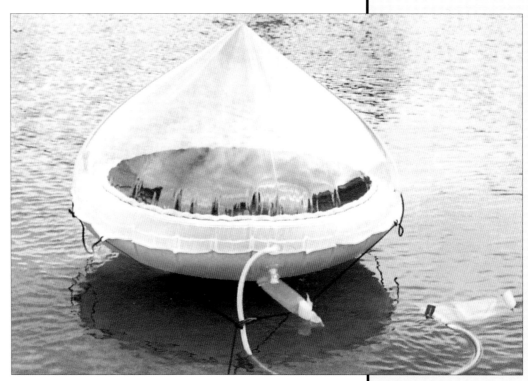

Although not as effective as a seawater pump, the solar still does work and should be put into operation immediately.

absorb rain, later squeezing it out into containers. Once all water containers are full, start drinking your fill. If the air temperature is warm enough, use the rainfall to wash salt off your body and rinse out clothing saturated with seawater. When the rain has stopped, resist drinking

for the following 12 hours.

Ice Sea ice loses its salt after a couple of years, and ice with a bluish tinge should produce salt-reduced water. While freezing seawater will dissipate its salt content, in such conditions surviving the cold will be a greater priority.

Modern seawater pumps have solved the water shortage problems associated with survival at sea.

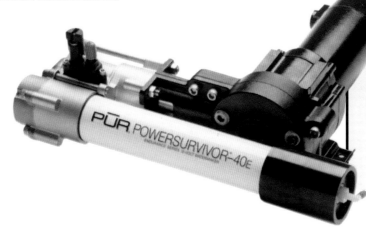

Sea Water Kills

Never drink sea water or urine unless distilled, as they will cause kidney failure. Do not drink alcohol or smoke – both cause dehydration.

Rationing

All liferafts carry water rations: these should be checked, and protected from seawater contamination. Water rationing should be calculated according to the number of survivors and what can realistically be produced from solar stills and seawater pumps. Fix the daily ration, with the exception of rain water, of which everyone should drink their fill after all storage vessels have been topped up.

NEARING COASTLINES AND ISLANDS

Cumulus clouds are one of the best signs of land, and can be seen long before the land itself. In the Arctic note any strange cloud reflections; they are normally grey, and lighter colours may indicate solid ice pack. Seabirds rarely venture more than 100km (62 miles) from land. Note their direction of travel – in the morning they will be outbound, while in the late afternoon they will be returning to nest on land. Deep ocean water is dark green to black, whereas shallow water is lighter in colour. Noises such as seabirds calling or surf crashing often indicate land, especially at night when sound further.

Beaching

Shorelines can vary from solid cliffs to muddy estuaries, pack ice or sandy beaches. If you are approaching land from the sea continue along the coast until you find a safe inlet, preferably one with a clean beach. Shores protected by cliffs are impenetrable and best avoided. Keep in mind that you may need to put out to sea again. Beaching in strong surf can be very dangerous; watch for breaks in the surf line, and avoid hidden coral reefs by using the paddles to steer. Some coral and beach rock formations are sharp enough to wound the strongest swimmer lethally, and all efforts should be made to avoid them. Tropical shorelines can often be muddy with thick root systems stretching out into the sea. While it is possible to land in such places you are better advised to search for a sand or pebble beach.

Waters along the Arctic shoreline are normally calmer, but you may need to carry the raft over several smaller floes until you find one that is large enough to support you for some time. Ice floes disintegrate and break away without warning. Avoid any large ice cliffs, as they are impossible to land on and constantly send large chunks of ice crashing into the sea. Keep the raft inflated on the ice and use it as your accommodation. Avoid getting the raft trapped between the ice floes.

Islands If, after drifting at sea, you come across an island and landing is both possible and safe, you should do so. If there is a group of islands, proceed to the largest. There are few islands that have not been at least visited by man, and even a deserted island will usually retain some remnants that are useful to your survival. Explore the island; start by walking around the perimeter – this may take several days. Note any natural routes inland, any potential camp sites and shelter. Next make your way inland taking a spiral route up to the highest point. This should give you an overall view of what the island can contribute to your survival. Check and mark the direction of the prevailing wind, and look for any sign of bird life. Check other nearby islands as soon as possible.

Shorelines Landing problems aside, the seashore offers excellent opportunities for survival, and is far safer than being at sea. Most coastlines are inhabited, and where they are not there is an ample supply of fish, seaweed, birds and molluscs. Fresh water can normally be found along the seashore, and more often than not you will find sufficient materials to build a fire or construct a shelter. Your liferaft can also be used as a temporary home, or for coastal navigation if the terrain makes walking around the coast impossible.

Fresh Water Sources of fresh water may be found next to the sea. If there are cliffs, look for faults in the rock strata where the layers may have become dislodged and tilted; pure ground water may seep from the lowest points. Also check any signs of green vegetation growing on or near the cliff. On a sandy shore you will have to dig to find out if fresh ground water is present. Choose a spot at least 100m (330ft) above the high tide line to avoid contamination by seawater. Dig down until the sand becomes damp; then wait and see if the hole begins to slowly fill with

By landing on as large an island as possible you will increase your chances of finding fresh water.

Long line fishing will produce a continuous supply of fish and crustacians.

water. If it does, stop digging; any greater depth may mean that salt water will begin to mix with the fresh. The water will anyway taste salty, but in the short term will pose no great problem. If you use a solar still you can vastly improve its drinking quality. Wells can be dug in the sea shore providing they are far enough away from the water's edge. This water will be salty and brackish but will support life.

Shoreline Food Food is fairly plentiful along the shoreline, which provides a range of seaweed and a host of crustaceans and fish. The best bait for fishing is the meat of shellfish. Limpets, mussels, clams, dog whelks and periwinkles can all be found and harvested in this environment. Provided they are cleaned and thoroughly cooked, the shellfish themselves can be eaten as a survival food.

Long-Line Fishing Long-line fishing at low tide is designed to catch demersal fish which flow with the returning tide in order to scavenge the beach for food. You simply need to stretch your main line along the water's edge. The line must be securely anchored to withstand the tide and the pulling of any catch. Attach small branch lines with as many hooks as possible, baited with lugworms, limpets, small crabs, etc. You must check your line as the tide recedes or your catch may spoil or be eaten by other predators. If a fishing net is available the same procedure will produce a much better catch.

Seaweeds Seaweeds provide a valuable source of food for any survivor within reach of a seashore. Although they can be found in the zone between high and low tide lines, the most plentiful and healthiest growths are to be harvested in the shallows just below the low tide line. Seaweed can start to deteriorate when exposed to the air, so look only for specimens which are either floating or are still attached to rocks near the low tide line. Choose species of red, green or brown colourings; all are very nutritious, containing high levels of vitamin C and iodine. (See page 238 for specific varieties.)

Once harvested, be sure to wash the seaweed thoroughly in clean water, changing it many times to get rid of any sand particles or minute crustaceans that may be caught within the weed. Seaweed can be dried for storage; this is best done by hanging it in a well-ventilated area for two or three days.

EDIBLE SEAWEEDS AND SHORELINE PLANTS

Bladder Wrack

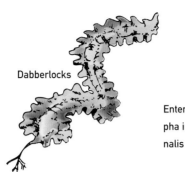

Dabberlocks

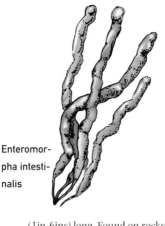

Enteromorpha intestinalis

Irish Moss

Enteromorpha Intestinalis Pale green, shape resembles an intestine – inflated, tubular construction constricted at intervals; 5cm-60cm (2ins-24ins) long. Wide distribution; found in rock pools or grouped on rocks near upper tide line and even in salty marshes in cooler climates. Can be eaten raw, or dried, pulverised and added to soups.

Bladder Wrack (Fucus vesiculosus) Thick, leathery, greenish-brown or greenish-yellow, the fronds covered in paired air bladders; stalks have distinct mid-rib; 15cm-90cm (6ins-36ins) long. Commonly found at mid-tide level on northern temperate coastlines, especially if rocky or stony. Can be used fresh or dried, boiled with fish or meat or used in soups; or dried and infused as a tea, but this should not be taken for more than a few days at a time. Medicinally, it can be boiled to make a soothing poultice for rheumatic wrists and knees.

Sea Lettuce (Ulva lactuta) Pale to dark green, resembling lettuce leaf. Found on rocky and stony shores of both Atlantic and Pacific, usually in mid-tide zone. Best harvested in early to late spring; can be eaten raw as a salad plant or added to soups and stews.

Dulse (Rhodomenia palmata) Dark red to red-brown; single tough, leathery, deeply divided frond; 8cm-40cm (3ins-16ins) long. Found on Atlantic, Pacific and Mediterranean coasts; prefers rocky shores and mid- to low-tide zones or shallows. Has a sweet taste and is easily digested – a very desirable food plant. Tastes best raw, but can be boiled as a vegetable or added to soups and stews. Dulse can also be dried, either for storage for later frying or boiling, or as a tobacco substitute. When drying, rinse thoroughly first in seawater and dry in the sun; during the process it will shrink and temporarily turn black.

Laver (Porphyra umbilicus) Red, purple or brown; irregularly shaped, leaf-like and folded in appearance; gelatinous to the touch. Found on large rocks between mid- and low-tide zones around Atlantic, Pacific and Mediterranean; will grow on rocks covered in sand. Can be eaten raw, fried, or boiled gently for a long time before being mashed.

Irish Moss, Carragheen (Chondrus crispus) Red-purple or purple-brown, or green if exposed to bright light; tough leathery, intensely forked and divided fronds; 3cm-16cm

(1in-6ins) long. Found on rocks on lower shore and in shallows on temperate Atlantic coastlines. Best boiled, or added to stews, either with meat or other vegetables. Becomes gelatinous if cooked and then cooled. Can also be dried for storage. Soothing medicinal properties – an infusion helps bronchial coughs, and kidney and bladder inflammations.

Dabberlocks (Alaria esculenta) Olive green to dark brown; short stem with finger-like projections which produce spores, frond often up to 90cm (36ins) long. Grows at low-tide mark and in shallows on N.Atlantic coastlines. Stem and mid-rib can be eaten raw, but taste better when boiled or used in soups and stews. The frond, without the mid-rib, should be soaked in fresh water for 24 hours before being boiled.

Oarweed, Tangle (Laminaria digitata) Olive to dark brown; thick, leathery fronds divided into strap-like segments, overall shape suggestive of a thick oar; up to 25m (82ft) long. Often found in large groups on temperate Atlantic and Baltic coasts, on rocks at low-tide line and also in water as deep as 7m (23 feet). Inedible raw, it can be used in soups or for making a stock after sufficient boiling.

Sugar Kelp (Laminaria saccharina) Chestnut to olive brown; blade-like, very crinkled fronds; up to 40cm (16ins) long. Wide Atlantic and Pacific distribution; grows on rocks below the tide line, in depths up to 20m (65 feet). Small plants and young stems can be eaten raw, and whole plant if boiled; sweet taste.

Sea Kale (Crambe maritima) Not seaweed – perennial member of cabbage family, found on cliffs, rocks, shingle and dunes on northern temperate coasts. Blue-green, smooth, cabbage-like leaves, large at base of plant and smaller at top; up to 60cm (24ins) tall. Small, white, clustered flowers February/May. Cook by blanching shoots and young leaves briefly in boiling water; then chop them up, and boil for about 20 minutes in clean water.

Sea Arrow Grass (Triglochin maritima) Grows near most coasts in northern temperate regions, in salt marshes and grassy areas near shoreline. Narrow, erect leaves issue straight from base and grow to 30cm (12ins) tall; stem, up to 45cm (18ins) tall, carries small green flowers on a loose spike. Whole plant edible but must be harvested before flowers appear. Can be eaten raw, but better cooked as a vegetable or added to soups and stews.

Laver

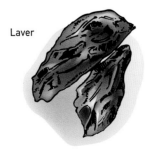

Sea Kale

Sea Lettuce

Rescue

Rescue at sea normally comes suddenly; however, the search aircraft may only drop you supplies when they first spot your position, and it may be several hours or even the next day before a pick-up can be organized. Prepare for your rescue by taking down any sail or overhead protection, and reel in any fishing lines, etc, thus avoiding any snagging problems when a winch is lowered or a line thrown.

In an assisted helicopter recovery, follow the instructions given by the winchman – these will include a request that you do not cling on to him, hampering him in doing his job. Wait calmly while he fits the lifting strop. If the winch recovery is unassisted, wait until the recovery harness has 'grounded out' by touching the sea, or you may get an electric shock when you grab it. Help those who are injured or sick into the harness and let them be winched out first. Once you are ready, signal the winch operator with the 'all clear' signal.

Signals All the normal signalling devices should be used to attract the attention of any search and rescue craft (see Survival Essentials). As always, due to their limitated life once ignited, flares should not be launched unless it is clear that rescue is at hand. Items such as the heliograph should be used constantly to scan the horizon. The moment you hit land, build a driftwood fire ready for use. Mark out a distress code on the sand using the contrast method. On the ice pack, mark the snow using panels or shark dye.

Helicopter Rescue

• In an assisted helicopter recovery, follow the instructions given by the winchman.

• These will include a request that you do not grab on to him. He has done this many times, so let him get on with his job. He will tell you what he wants you to grab, and when.

• Wait calmly while he fits the lifting strop.

• All aircraft carry an electronic charge in their structure. Don't grab the cable until it has 'earthed' by touching the ground or water.

Listen to and obey the winchman's instructions – and don't grab him.

MILITARY
SURVIVAL

EQUIPPED, TRAINED AND HUNTED

Psychological Battle

Short Term Survival

Equipment

Concealment

Long Term Survival

Escape Techniques

Lock Picking

Escape Tools

Escape and Evasion

EQUIPPED, TRAINED – AND HUNTED

A number of essential differences separate the experiences of civilians and military personnel in survival situations. Civilians usually find themselves in a survival scenario due to unforeseen circumstances and relatively unprepared; military personnel can predict problems and plan to overcome them. For personnel who fly over or infiltrate enemy territory the destination is always known. Contingency plans take account of the possibility of an unintended encounter with the enemy. Escape equipment is issued, intensive survival training is given, and escape lines and procedures are allocated. One serious disadvantage must be set against these positive advantages: the military survivor is usually being actively hunted by large numbers of determined enemies. Two clear illustrations of such scenarios in recent years were the actions of the British SAS patrol Bravo Two Zero behind Iraqi lines during the Gulf War of 1991, and the American pilot Lt.Scott O'Grady shot down over Bosnia in 1995.

The Psychological Battle

The immediate impact of finding yourself in an unfamiliar environment, behind enemy lines, with no obvious avenue of escape or rescue, can be emotionally devastating. The threat to your safety will increase if you are captured; it is therefore in your interest to stay free, and able to control your own immediate destiny.

One of the most frightening ordeals that a soldier can face is being taken prisoner. He faces an unknown fate at the hands of others, with a possibility of death or torture; beatings are common, as are psychological measures designed to destroy the captive's willpower. These fears must be put in perspective if the soldier is to control his feelings of isolation and abandonment.

Modern high technology warfare has reduced the number of men needed on the battlefield. Even in large-scale conflicts the West is reluctant to commit and lose manpower. This reduces the number of soldiers captured, which on the whole is a good thing. However, it does allow the enemy to employ a larger ratio of guards to prisoners, making immediate escape more difficult. Again, aircrew who deliver 'smart bombs' from a distance are accustomed to an impersonal level of warfare. When captured their harsh, individually focused treatment at the hands of individual enemies will be psychologically shocking. Under such conditions escape will seem impossible, but if an opportunity to abscond arises it should be pursued at all costs. At the very worst, the thought of escape will keep the prisoner's mind engaged.

Escape Plan All those who operate over or behind the enemy lines have a delivery and recovery route. If things go wrong and these routes are disrupted, they have a pre-arranged escape and evasion plan designed to increase their chances of survival and repatriation. Survival skills are learnt during escape and evasion training, and are employed to keep the soldier 'running'. Repatriation is a process of communication, position establishment and the commitment of SAR teams.

Escape and evasion plans should assume that the survivor will endeavour to put himself in a position clear of enemy forces where an extraction is both feasable and not threatening to SAR troops. Likewise, recovery procedures can only be imple-

The psychological and physical effects of capture are harsh and very real. Hold yourself together by drawing on your personal resources and training.

Ejecting over Water You will be forced to survive in a one-man raft. Unless the enemy has shipping in the area you are probably free from the risk of capture, as your aircraft will sink and your raft presents a minimal signature. You should operate your beacon immediately and carry out a survival routine as trained.

Ejecting Over Land If forced to eject while flying over enemy-occupied territory you have two immediate concerns. The first is the enemy's report of your crippled aircraft, i.e. its mid-air explosion, smoke trail or ground impact. The second is the visibility of your parachute during its slow descent. Either will indicate your presence and your general landing location. However, the time spent descending, determined by the ejection height, can be extremely valuable as well as making you vulnerable.

The moment you have checked your canopy, estimate your direction and drift and pinpoint, if possible, your final landing area. If height permits, do a 360° sweep of the area for signs of the enemy and of any civilian population. Use your height to note topographical features such as rivers, roads, forests, mountains and villages. If you have been spotted by the enemy, look for some

terrain feature which will either provide cover, or put an obstacle between you and imminent capture. Injuries permitting, you should distance yourself from your landing zone and any aircraft wreckage the moment you hit the ground; both the burning plane and the parachute canopy will give the enemy a clear fix on your position.

In many instances the first people at the scene will be militia or local civilians, who are normally drawn first to the crash site, where they will confirm your ejection. This time should be used to put as much distance as possible between yourself and the enemy. Only when you are in a secure hide should you consider your survival plan.

Ejecting from an aircraft hails the start of genuine escape and evasion – switch on immediately your canopy opens

mented if the resources are available, and the survivor's location is known. If communication with friendly forces is not possible, then the alternative is to make your way towards the border of a friendly or neutral country.

For those soldiers who have deliberately been inserted into enemy territory and who have become separated from their unit, the first task is to execute Standard Operating Procedures (SOPs). This will mean moving to the last patrol rendezvous (RV). If this is unoccupied after the stipulated time then the survivor must move to the designated war RV. If no contact is established with the unit, the next step is to make communications contact using the SAR beacon; or, if this is not available, to walk out to the nearest friendly forces.

Assessing Your Situation

As a military survivor or escaper your situation will depend on a number of factors:

• The distance between you and friendly forces
• The communications available
• Your physical condition
• Is the enemy aware of your presence?
• Were you deliberately inserted or forcibly trapped behind enemy lines?
• Were you forced to eject?
• Are you escaping from a prisoner-of-war camp?

Recent events have clearly shown that soldiers who follow their survival training 'by the book' have an excellent chance of rescue or repatriation.

Short-Term Survival

Short-term survival can be defined as temporary separation from the direct support of friendly forces. The duration can be anything from a few hours to several days, and separation distance anything from a mile or two to a hundred miles. If the distance is short, i.e. a soldier is temporarily trapped behind the enemy's forward lines, then he may be able to work his way stealthily back. Likewise, a pilot who has ejected and whose position has been established has an excellent chance of a rapid SAR pick-up.

The first priority is to establish your physical condition. Were you injured during ejection or landing, or have you been wounded? The extent of any injuries will be a deciding factor in determining your survival plan. The main problem arising is immobility when the enemy is aware of your presence in the area. In such a case concealment is your only means of avoiding detection, and you will be forced to remain hidden until fit enough to move or friendly forces have overtaken your position.

For those who are able to move, passing through the forward battle area will be extremely dangerous. The enemy will be heavily concentrated and troops on both sides will be exchanging fire. Avoiding being wounding or captured so close to freedom demands the utmost vigilance, and strict employment of military skills of movement and concealment. Timing is also crucial. Whether you need to pass near a concentration of enemy troops or simply to make radio contact, picking the best time can make the difference between success and failure.

Modern warfare techniques demand that most battles are fought at night. While there will be sentries, normal infantry are at their most vulnerable between the hours of 3am and 4am, allowing you to slip past. At around the same time bomber aircraft, most of which can receive signals from an SAR beacon, will be returning to base

Military Survival Equipment

Survival equipment was mainly developed by the military (see Survival Essentials), and there are several specialist items not commonly available to civilians. These include button compass, silk maps, lock-picking tools, blood chits and gold coins. Pilots flying over enemy territory and Special Forces operating behind the lines will be issued such equipment in addition to SAR beacons and radios. The down side is that if a soldier is captured with specialist survival equipment on his person, this is an immediate indicator to interrogators that he is a member of Special Forces.

Communications See SARBE in Survival Essentials.

Button Compass A small navigational device which can be secreted about the person, or sometimes swallowed if capture is imminent. Size can vary from 1cm to 3cm (0.4in-1.2ins). Button compasses normally indicate only the four cardinal points.

Escape Map These are large-scale maps covering the theatre of war. They were traditionally printed on silk, but modern cloths are now used. Printing on cloth makes the map less vulnerable to wet, and allows it to be hidden in the lining of clothing.

Lock-Picking Tools Some individuals may choose to include

Issued escape and evasion equipment is designed to keep you free, communicate and guide you back to friendly forces. The equipment is only useful while you remain uncaptured.

the basic items for lock-picking within their survival pack. The main tools required are a tension bar and a double-ended pick and rake (see Lock-Picking, below). Tools and devices for opening doors and windows are not difficult to make.

Escape Money 'Blood chits' are letters in the language of the country of operation; each soldier has a copy stamped with an individual number. The letter simply states that anyone helping the escaping soldier to safety will be rewarded. The soldier keeps the blood chit but gives the unique serial number to those assisting him; upon revealing this number to any embassy it is a simple matter to identify a particular soldier. Many Special Forces soldiers and pilots are also issued with money, either in the form of US dollars or gold coins, and this has proved to be a much more tangible inducement when soliciting help. However, it can also attract greed to raise its ugly head, and the escapee should be careful not to flash the money around.

Concealment

Camouflage means not being seen or detected. This can be achieved by hiding while static or transforming yourself while moving. The basics of camouflage are shape, shine, shadow, silhouette and movement, but you must also add noise and smell to this list. Disrupting a defined outline can change any shape; this is best done by draping some form of cloth or vegetation over your whole outline. Remember to blend with the climatic conditions (Arctic, desert, jungle) and the prevailing colour patterns and textures that are natural for that area. Covering your face, hands and any exposed skin with charcoal or camouflage cream can prevent shine. Make sure you conceal watches, dog-tags and any other bright metal objects by painting them with mud, or wrapping with cloth or tape.

Movement will give your position away quicker than anything else. If you spot the enemy, go to ground and avoid all movement until it is dark or the enemy has gone. If you must move to avoid possible capture, do so slowly. Move around objects and exposed terrain, staying in the low ground to avoid silhouetting yourself. If in the open, try to walk in the shadows of any hills, hedges or trees. Noise and smell also attract unwanted attention. Make any unavoidable movement over noisy ground (e.g. a carpet of dry leaves) when there is some background noise – such as rain – to cover it.

Although hygiene is important, avoid using soap while the enemy is around. Likewise do not cook when the enemy is near as the smell of the fire and food will travel for several hundred metres.

Night Vision The only way to achieve night vision is by waiting until the eyes have become accustomed to the darkness. Maintain it by shutting out any bright light source such as a torch or a car headlight. If you must look at a bright light once you have your night vision, always cover one eye to protect it. Remember, however, that low light conditions can be deceptive to the eye, especially at a distance. It is vital to use all the senses when walking at night.

Long-Term Survival

Treatment on Capture
Despite the Geneva Convention and other laws governing the correct treatment of POWs, the captured serviceman cannot expect any particular adherence to these codes. You may be treated in accordance with international law; or you may be subjected to inhumane treatment or execution. The factors which influence the treatment of prisoners vary. A captured soldier may be seen as the representative of the opposing

Make A Break – Or Wait?

If captured in a forward area you have a choice: try to escape immediately – or wait for a chance further back down the line leading eventually to a prison camp? Arguments for making a break for it include:

• You are still near your own front lines.

• Your unit is probably still close to its last known location.

• Unless wounded, you are still in good physical and mental condition.

• You may even still have some useful equipment on your person.

But:
• Your captors are probably still highly tense from combat. If you try to escape they are entitled to shoot you on the spot, and may well do so.

• Escaping across the front lines during battle carries a high risk of injury or death.

Remember your basic training of camouflage and concealment.

Take extra care when passing through the forward battle area.

army and may therefore be treated as a scapegoat for the enemy's military casualties or for war crimes, real or alleged (e.g. the bombing of civilians). Aircrew taking part in an airstrike against enemy troops and subsequently shot down and captured may take the brunt of their captors' anger. Another deciding factor in the treatment of a prisoner is the professionalism of his captors. In general, a professional soldier will act in a professional (i.e. relatively humane) way; members of local militia forces may behave with far less restraint.

Early Escape Your reaction to capture, and therefore your chances of survival and escape, will be heavily influenced by your physical state, your attitude, and the exact location of your capture and imprisonment. It is the duty of every captured soldier to try to escape as soon as an opportu-

nity presents itself. The sooner this is done, the more likely it is that he will still be close to his own lines and aware of the position of his troops. Unless he has been wounded he should still be fit, both physically and mentally. However, if he has been captured close to the front line then the dangers of an escape will be high. Enemy combat troops will be present in strength, and many will be working under high levels of stress; attempts to escape under these conditions increase the danger of being shot, and should be avoided unless the perfect opportunity to make a clean getaway arises.

Ultimately, your individual character, training and fitness will have the strongest bearing on your chances of survival. This is especially true if you are surviving on your own for a long time, with no chance of rescue in the foreseeable future.

Psychological Effects of Capture When his existence is under threat a man is often psychologically incapable of making decisions in his own best interests. The only way to control these natural negative reactions – e.g. to fear, pain, boredom, loneliness, cold, fatigue, thirst and hunger – is to recognize their symptoms and understand how they work on your mind.

Interrogation The type and severity of the interrogation of a captured soldier or airman can vary dramatically, from general questioning under cool but controlled conditions, to continuous brutal beatings which lead to death. Although some countries employ methods of torture, military prisoners-of-war are rarely killed during interrogation. Modern experience shows that the interrogation period is usually restricted to about two weeks, after which the prisoner is kept in solitary confinement.

Fear The greatest enemy for the interrogated prisoner is fear. This normal and necessary reaction during times of danger releases high levels of the hormone adrenaline into the system to help the body cope with the greater demands put upon it. Trying to deny that you feel fear may put you at a disadvantage; accepting the emotion as natural brings two benefits. By admitting to your fear, you will get rid of any

'fear of being afraid'. The adrenaline released by fear often gives a person certain advantages, e.g. greater strength and stamina, reduced pain sensation, and the ability to think more clearly and act in a co-ordinated manner.

Pain Pain is the natural protective phenomenon which tells you that something is wrong with your body. However, even when you are aware of the situation the message refuses to switch off, becoming a distraction and even draining the will to survive. Nevertheless, it is possible to lessen its hold if you occupy your mind with planning for escape or survival, and carry out various tasks to keep yourself busy. If pain is not to get the better of you it is essential to focus the mind away from it and on to something more positive and useful.

The prisoner will be under constant duress, not just from interrogation, beatings, and political exposure, but also from the mundane pattern of prison life. Boredom and isolation numb the mind into a state of hopelessness. Quite often the prisoner can have his hopes raised only to be disappointed time and again. Darkness and loneliness also increase feelings of isolation and self-doubt. At times like this it is important to keep your mind occupied so that boredom and isolation will not be able to take hold.

Escape Techniques

A successful escape depends on making the most of any opportunity. If nothing else, the thought of escape stimulates the mind into considering the possibilities that might arise. Look at all problems in a logical manner. For example: all prisoners will be kept enclosed in some kind of structure. Many of these enclosures can be overcome if analysed for their strengths and weaknesses. You must decide the best way to get out – whether it is easier to go over, under, or through. The logical choice is governed by the structure of your prison and its routine. There are six basic types of structure: brick, stone, block, timber, reinforced concrete and wire.

Brick One of the commonest types of structure, a brick wall is also the easiest to break through. Walls depend on the strength of the bond between the individual bricks. Once this bond has been broken it is relatively easy to remove as many bricks as you need. To break through a wall, select your escape point, choose a brick in the middle of this space, and start to scrape away the mortar around it. Carry out this work only when there are no guards around, as the whole process could take a few days.

To conceal your handiwork, collect up the mortar dust at the end of each session, wet it with a little water or urine (plus some soap if you have any), and refill the gaps with this weakened mixture. It won't take long to scrape it out again the next day. Hide your work with some object in your cell, such as a bed. Once the first brick has been removed things should get easier, although it may take the removal of a few more before the bond has been broken enough to take the rest out by hand.

Blocks Modern buildings are often built of concrete blocks. Although larger and heavier than bricks, they still rely on the mortar bond between them for strength. The same method as for bricks will work, but may prove quite difficult. It is worth considering breaking through the block itself, particularly if it has a hollow internal construction. A single skin of such blocks may be smashed through in very little time. The only disadvantage with this method is noise, and this should be taken into account in your escape plan.

It is possible to break out of any structure, however this can take time and stealth. Make sure you conceal any escape attempt.

Wire fences come in a variety of forms; study the design to find the easiest method of escape. Start by deciding whether to go through, over or under.

Stone Older buildings built of stone often have very thick walls. For this reason, although the same method as for bricks could be used, it would take an unreasonably long time. In these circumstances carefully study all the other openings. Windows and doors in an old building may also be old themselves and therefore not in good repair. Look for weaknesses and exploit them.

Timber Escape from buildings constructed of wood is relatively easy, provided they are not made from solid logs. Overlapping joints are a weak point and may be forced apart. If panels are held together with nails, these may be removed to make a good escape hole. Don't consider the walls alone; the roof may also offer good possibilities. Some wooden buildings are built directly on to earth floors; if so, this may open up an opportunity for tunnelling out.

Reinforced Concrete Reinforced concrete walls tend to be thick and impenetrable, and it is wise not to waste time even thinking about getting through them. Instead search out other possible weaknesses, such as air vents, windows, doors or even sewers. Luckily this kind of wall is rare, and is usually only found in special high security buildings and structures such as foundations and cellars.

Fences Although the many kinds of fences are not as solid as walls they still pose a problem to the escaper. Fences may be used either for a primary enclosure (although this is generally temporary), or may form a secondary line of obstruction. Fences need the same kind of study and analysis as walls before any kind of escape is attempted, or it will probably fail. Some fences are constructed so that severing certain key links will destroy a large section without too much effort. If the wire is too thick for the prisoner to cut, or he has no cutting tools, he may have to consider climbing over it; however, before doing this he must make sure that it will bear his weight. Razor and barbed wire will require some kind of padding to cross without injury. Remember, depending on the type of fence, only you can decide whether it is best to go over, under or through.

Links The most common type of fence is constructed from metal links. Loose link fences can usually be cut through fairly easily, and if the links are cut to a planned pattern a hole can be made simply and quickly. Trying to cut through solid mesh fences, as used in modern prisons, is not recommended. These types of fences are best climbed over, although you will need a makeshift claw grip (see Escape Tools). Climbable fences will usually have a secondary barrier at the top in the form of razor wire, barbed wire or rolling drums. To cross the sharp wires use a 'batman cloak', fashioned from a thick piece of canvas, carpet or any other heavy material. Wear it like a cloak while you are climbing so that it does not get caught up; when you get to the top throw it over your head and over the wire and release it from around your neck. Rolling drums require even more forethought as they will need to be fixed before you can get over them.

Electric Fences It is best to check any fence that you are unsure of for electrification. Take a small piece of grass and place its tip on the fence, making sure that your skin does not come into contact with the wire. If nothing is felt when the tip of the grass is placed on the wire, slowly move the blade up the wire, bringing your hand closer to the fence. By the time your hand is within half an inch of the fence, if no tingling is felt, then the fence is safe.

Tunnels In the prison camps of the Second World War some Allied POWs almost made a career out of escaping by tunnelling. This method was suited to their particular circumstances. Firstly, their barracks were often made of wood on a dirt floor. Secondly, they had the necessary manpower – many men were needed not only to dig but also to distribute the excavated earth. Thirdly, they had the uninterrupted time needed to dig long tunnels. Although this escape method could still be used today, tunnels are best confined to short lengths under fences which require only one person and a very short time to excavate.

Lock-Picking

It is said that during the Second World War the Allied prisoners held in Colditz Castle in Germany were able to open the internal doors on a regular basis by means of skeleton keys or picking the locks, and therefore had the run of much of the castle. Although the principles seem fairly elementary, however, lock-picking is a skill which takes many years to master. Long and constant practice is needed to achieve what is known as 'the feel'. This expertise combines a practised and focused sense of touch, and the ability to concentrate on a mental picture of what the picks are doing inside the lock at any given moment. A lock can only be opened by a key or by mimicking the actions of that key. The aim of the following entries is to give the briefest of guides as to how this can be done.

Pin Tumbler Lock The most common type of lock that a prisoner is likely to encounter, this accounts for 85% of all locks world-wide. A series of small pins fit into the inner barrel of a cylinder. These pins are split in the middle, usually at different lengths, and are forced into recesses within the inner barrel by a small spring. Upon the correct key being inserted into the lock, the different size pins are brought into line at the point where their split meets the outer casing of the barrel. This alignment then allows the inner barrel to turn freely within the casing and release the lock.

To open this type of lock without a key requires the pins to be aligned in the same manner as above, and this can be achieved by two methods: raking, or picking the pins. The tools required are a lock pick/rake and a tension bar. It is not easy to purchase these tools in most countries, but it is possible to make your own (see Escape Tools). The pick or rake is simply a flat strip of hardened metal with its end shaped in order to fit into the lock and press the pins to the depth needed to align them. The tension bar is also a flat strip of metal. This is placed into the mouth of the barrel in order to exert a small amount of tension. This action helps to seat the pins and turn the barrel.

Raking and Seating The quickest method of opening a

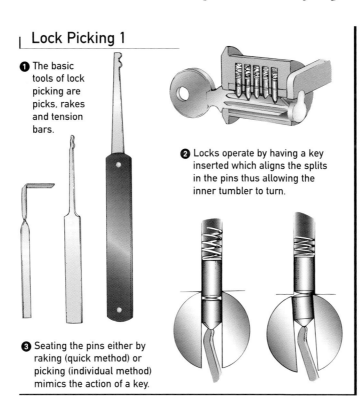

Lock Picking 1

❶ The basic tools of lock picking are picks, rakes and tension bars.

❷ Locks operate by having a key inserted which aligns the splits in the pins thus allowing the inner tumbler to turn.

❸ Seating the pins either by raking (quick method) or picking (individual method) mimics the action of a key.

By Any Means

Desperate people will often find desperate ways of escaping, and over the years there have been tales of many daring and ingenious attempts. These range from building gliders and balloons to hiding in vehicles, and even walking out the gates in improvised enemy uniform. Resourceful and unorthodox escapes can sometimes be the easiest way out of prison, and all avenues should be researched.

Defeating an Electric Fence

A fence surrounding a prison compound is best defeated by fooling the guards into turning it off.

• Acquire a length of line. Tie to one end a ferrous metal object light enough to throw and heavy enough to short-circuit the electric fence.

• Wait for a dark night with a high wind. If it is also raining, fit some form of insulator between your metal object and the throwing line – when this gets wet you will be in danger of electrocution.

• Throw the object at the fence to activate the alarm, and withdraw it immediately. Once the guards have investigated, found nothing, and returned to their posts, repeat the process.

• Keep going until the guards become convinced that the weather is causing the malfunction; to prevent any further call-outs they may well shut down the system.

• Warning: Some modern electric fences emit intermittent pulses which activate every five seconds or so.

249

Lock Picking 2

1 Fit the tension bar into the mouth of the keyhole. Apply pressure to see which way the inner barrel turns.

2 Insert a pick or rake to the far end of the barrel so that it sits below the pins.

3 Apply a small amount of pressure on the tension bar and quickly remove the rake/pick touching all the picks in sequence as you do so. Note any movement on the barrel.

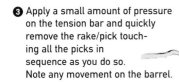

4 Gently relax the pressure on the tension bar and listen to the pins 'popping' back into place. Repeat the process until all the pins are seated.

lock is by 'raking'; this is a simple technique as long as the pin sizes do not change suddenly. The process consists of inserting the pick to the rear of the pins and then quickly snatching it outwards, so that its tip runs over the pins on the way. First of all, clean the lock and blow into it hard to dislodge any dirt. Then place a tension bar into the bottom of the keyway so that a slight pressure is put on the inner barrel. The amount of tension applied should be enough to turn the barrel once the pins are seated, but not so much as to hold the pins against the barrel.

Getting the 'feel' of a lock like this is the basis of all good lock-picking. Too heavy a tension, and the binding pins will not allow the breaking point to meet; too light a tension, and the pins will just go back into the locked position. When using the raking method it will be necessary to repeat the above process more than once. However, if it has not been successful by the fourth attempt you should check the amount of tension you are using. You can do this by holding the tension in place with the tension bar and placing your ear to the lock, slowly releasing the tension and listening as you do so. If you hear a pitting sound as the pins fall back into place, then you have used too much pressure. If you hear nothing at all then you have not used enough.

Three factors will determine whether or not a lock will be easily opened: the length and position of the pins; the type of tools you use; and the way the lock has been manufactured. In general, expensive locks are harder to open than cheaper ones as they usually have less clearance between the barrel and the body. Cheaper locks tend to have poor barrel alignment and oversized pin holes, making them far easier to pick.

Although similar to raking, lock 'picking' requires more skill and time. With this method the pins have to be seated one by one. Taking the pick, start at the rear of the barrel and feel for the furthermost pin. By gently pushing it up, the barrel should move a tiny fraction. Working in sequence, seat each pin in turn, and the barrel should release. Often the easiest method to release a lock is a combination of raking and picking: one quick rake, followed by picking.

Opening Cars and Windows

One simple method of getting into some models of locked car is to use a strip of strong, flexible plastic banding. Fold it in two, and force the loop end through the rubber seal around the door. The plastic strip can be slid down and manipulated to fit over the door button release. Once the button is trapped, manoeuvre the plastic strip carefully upwards to release the lock. The same approach can be use to retrieve keys left in the lock on the outside of the door, and to open house windows secured by ram-and-pin devices.

Padlocks One useful tip for opening padlocks is to sharpen one end of your pick to a needle point. Push the point all the way to the end of the lock so that it touches the rear plate. The sharp end of the pick will bind on the metal. Use this grip to try to force the back plate up and down, as this will sometimes release the mechanism without any need for picking or raking.

Escape Tools

Boredom is one of the great enemies of the prisoner-of-war. To overcome this the mind needs to be kept occupied with challenges. One good challenge is to devise ways of making simple escape tools, or anything else that may improve your standard of living. Any tools that you make, any items that you still have – including clothing and boots – should always be well looked after. This also includes your body, so any attempt at keeping up some level of personal hygiene will always increase your wellbeing. Whatever you make, practise using your own resourcefulness and ingenuity. These will always be the key to survival in any situation.

Maps Maps can be a vital aid if you are planning to escape. Try to obtain one by any means – steal one if you can, or try to make your own from information gleaned from guards or other prisoners. It can be drawn on the inside of your coat, jacket or shirt, or even memorized. Once you have escaped, look for any form of map on your route. These may be found in cars, telephone boxes, on dead soldiers, and in many other places.

Lock Picks A lock-picking set may be improvised from many items: safety pins, tempered wire flattened at one end, or even hard plastic cut into the right shape. Heavy duty feeler gauges obtained from a machine shop can also be fashioned into a good set. A one-metre section of flat plastic banding tape of the type used to secure packages is also very handy, especially when acquiring a car.

Chisel A basic chisel can be made from anything metal. A spoon or other kitchen utensil, the metal tip of a boot sole – all will perform as chisels to scrape mortar from between bricks. If you intend hammering, a 15cm (6in) section of metal pipe which has been flattened at one end will serve you well.

Ladder Sheeting and blankets have been made into climbing ropes to aid escape from many prisons, but the bed itself should not be overlooked. Many beds used in prisons have a chain-link metal base which can be broken down and reformed into a ladder. Always test the strength of any improvised lowering device before trusting your weight to it.

Compass A compass will be needed after the escape, when attempting to travel to safety. A compass is simple enough to make; all that is needed is a magnetized needle and something to balance it on which will allow it to turn freely towards the North. This need not be a solid object – the needle can also be floated in water or suspended in the air (see Survival Essentials).

Food and Bones All bones, no matter what animal they come from, can be useful. They can be fashioned into sewing needles, buttons, scrapers, and handles for home-made tools. Bones are one item not missed by the guards once you have eaten your food, but you are advised to leave some bones in the waste to avoid suspicion. Food given to you in captivity should always be eaten, as you can never be sure of when you will next be fed. However, if you are

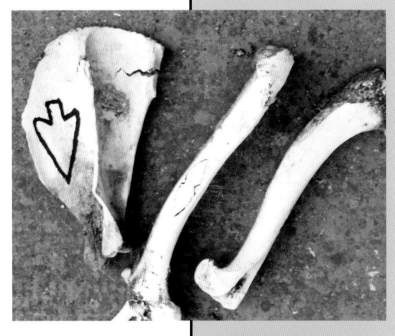

planning an escape, try and keep a few scraps back. Make sure that they are not perishable. Sugar is a good food to store, as by adding a little water and heating to dissolve it the sugar, upon cooling, will form a solid, transportable block. Eggs can be baked hard by placing then on a metal spoon held over a candle.

A metal pipe will serve you well as a chisel.

Escape

No escape should be attempted without some knowledge of the immediate surroundings and the intended route. Gather as much intelligence as possible by coaxing or eavesdropping snippets of information from the guards. Incorporate these into your escape plan. Your chances of staying free will depend upon the accuracy of your information.

If the enemy cannot find you he will search the most obvious routes; take the opposite choice. Streams and rivers make good escape routes, but travel only at night and avoid contact with any other river users. Avoid trains and other direct lines of communication. If you plan to escape in a group, make sure that any supplies of first aid materials, water, purification tablets, matches, etc, are divided up equally among you – even if one escaper or one pack is lost it will not leave the rest of the group without vital resources. Essential items such as your knife, compass, flint and steel, etc, should be securely attached to your person.

Evasion

Evasion principles apply to both short and long-term survival. A short-term evasion may be measured in hours, or at the worst, days; survival and return to friendly forces will depend on stealth and alertness rather than food and water. Evasion in the long term is another matter. An escaped prisoner or a downed pilot may be deep within enemy territory, far from friendly forces, for weeks or even months. All this time he will have to worry about not only avoiding capture, but also his own survival with regard to food, water, shelter and warmth. He must also be prepared to navigate and travel great distances through hostile terrain.

Military survival is not simply a matter of finding enough food and water and a place to shelter; the escaper must also hide in daylight hours and run by night. Throughout the whole evasion stage he will be surrounded by hostiles, both military and civilian, all charged with looking out for him. He must stay unseen and avoid any contact with the local population. This is not easy when the people of a country are in conflict, and suspicious about every stranger.

War means shortage of food, lack of public law and order, and easy death for many. The poorer peoples of the world may resort to turning a prisoner-of-war into a hostage held for ransom. In such an instance, where the local military or police have not been informed, you should use your gold or blood chit to gain assistance. One of the best ways of remaining free is to collect information that will help decide your escape route. Remember the essence of evasion: 'once free, stay free.'

Contact Rapid rescue from hostile environments requires a location and distress radio on whose signal the SAR crews can home in. Ideally the radio should be capable of automatic operation and manual transmission. Such radios as the SARBE 6 (see Survival Essentials) and the Tacbe BE499 are well suited to this task, and are compatible with the SARSAT (Search And Rescue Satellite-Aided Tracking) system. Where military issue radios are not available, look for alternatives.

While military communications are prime targets,

civilian telephone systems may still be operating. Using a public telephone box will mean exposing yourself and, if the enemy is on the ball, possibly giving away your position (although most exchanges are now totally automated). Many mobile telephones operate on GSM, thus giving access to the whole world. The acquisition of a mobile phone during a conflict is not as difficult as one would imagine. If the opportunity arises where you are in a position to make a call, consider the following – you may only have one shot at it:

- Who you will call?
- Do you remember any time zone difference?
- Do you have the correct code and number?
- How can you identify yourself beyond doubt?
- Have you thought what words to use? You need a quick, safe, unmistakable way of conveying your intentions, and a time and place for a possible SAR pick-up.

Run or Hide? Once you have escaped your primary goal is to stay free. Recapture will certainly result in punishment, and sometimes in death. When the escape is discovered a search party will be sent out. This may include dog-handlers, and perhaps armed civilians as well as the local militia – dangerous, and trigger-happy. The escaper has two options: lie low in the immediate vicinity until the search has died down, or get out of the area as quickly as possible.

Hiding has a lot of merit, provided that the hide is indetectable – even to dogs – and you have enough food and water with you that you do not have to expose yourself in search of more. This option is more likely to be adopted by Special Forces, who undergo extensive training in hide construction as part of their surveillance role. Hiding also has the advantage of putting the search troops in front of you rather than behind you.

Grave Hide For a simple but effective hide for short-term survival, dig a shallow 'grave'. Avoiding detection depends on the strength and concealment of the top cover you construct. Obviously, it should not be sited where anyone is liable to walk directly over it. Take care over making it waterproof and comfortable; but except in times of immediate danger from the enemy you should occupy it only for daytime rest and sleeping. Ensure that it has easy access. The entrance should be at the head end, where a dirt-sealed hatch can be fitted once the occupant is inside. Make sure you leave no tell-tale signs on the ground outside.

Movement If you decide to run, then do so with vigour, putting as much distance as you can between yourself and the search effort. Time your escape for the period of a full moon, as this will help you navigate at night and move quickly through forest and other obstacles. Remain hidden during the day; avoid barns and houses; watch what sign you are leaving for the enemy to follow. Use your time in the hide to take stock of your situation. If you are cold, consider whether or not it is safe to light a fire. A fire may expose your position – why build one if you may have to move shortly?

Daytime travel can be risked if you have an appropriate disguise, but remember

Using a Hide

Whether a hide is a natural refuge, or deliberately constructed to blend with the terrain, the same considerations apply:

- It must prevent discovery.

- It must offer protection from the elements.

- It must not be in a danger area.

- Enter and leave it only under cover of darkness.

- In hot areas, remain hidden during daylight.

- Relieve bladder and bowels before entering.

If you decide to run use whatever shelter you can find.

The Grave Hide

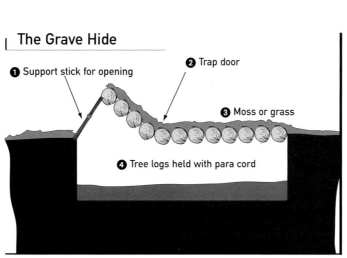

❶ Support stick for opening

❷ Trap door

❸ Moss or grass

❹ Tree logs held with para cord

that you may be stopped at roadblocks and challenged in a language you cannot speak. If you are going to bluff your way through, make sure your cover will fool everyone.

Intelligence The type of information obtained will be determined by the source; e.g. schools, libraries, and telephone boxes will all contain local area maps, as may abandoned cars. Newspapers, magazines and broadcasts, although normally censored during wartime, may suggest how to avoid enemy concentrations. During any war homes are often abandoned fairly intact. Do not approach houses unless absolutely necessary: they may be used by enemy soldiers as a temporary resting place; the family may return; and if caught you can legitimately be charged with looting.

SAS Tip: If you ever need to know who is living in a house, check out the washing line – an excellent indicator to both the number and size of male, female and child occupants.

Military Obstacles Military survivors moving back towards their own lines will face continuous natural obstacles (see Survival Essentials) and relevant climatic/terrain sections). They will also encounter obstacles associated with the state of war – anything from troop activity to mines, border fencing, and even contaminated areas. The latter are not always easily visible to the naked eye. Bear in mind that the contamination could be due to chemical, biological, nuclear or human waste sources. Such obstacles can stop you and trap you. Learn to recognize them quickly, and if you feel that an area does not look right, avoid it. Signs to look for include:

- Fenced-off military areas and/or warning signs.
- Dead animals and birds.
- Areas of dead vegetation or unseasonable discoloration.

Dogs are used to either keep a captive or hunt you if you escape. Remember, the dog is only as good as its handler.

Dogs

Dogs pose two threats to the escaper. Firstly, watchdogs may give the escaper away to the civilian population by their barking and their interest in a stranger on their territory. Secondly, the enemy may use professionally trained dogs to detect the escaper's scent and pursue him. The latter is by far the more dangerous situation.

Irrespective of breed, all dogs used for military purposes will meet certain requirements. They will be 55cm-66cm (22ins-26ins) high at the shoulder; will weigh 20kg-45kg (45lbs-100lbs); and will be capable of speeds of 40kmh-48kmh (25mph-30mph) for short distances. They are also chosen for their temperament: brave, intelligent, faithful, adaptable, and energetic. Typical breeds include the Alsatian, Dobermann, Rotweiler, Mastiff and Labrador.

Guard Dogs Guard dogs are trained to guard a certain territory against intruders getting in or out. They may run loose in a compound, on a running perimeter wire, or be held on a lead by their handler. These dogs are normally trained to be aggressive.

Sensory Characteristics A dog's primary sense is not sight, but smell, followed closely by hearing. However, if a dog's attention is caught by movement it will certainly investigate with its nose and ears. Although often stated, it has not been proved that a dog has better night vision than a man; but the dog's relatively lower position to the ground may enable it to see more silhouettes against the skyline. A dog's hearing range is twice that of a human; but whether or not it hears a sound will depend upon the weather, particularly with regard to wind and rain.

The Scent Picture The dog's sense of smell is estimated to be 700 to 900 times more acute than that of a human. The information that a dog receives from its nose is known as the 'scent picture'. This can be made up of substances from two sources. Air scent is suspended as vapour before finally falling to the ground. It can consist of body odour, perfume, deodorants, clothing, and even the detergents used to wash the clothes. The dog will also be able to detect the scent of an individual human: each of us produces our own scent depending on genetics, constitution, activity and mental state. The ground scent can be made up of two components: the air scent as it falls to the ground, and any disturbance of the ground caused by the pressure of feet. The latter consists of a mixture of gases released by crushed vegetation, dead insects and the breaking of the surface layer; less volatile than air scent, it may last up to 48 hours in favourable conditions. Favourable scent

conditions include moist ground, vegetation, humidity, forest areas, light rain, mist or fog. Conditions which work against the preservation of ground scent include high winds and heavy rain, arid areas, stone, sand, roads and streets.

Tracker Dogs Tracker dogs are trained to locate and follow a certain scent, usually that of a man on foot. To do this they use mainly ground scent, following the freshest source available. The dog will usually stay with its handler at all times, and much depends upon successful teamwork between them. Although the dog will follow a track invisible to its handler, it he who must ensure that it is the right one. Tracker dogs are not normally aggressive.

Dog Evasion If a dog has spotted your movement, it is important that you freeze immediately – the dog may lose interest. If the dog pursues you, then you have no option but to run, at once. Any delay in the time between your getting away and the pursuit, no matter how short, should be used productively to introduce some countermeasures and therefore increase the distance between you and the dog.

❶ Run steadily.

❷ Climb up or jump down vertical features.

❸ Swim rivers.

❹ If in a group, split up.

❺ Run downwind – this will make it harder for the dog to pick up any air scent.

❻ Do things to confuse the handler. Try to make him think that the dog has lost the scent by, e.g. crossing and recrossing an obstacle (such as water) several times within a short distance. This will cause the dog to look as if he is confused – when the only confused party will actually be the handler.

Warning: Using a chemical substance such as pepper in the hope of disguising your trail is definitely not recommended. This will only increase the scent picture that you leave.

Dog Attack It is no use running from an attacking dog unless you are sure you can reach a place of safety quickly – dogs can easily outrun humans. Instead, stand your ground and bar his path with something like a strong stick. It is a dog's instinct to paw down anything that gets in its way, and doing this will slow him down and break his momentum. Once the dog has reached you it will normally attempt to bite and lock on. If you have a body area that is padded, offer that to the dog and let him get a firm grip. Then you should be able to either stab him in the chest or hit him on the head with a rock or some other heavy object. Make sure that the injury is permanently disabling, or else the dog may become even more angry and violent.

A charging dog relies on its

momentum to knock you to the ground. Therefore any way of breaking his speed will be to your advantage. One way of doing this is to stand next to a tree, but exposed to the dog until the last moment; just as he reaches you, move rapidly behind the tree. This will force the dog to stop in order to change direction; this unexpected change in pace should give the escaper a chance to take advantage of the situation. If the handler is not present there is a chance that the dog can be intimidated. Charge towards him screaming, with your arms outstretched. Your larger size and aggressiveness may weaken the dog's confidence, causing him to run away.

If the dog is leashed to its handler then it will only be as fast as its master. If you are fit enough you could try to outrun them. If unarmed, give yourself up if you are cornered by a dog and its handler. Finally, unless you are forced to, never kill the handler's dog – this will only bring greater punishment for you if you are recaptured.

Essentials of a Good Evasion Plan

• Careful prior preparation and planning. Formulate a workable plan; make sure you are prepared mentally and physically for the challenges ahead.

• Decide direction of travel and route. Consider contingency plans for any of the many things that could go wrong. Be patient, and confident in your abilities.

• Stockpile escape rations by conserving food wherever possible. Find a use for everything – never throw anything away. Obtain local high denomination coins if possible.

• Once free, make full use of military skills e.g. camouflage and concealment. Choose routes that give the greatest cover; if you must cross open ground, try to do so only by night. Never take chances if there is a safe, slower way of achieving the same aim. Stay alert.

If you find yourself in a survival situation, whether by design or by accident, remember

FIVE GOLDEN RULES OF SURVIVAL

1 Life itself is survival, all that changes is the environment or the conditions under which you live. When crossing a wilderness area or entering a dangerous environment do so properly equipped.

2 A quick rescue is the best rescue. Use every modern aid to make others aware of your plight and location. No matter what the danger, good communications will prevent a survival situation evolving.

3 We only need the basics. Given that you are uninjured and functioning properly, you need only air to breath, water to drink, food to eat and shelter from the environment. However scarce, nature supplies all these elements but you cannot expect nature to change in order to accommodate your requirements, You must learn to adapt to use whatever she provides.

4 Plan your survival. When disaster strikes think about your situation and make a plan of your basic needs. Through the practical applications of survival you will maintain hope and give hope to others. Maintain your health, care for the injured, build a fire if you are cold, eat if hungry and sleep when tired. Do not needlessly expend energy or put yourself in danger without good reason.

5 Recognise that danger is everywhere. The cold can kill. The heat can kill. The sea can kill. Wild beasts can kill. Despondency can kill. Lack of nourishment can kill. Watch, listen, think and determine the problem – learn to survive.

Acknowledgments

The information contained in this book was researched from the world's elite survival schools, both civilian and military. The use of photography as opposed to illustrations has been adopted to indicate that the processes and methods actually work. Although the photographs are from various sources world-wide the contributions of Guy Croisiaux and Neil Devine are especially outstanding. The visit and introduction by Brig. Gen. Dato Modh Azumi bin Mohamed, to the survival school in Malaca was very much appreciated, supplying in the process some outstanding jungle photography. As always, without the skillful work of Julie Pembridge in coordinating the written material and helping this book develop, attainment would not have been possible. Finally the author would like to express his gratitude to the CEO of BCB International Ltd. , Andrew Howell, through whose office many of the contributing companies and individuals were contacted for their support.

BCB International Ltd. UK
Beaufort. UK
Special Forces Survival School Malaca. Malaysia
International Long Range Patrol School. Germany
The Survival School. Belgium
The Royal Navy Survival School. UK

Director of Public Communication, Pentagon. USA
Manchester Airport Security Training. UK
Martin Baker. UK
GQ Parachutes. UK
Marinair Holdings. Malaysia